WHO'S THE
B*****D
IN THE BLACK?

WHO'S THE B*****D IN THE BLACK?

Confessions of a Premiership Referee

JEFF WINTER

WITH RAY SIMPSON AND ANDREW WILKINSON

EBURY
PRESS

9 10

This edition published in 2006
First published in 2006 by Ebury Press, an imprint of Ebury Publishing

Ebury Publishing is a division of the Random House Group

The Random House Group Limited Reg. No. 954009

Addresses for companies within the Random House Group
can be found at www.randomhouse.co.uk

A CIP catalogue record for this book is available from the British Library

The Random House Group Limited supports The Forest Stewardship
Council® (FSC®), the leading international forest-certification organisation.
Our books carrying the FSC label are printed on FSC®-certified paper.
FSC is the only forest-certification scheme supported by the leading
environmental organisations, including Greenpeace. Our
paper procurement policy can be found at
www.randomhouse.co.uk/environment

Printed and bound in Great Britain by Clays Ltd, St Ives plc

Cover design by Two Associates

ISBN 9780091909178

To all those hardy souls in black
(or yellow or green) much maligned,
unloved, and the scapegoat for every player,
manager and supporter's feelings.

Remember that without a ref
they wouldn't have a game.

Keep smiling, stay calm and enjoy,
don't let the bastards get you down.

ACKNOWLEDGEMENTS

Surround yourself with good people and you won't go far wrong. Either through luck or good judgement I have been helped throughout my career and private life by some great friends and colleagues – and of course family.

I have needed every one of them at times, and they are too numerous to mention.

I still fondly remember the boys on the terraces back in the early 1970s, and the characters from the local leagues who helped me on the journey up the refereeing ladder. Special thanks to those who helped keep me on the pitch, including physiotherapists Ronnie Gomer and Barry Phillipson, chiropodist Richie Lawson, and physical training instructors Matt Weston and Steve McArten – and to my many fellow referees, the "good guys" whose honesty and strength of character is vital to the game. Thanks to Ray Simpson and Andrew Wilkinson for their help in writing this book. Their enthusiasm for the project fully vindicated my decision to work with two local writers who share my passion for football and understanding of the Teesside area. I am also indebted to Andrew Goodfellow at Ebury for his patience and sound advice, Phil Hughes for getting me the introduction to Ebury and to Jeff Weston, my agent at SEM, for helping me keep the wolf from the door.

And most importantly of all, my wife Lynette and my children Emma, Craig and Mark who are more special to me than words can describe. Perhaps I don't always show it but you are to me the reason to live. In fact only one person comes anywhere near them in terms of the inspiration they have given me. Steve Gibson is, like me, a Boro lad made good. He loved Middlesbrough FC so much that he bought it, and gave it the status it enjoys today. He didn't do it for himself, but for the thousands of fans like him. The joy he has brought them is without measure. And he did it without ever turning his back on his roots.

Keep it going Steve, "We shall overcome some day."

1

YOU ARE MY BORO

The cold steel blade was flashed menacingly in my direction, and suddenly the rest of the world seemed to cease to exist. I knew instantly how it felt to be isolated in a crowd. The only thing I was aware of, the blade apart, was the thug attached to its handle. He conformed to the typical image of a Scottish football hooligan, clad in a Celtic shirt, and sporting the obligatory ginger hair.

In a split second I learnt two things. One was that I had developed a sudden affinity with Rangers, and the other that this fight should be put on hold. I turned, shot up the wall at the back of the terrace, and clambered out of the football ground. The feeling of relief was almost tangible, and I could sense the blood draining from me as surely as if the knife had been plunged into my flesh. I felt as if I had turned as white as a sheet. But I probably turned whiter still – if that's possible – when I realised that I would have to pay again to get back in to see the match. I reached for my cash, happy to be in one piece, and headed back into the Kippax End of Manchester City's Maine Road ground.

It was commonplace for hordes of Middlesbrough fans, with me in their midst, to storm into the "home" end of football venues across the country. But it was rare for the home fans to stand their ground, let alone produce weapons, for we usually caught them by surprise, before they scattered in all directions, faced with up to five hundred fans coming at them in one surge. But on this occasion the City supporters, including the one with Scottish roots, didn't flinch, and it was we who beat a hasty retreat. I was looking after number one, but several other Boro fans had followed my lead and scrambled to safety.

As fate would have it, when we played the return game against Manchester City at Boro's Ayresome Park, I saw the lad again, and instantly recognised him. We knew some of the local police officers and I told one of them – who I had better not name, for it may put his pension in jeopardy – what had happened in Manchester. The officer grabbed the Celtic lad, and winked at me. I followed the officer to a quiet area behind the terrace and he whispered, "I'll turn a blind eye for five minutes while you get your own back." Let's just say that revenge was sweet.

Despite this incident, and others of a similar nature, let me make one thing clear. I did not consider myself to be a soccer hooligan in my days on the Boro terraces. I stress that because to this day local Middlesbrough folklore has it that I was. The truth is that I ran with the gang, no more, no less. I threw and took a few punches, frightened a few opposition fans, and was in turn sometimes frightened by them. We were boot boys rather than hooligans. You might wonder what the difference is, so I'll explain how I see it. My image of a football hooligan is someone who belonged to a much later era, the 1990s. The word "hooligan" conjures up images of fans abroad, rampaging through the streets and squares of a town, cracking chairs over the heads of rivals. Inside grounds I see hooligans as gangs hurling bricks and bottles at police and rival fans. We never did that – at least not so far as I can remember. A boot boy was more bravado than violence. Put it this way. I was never in much danger of being sent to prison, but neither was I an innocent caught up in trouble.

I enjoyed those days with a passion and remember them with fondness. I would not seek to wipe them from the records, simply because I later became a figure of authority within football, as a Premiership referee. To do so would be dishonest, for following my beloved Boro home and away was the centre of my world. Without it life would have been rather empty and meaningless.

Football, and Boro in particular, was an antidote to a painful home life. I wish I could report that I was surrounded by the love of a big family. But that was not the case.

My mother Betty (christened Betty and not Elizabeth) and my father Jim were old in comparison with the parents of other youngsters my age. I was a second son, my elder brother Peter having died aged just a few months. My father, who was around fifty when I was born, was too old to play football with me as other dads did with their sons, and I badly missed not having a bigger brother around.

My father was a character to be wary of at the best of times, and feared at the worst. His mood swings and heavy drinking created a tension within the household and my mother, though kind and loving to me, lived under a cloud. It was only after my father died, and I grew to know a liberated mother, that I fully realised how bad things had been for her. My mother was from Hartlepool, just a few miles up the bleak North East coast, and my father a skinhead from London, with a forces background. I believe that when he settled down in Middlesbrough with my mother it was his second marriage, though such things were not talked of, at least not within earshot of me.

I was born on 18 April 1955, half a mile from Ayresome Park, in a maternity home, and was raised in Jedburgh Street, a terrace of very modest houses, different from the hundreds of similar streets that surrounded ours only in that it boasted then – as it does now – a fish and chip shop reputed to be among the finest on Teesside. The chippie may have had something to do with my physique in later years, though as a youngster the weight never had time to pile on, for I was always on the go, playing football in the streets or on the nearest patch of grass, where so many youngsters would turn up that there were three or four games going on at once, with jumpers for goalposts of course.

The nearest decent pitch was at Breckon Hill, a mile and a half away from my house. I would play for three hours, run home for lunch, then return and play for another long spell. I fancied myself as a striker who would one day make the professional grade. I was tall for my age and could push the smaller kids around. Once they grew, I realised I would never be a footballer, for the skill deficiency became obvious. However, I did once score in a cup final for the Cubs' team. Some remember it as a tap-in, but I say that it was a 25-yard scorcher.

I loved playing football with my pals so much that I hated going away on holiday with my parents. Until we got there, that was. We would take the train to Newcastle, then the bus from Marlborough Crescent to Sunniside, outside the city, where an uncle and two aunts had a farm. While my dad helped on the farm, I rode Charlie the big carthorse. The countryside made a change, though I was a town kid at heart, and was never attracted to fishing, shooting, or other countryside hobbies.

Money was not plentiful, but my mum, who had worked in the Post Office, was organised enough to make it stretch and I was brought up to know the value of money. If I wanted a new Subbuteo team I had to save up, or wait for my birthday or Christmas to come along.

Teessiders were known as Smoggies, more so now than then, though the name was more appropriate when I was young, for the chemical and steelworks on which the town developed churned out more smog than they do today. At times the air was thick with it. If you have to be born within the sound of Bow Bells to be considered a true Cockney, then you have to arrive in this world within the sound of Middlesbrough town hall clock to be a "Smoggy". I was, and am proud of it.

My father had worked in the steelworks further down the River Tees at the Dorman Long plant, until he was crushed by heavy machinery in a near fatal accident. Unable to work again, and in those days there being no compensation for industrial mishaps as far as I was aware, the accident crushed his soul as well as his body. His drinking and his moods worsened, and what had been a tolerable existence in my early years (for I knew no better), became near intolerable as I entered my teens.

Following the Boro was a lifeline. My father did not come with me to games. He hated northerners, which didn't endear him to some of the locals, and used to harp on about the football teams from London, even though they were of no interest to me. But all the young lads my age went to watch the Boro, and a camaraderie grew from the moment we entered the Ayresome "boys' end". I went with Geoff Mullins, who was a couple of years older, and deemed responsible enough to look after me. The boys' end was set high up in the corner between the main stand and the terrace behind the goal. Because I was tall, and it was a boys' only enclosure, I had a good view of the pitch.

We later used to run a scam, thanks to a friendly gateman. I would collect a token amount from the gang, pass it to him, and he would let us in through a side door. What we saved went towards paying travel costs to away games. We often used to think that the crowd figures were fiddled by clubs, so that money could be salted away. The fact is, if people enjoyed the scam that we perfected, then the official attendance would not reflect the true crowd. I used to raise a wry smile when Ayresome was full to the rafters, and the attendance figure was given out as well short of capacity. Teesside society was just naturally rebellious, and people would get away with whatever they could without batting an eyelid. It was all in the game, and the successful ones would consider themselves entrepreneurs. The meagre income that enabled me to attend the games came from the newsagent's in

Borough Road, just round the corner from Jedburgh Street. I didn't do a paper round. I was too much of a wimp to go out in the cold, but I organised the rounds for the other boys and girls, and was even entrusted to open the shop on Sunday mornings, a responsibility I appreciated, and never abused. Even if I had not got back from a game at Ipswich or Norwich until the early hours of the morning, I would still be there, bleary-eyed, to open the shop at 6.30am. Dave Longstaff, like me a big Boro fan, used to work in the shop, and owns it now.

My teenage years were spent at Middlesbrough High School, which I went to after having passed my 11-plus and moved up from Marton Road Junior School. I was to gain a few O levels, and fancied a career in journalism, though that would have involved staying on for further education, which didn't appeal. Woodwork and sport were my favourite subjects. It was a rugby-playing school, and I preferred football, though I did play rugby, and because I was one of the tallest and strongest lads I was wanted in the scrum. But from an early age I had no desire to put my head between other men's legs.

I was a little rebellious at school, and was no stranger to corporal punishment. I remember that the maths teacher had a slipper, the headmaster a cane, while the physics teacher possessed a lump of wood. I was well acquainted with all three teachers and all three implements. I never did anything much worse than act the fool, but I was so pleased to be out of the house that school felt like freedom, and I was bound to let loose a bit. I was almost expelled once after a fist fight, but the deputy headmaster, Albert Watson, decided that punishment would come soon enough without him having to administer it. "You'll be in jail within a couple of years, Winter," he said.

I returned to visit the school two years later, by then a member of the Institute of Bankers, and rammed the words down his throat. It's strange that I ended up in banking, as I didn't pass my maths O level. I put this down largely to not having been given any encouragement by my dad. On the rare occasions that I got nine out of ten, he wanted to know why I'd got one wrong. That was almost as annoying as the 10pm curfews he imposed – even after I had left school at sixteen. My dad was the dominant force in the house, and he set the rules. Whether my mum agreed or disagreed with him didn't matter, it was my dad I had to answer to.

In any case, academic achievements were never my priority. The next Boro match was all that mattered. If you couldn't go, you felt like an outcast, because all your mates would be at the game. There were never any discussions about what we would do at the weekend, because everybody would go to the match. I had fallen in love with the club on my first visit. The noise, smell, and entire atmosphere captivated me. Success for the team was limited until World Cup winner Jack Charlton took over as manager in 1973 and "Charlton's Champions", as they were known, began to win, and win well, on a regular basis.

By the early 1970s, in my mid-teens, I was attending away games as well, and was as passionate a fan as it was possible to be. I vividly recall the thrill of making my first away trip. It was to Hull City on the "football special" train. There was nothing memorable about the trip, other than the fact that I was "on tour" with the Boro, but the feeling of speeding away from home on the train to follow my team gave me a huge glow of satisfaction, tinged with apprehension. It was a heady cocktail that got my adrenalin pumping and made me feel I was embarking on a great adventure. It gave a new dimension to being a football fan. I was now dedicated, rather than being a part-time supporter.

Soon afterwards I went to Sunderland, our arch-rivals, for my first derby experience away from home. To be with the Boro masses in enemy territory made me bristle with pride. Thousands of fans travelled to away games and it seemed that every pub and club was running a coach to games. Especially the local ones like Sunderland. I soon went from being a passenger to an organiser; my final school report was rather more accurate than I dared to admit. It read, "Not unintelligent, but talks too much. He also likes to be the centre of attention." Most football fans would agree that I was perfectly qualified to be a referee.

I wince at the memory of my first day at work in the Yorkshire County Savings Bank (now Lloyds TSB) in the High Street, Thornaby, just a few miles from Middlesbrough. It was a Tuesday, just after the August Bank Holiday, and I was tired when I arrived, having had very little sleep that weekend. I had arrived home late from the annual funfair at Eston Recreation Ground on Friday night to find the front door locked. Instead of knocking until I woke my parents and so face the inevitable leathering from my dad, I went down to the local café and spent the night drinking coffee with the various characters who assembled there on a regular basis. My mum was in tears with worry the next morning, and of course the punishment from my father had simply been postponed and not abandoned.

So it was hardly with the perfect preparation that a young, immature and rather nervous young man stepped, on 31 August 1971, into what was perceived to be the rather serious world of banking. I expected to be home at around 5pm, for the banks closed at 3.30pm. By lunchtime I was so tired that 5pm seemed a lifetime away. However, I knew that I would have perked up by late afternoon, for tea would be on the table, and Boro were at home to Sheffield Wednesday that evening. Boro had just signed John Craggs – many years later I was to run the line at his testimonial match – and I was looking forward to seeing our new full back in action.

What I didn't realise, however, was not only that Tuesday was the busiest day, because that's when the weekly accounts were done, but it was also the month end, and in the case of our bank, August was when the quarterly accounts were processed. That may seem unusual, but I distinctly remember that accounting dates were the ends of February, May, August and November. It was a stark welcome to the world of work, and the clock said 6.30pm by the time I rushed from the bank, scrambled on to the bus, and sprinted into the house to find my meal in the bin. My dad thought that I had deliberately come in late, having failed to learn the lesson of the previous Friday. I was sent straight to bed.

But the Boro beckoned, so I crept downstairs, slipped through the back door and scaled the wall in the yard, before running as fast as I could the mile or so to Ayresome Park. I can't remember whether or not I was punished when I got home, but it's a safe bet that I would have been. These days you would run to social services. But for all his failings my dad had his standards, even though they weren't mine. He was Victorian in his outlook, and dictated what we could and couldn't wear on a Sunday, as well as applying other rules and regulations. I didn't argue, possibly out of fear as much as respect. When I look back, I have some sympathy. Like all fathers he was of a different generation, but especially so in his case as he was so very much older than me. War years, two marriages, the death of a son, life in the forces, and his industrial injury had all taken their toll. In contrast I was doing well, with a respectable job and Charlton's Champions to watch. In the 1973–4 season I didn't miss a game, home or away.

My determination to see every game became a standing joke at the bank and Eric Andrew, the manager, reaped the benefits. In those days, whenever we drew in a cup game, the replay would take place three or four days later. I queued for tickets on the Sunday morning, and was in the bank bright and early on the Monday. I made coffee for the Eric, dealt with the post, and was a model of courtesy. After an hour or two he would say, "What time do you need to be away for the replay?" I don't know why he asked, because whatever time I said, he always let me go. He knew that wherever the Boro went, I went too, even, on one occasion, to a midweek cup tie in Portsmouth, despite it being a 650-mile round trip, with work in the morning. But I was not alone. If you weren't at a game you were considered to be either a swot or a freak. None of my gang ever came out with "I think I'll give this one a miss."

Police segregation at grounds back then wasn't the military operation it is today, and we took advantage of that. The thrill of fifty coachloads of fans converging on an away ground and piling into the "home" end never waned. It wasn't organised hooliganism, just spontaneous behaviour. I was once thrown out of a game at Ayresome Park. Police, in response to the increasing trouble which football was beginning to attract, had zoom-lens cameras fixed on sections of the crowd. They closed in on a group of us behind the goal, and while I can't recall doing anything more serious than messing around, I was ejected. Perhaps they felt they had to justify their new expensive camera equipment. I complained, but there was no point in arguing with them. I didn't dare tell my dad.

I suppose our "uniform" of scarves, hats, Ben Sherman shirts, Levi's trousers, Doc Marten boots, maybe a Crombie coat, and skinhead haircuts, immediately branded us. That was the intention, so I guess you had to take the rough with the smooth. Ironically, my dad thought that our football uniform was smart. Even acceptable for a Sunday!

The pride at following the Boro to one of the really big clubs beat any other feeling. I have always believed that you should support your local team. If you are from Darlington, then support Darlington; if fate decreed you be born in Rochdale, then Rochdale should be in your blood. So it was with Boro. But we were luckier than the small-town fans, for we got the chance to visit places like Highbury, Stamford Bridge and Old Trafford. The first time I went to the home of Manchester United was for a League Cup tie. We won 1–0 with a goal from Malcolm Smith. United had a big hooligan following at the time, and with this being a midweek game the Boro contingent was not as substantial as usual, though every member of my gang was there.

When we returned to board the four or five coaches that had made the trip, the windows were smashed, and a "welcome party" was awaiting us. We were seriously outnumbered, so we turned and ran. Three laps of Salford Docks later and we were clear of the United mafia. Dripping with sweat we jumped on to the coaches and endured a cold trip home as the wind roared in through the broken windows.

There are many occasions from my gang days that stick in my mind. I remember once hitch-hiking a lift to a game at Derby when I was ill with a nasty throat infection, and was taking antibiotics. A few days before the game it became clear that I was allergic to penicillin, for my condition suddenly worsened. I thought there was no chance of making the game, so I didn't book a seat on any of the coaches. But by Saturday morning the symptoms had eased a little, so I climbed out of my sick bed and hitched, getting there in time for kick-off. I spent the second half trying to scrounge a lift home, and was eventually promised a place in the back of a Transit van. I can't remember how many people were crammed in there, but we were like sardines. It's a good job the police didn't stop us. Even they wouldn't have believed how many people could fit in the back of a van.

I remember some classic matches too, including a 7–2 win over Chelsea. Our Irish winger Terry Cochrane shone that day, and became an instant hero of mine. These days we are colleagues on local radio, summarising at matches, and we fight like cat and dog. Another match that sticks in the mind is when we were 2–0 down to QPR around six minutes into the game, but roared back to win 6–2. I admit that sometimes I forgot the scrapes I got in, and the aggressive behaviour, and simply revelled in the joy that the team brought me.

We were genuine fans, but there was a clear divide between those who went on the official Supporters' Club coaches and those, like the boot boys, who booked their own coaches. Fans who travelled with the Supporters' Club were never involved in trouble. They parked up outside the ground, went in, watched the game, and travelled home. It was an unwritten rule at all clubs that the boot boys left them alone. That's another reason why I did not consider us to be hooligans. In later years, when hooliganism reached its height, nobody was safe, but that was not the case in our day.

We felt that we were carrying the reputation of our town. While the team battled for two points (as it was then) on the pitch, we fought for the pride of Middlesbrough. We did it by taking over the terraces by sheer weight of numbers, rather than by fighting. We would charge into the "home" end, drive the opposition fans back, and stand our ground. Games often took place with visiting and home fans in one end, with a line of coppers keeping each section apart. In between was the empty terrace of no-man's-land. Taunts and chants would fly from one section to the other, but it was very rare for a bottle or coins to be lobbed over the divide.

Often we were fuelled by drink, so no wonder we displayed a certain bravado. The police never checked the coaches for alcohol. Some of us would take strong cider, and others would be armed with bottles of Newcastle Brown Ale – in those days we thought that the ale was the only good thing to come out of Newcastle. Some of us still do. We took Tupperware jugs and at the back of the coach mixed the drinks into a cocktail known as a Snakebite. I was never a heavy drinker, but a few swigs of that stuff removed any inhibitions. When we reached our destination, we drove into terraced streets packed with coaches full of fellow Boro boot boys.

Along with my mate Tony Smith I organised our coach. We would collect the cash at the previous week's home game. The coach company we used was Begg's, the family firm of Barbara Begg, one of my colleagues at the bank. I was always worried that our escapades would filter back to her, but as we used the same driver week after week he almost became one of the lads and we knew we could trust him – at least in terms of keeping quiet.

The stops on the way home were pre-arranged with other coaches, so that we could all meet up, have a drink and admire the local talent of Doncaster or Sheffield when we came back up the A1, or Skipton when we had travelled to the north-west. But on one trip back from Norwich, the coach driver, Ken, suggested Newark for our stop. He said that when he was stationed there in the war women outnumbered men by two to one. It was probably true, because there was still a saying at the time that there were many more women than men in Nottinghamshire. So that settled it. Newark it was.

It was a mistake. Not only was there a large gypsy encampment on the outskirts, with most of them in town for a Saturday night drink, but a sizeable contingent of Newark's Irish population were out on the town too. Not to mention that several coaches of Nottingham Forest fans had stopped off on the way home from a game. There were only fifty of us, and we split up to go into different pubs. We didn't last long. We shot out of the pubs quicker than we went in, and scrambled back on the bus. It was the last time we listened to Ken.

Whenever we arrived at our stops we would meet up with fans from all parts of Teesside – Redcar, Billingham, Stockton, South Bank. Our gang was called the Central Boro crew. When enough of us travelled, especially on reasonably short journeys to Blackpool, Preston and Hull, we took over the pubs in the town. The police presence was there, but they never tried to keep fans out of the pubs, and were only concerned with preventing trouble on the streets. In any case, the beer tasted weak compared to the Snakebites. Then it was off to the ground in chanting hordes, the noise reverberating along the terraced streets.

The home fans would arrive in dribs and drabs, so it was easy to take over their end of the ground, especially given there could be over two thousand of us. But sometimes we made mistakes. At Sheffield Wednesday we once arrived at the ground around an hour before kick-off. Although there were around five hundred of us, half went into the Leppings Lane End, and the other half, including me, made for the huge Kop behind the opposite goal. Normally when we charged in from one side, the home fans would run the other way. But Wednesday's terrace is huge. Gradually the Wednesday fans collected behind us at the back of the terrace. When there were enough of them they charged down. It's very hard to defend yourself from an attack from above. We suffered a heavy defeat, and while I escaped relatively unscathed a few of our lads, who didn't retreat quickly enough, took a beating.

The Wednesday lads had been a step ahead of us, and we learnt from that. Shortly afterwards we tried to take the Fulwell End at

Sunderland, which was a bit ambitious even for our hardy crew, despite the pre-planning. But we wanted to have the notoriety of at least having a major presence in the home end of our biggest rivals. We hid our red and white scarves, which were normally tied round our wrists, and queued for the Fulwell End turnstiles. The plan was to congregate at the back right of the terrace, then swoop as the Wednesday fans had done.

But we had overlooked one thing. In the northern part of Teesside, around Billingham in particular, there is a strong base of Sunderland fans. They had got wind of our scheme, and were ready for us. They had deliberately got to the ground early, and attacked while half of us were still queuing outside the stadium. I was one of the ones outside, and heard a sudden roar as the fight broke out. The Boro fans were in the minority. Our aerial position was no advantage against such weight of numbers. Fortunately not many of our lads were hurt, as the police (who were a major presence, given it was a derby game) quickly stepped in. Our fans were led away and Sunderland could claim a major victory. Sunderland still had to come to Ayresome Park, however. Away fans who travelled to Boro often came by train, and faced quite a long walk, much of it through terraced streets. They had to run the gauntlet as Boro fans ambushed them from pubs and back alleys.

We were tough, but so were other fans, and West Ham was the toughest trip of all. Our buses used to stop near King's Cross, and we had to make our own way to Upton Park. There was safety in numbers to an extent, but tube travel was alien to us and made me feel uneasy. Opposing fans would ask what time it was, just so that they could check our accents. I was always relieved to get away from the underground and back on to the streets, though the East End streets and markets felt more alien than any other away territory.

Even when we arrived unscathed back at King's Cross, there were times when Millwall, Chelsea or Spurs fans were waiting. We were impressed with the West Ham fans who came to Ayresome, because they were so well organised. Their Inter City Firm had almost military organisation. They stayed tight-knit and held their ranks. They set the standard in boot-boy behaviour, which was now taking on a whole new dimension and moving towards what I have earlier described as hooliganism. We began to discuss our behaviour in a serious way. I remember one lad suggesting that we should organise ourselves properly as hooligans. A season or so earlier we would have laughed at him, but he was right. The boot-boy culture was changing, and I began to distance myself from it.

Travelling changed too, because the police became organised and would no longer let us stop on the way home, except when approved by them. Motorway services started displaying signs saying that football coaches could stop only by appointment, while a police presence began to appear on motorway slip roads to stop coaches calling into towns. My time as a boot boy was coming to an end, and perhaps with a new era on the horizon, it was just as well.

My dad's health was in decline. He was increasingly house-bound, more morose and wrapped up in his own problems. Much of my mum's time was spent looking after him. I cannot fault her. She stood by her man. But I was looking to spread my wings away from home. One night when I went to Dorman Long social club, where my mates and I would head to every Friday evening, I met a sixteen-year-old girl, Elaine. Many years later, on the after-dinner speaking circuit, I met up with some of the entertainers who used to perform at the Dorman Long club. A lot of them are still in the business, doing the circuit.

Elaine and I formed more than a passing relationship, as we married three years later. Looking back on it we were incredibly young to be making such a commitment. Even though three years is a long time to be together, I was no more mature than she was, even though I was three years older. As a child Elaine had everything I didn't. Her family of mum, dad, grandparents and brother were very close-knit, something I envied. She lived in a semi-detached house in Linthorpe around a mile from where we set up home together after marrying in November 1977.

I picked the wedding date to coincide with a break in domestic football, because England were playing Italy in midweek. But for some reason Boro rearranged a game – on my wedding day. It crossed my mind to postpone the wedding, but that was an argument I would definitely have lost so I had to miss the match. The wedding memories are hazy now, but Boro beat Aston Villa 1–0 with a Stan Cummins goal. Elaine and I went to London for our honeymoon, and I took her to see England at Wembley, where Kevin Keegan and Trevor Brooking scored in a 2–1 win.

The maturity required for married life led to me settling down. The wild, skinhead football fan who lived on the edge of the law – and sometimes beyond the edge – had turned his back on the crazy days. Well, almost. Even though my days as a regular Boro fan were drifting towards an end, I will never forget the gang I travelled to matches with. Some of them are still going to games together.

Kenny Hall was one of them, but as was the case with me, his early years did nothing to harm him, and he ended up as leader of Middlesbrough Council shortly before "Zero Tolerance" police officer Ray Mallon was elected mayor of the town. Dicky Dotchin and Stevo were two more of the lads I remember, and the last I heard of Stevo was that he had got a two-year banning order following Boro's first game in the UEFA Cup at Banik Ostrava in September 2004. That was the first time his name had cropped up in many a year, and all I can say is that he had a good run for his money before the authorities finally caught up with him. Sadly, one of the lads, Shaun Simpson, was killed in a car accident while travelling to watch a game.

Another, who, like me, had been a Boro fan from as early as he could remember, died in his mid-40s. His name was Eric Robinson, but he became known as Ernie Ragbo. That's what the rag and bone men, so commonplace in our youth, used to shout. At least that's it what it sounded like when they rode into the streets on their carts shouting "Any rags or bones". When a memorial trip for Ernie was held at a working men's club near Villa Park a dozen coaches full of his fellow fans arrived to raise a glass or three in his memory, before spilling out of the club and making their way to the game. I would have loved to have been with that throng of forty-somethings. I was refereeing somewhere, though my heart was at Villa that day.

Another of the lads was Frankie Bam Bam, famed for being the loudest supporter imaginable. I know for a fact that he still goes to games. I've heard him! I remember him being arrested at one game, but by the time he came to court, he had "lost" his loud voice, limped in, and told a sob story. It worked, and he escaped with a light fine. No doubt by the Saturday he was back to full volume and fearsome appearance.

These were salt of the earth people and no different from me. We loved football then, and those of us still around do now. And we loved the town of Middlesbrough.

And yes, I did join in with the singing of "The referee's a bastard".

2

TAKING UP THE WHISTLE

A mong my key tasks at the bank was establishing good rela-
tionships with customers, a job made considerably easier if
they shared my love of football. One such regular visitor was
Tommy Harper from the North Riding Football Association. He
was the secretary of the County Association, running it not from
some plush office, but from the front room of his house. After I
was married he gave me a terrible ribbing about the responsibility
of running a home and paying a mortgage, and how it was incompatible with being a diehard Boro fan.

I smiled back and took it in good heart, especially after it
dawned on me that he was a good means of obtaining a cup final
ticket, or a ticket to an England international. If Boro ever reached
the FA Cup or League Cup final, then Tommy would perhaps be
able to sort me out, and save me the trouble of queuing up with
thousands of other supporters. Unfortunately I never got the opportunity, because Boro never got to either major final until 1997, and
by then I was a top referee and could get my own tickets. Every time

Tommy came into the bank, we chatted about football, from the latest Boro performance to the previous night's results.

One day, there had been a highly controversial decision by a referee in a game on television – I can't remember which match – and after Tommy and I debated it, he said, "Look, why don't you think about becoming a referee?" The idea appealed to me. I wasn't doing too well in my own playing career. In fact that was an understatement. I started the 1978–9 season on the bench for my Sunday team, St Cuthbert's Boys' Club, not that we were boys any more. I'm sure I'm not the only married man to play for a boys' club, but it can't be common. As it became obvious that we weren't going to win the league – or finish in the top six for that matter – the better players drifted away, which meant me being picked to play. But whenever a cup tie came along, like the prodigal sons those better players returned, and I was back on the substitutes' bench. It quickly dawned on me that I was only making the numbers up.

There were other factors in my decision to take Tommy's suggestion seriously. I was now in my early twenties, the tearaway days were over, and the skinhead look had long gone. The thrill of going to Boro away games wasn't as great, because I had been to most of the grounds at least once before – though I was still going to every home game. What's more, in the late seventies, the likelihood of being unwittingly involved in trouble at football grounds had greatly increased. By now it was a blight on football, and there was an air of hostility at some away grounds that was off-putting. The number of hardened trouble-makers was growing.

So, encouraged by Tommy, I went along to a referees' course, which was organised by two local referees, Dave Bodley and Peter

Baldwin. The meetings were mainly about the laws of the game, with illustrations and explanations about certain situations on the pitch. One week, Dave wasn't at the course, and when I got home and put on *Sportsnight* I realised why. There he was running the line (if memory serves me correctly) at Leeds United. I was most impressed, being able to speak to people like Dave one week, and then see him on television the next.

In early 1979, I passed my first referee's exam in Peter Baldwin's front room, in Kirkleatham Lane, Redcar. Nothing too difficult, just questions about pitch dimensions, the air pressure in the ball, the offside law and pitch markings. I was now a Class 3 referee, although what I was going to do with this new qualification I didn't rightly know. I'd been on the course and enjoyed it, but I hadn't considered whether to take it any further.

I must admit that I became a bit of a bore to my friends at Boro matches. Earlier I had lambasted the referee, just like most other supporters, at every opportunity when he'd made a decision that had gone against us. But now I defended him because I could see the reasoning behind his decisions. My stance didn't go down too well with the rest of the lads, because they couldn't agree with me. Not all the people on the course with me were from a football background. There were people from the Duke of Edinburgh award scheme and schoolteachers, who used a referee's qualification to pursue their own careers outside football.

The day after I passed my exam, and was wondering what I was going to do with this piece of paper, I received a phone call from a chap called Harry Bage – nicknamed "Old Blue Eyes" – of the North Riding FA.

"Here are the details of a game you're refereeing this Saturday," he said in an abrupt manner.

"What game?" I asked.

"You've just qualified as a referee, haven't you? Well, here's a game you can do on Saturday."

I thought, I can't do it, Boro are at home. I'm not going to miss a Boro game.

"I'm sorry," I blurted out. "I'm not available this Saturday. I've got family commitments."

There was an explosion at the other end of the phone.

"Not available! I hope you're not one of these timewasters who come on a course, gain the qualification and then disappear. Do you want to be a referee or not?"

"Well, yes I do," I whimpered.

"If you can't make it Saturday, I'll put you down for a Sunday game. Yarm versus Cleveland Nomads."

"OK, then, thank you," I said, realising that my refereeing career was about to start, and I could still watch the Boro. Harry sent me the details in the post, and that essential piece of refereeing kit, a notebook. But I didn't have any other kit, so I went to the local sports shop and bought a black top, shorts and socks, as well as a whistle. Fully kitted out and feeling both proud and nervous, I took charge of the Cleveland Sunday League Division Four game between the unsuspecting Yarm FC and Cleveland Nomads, at the Harold Wilson Recreation Ground in Thornaby on Sunday 4 February 1979.

Yarm won 6–2, and you may, or may not, be surprised to hear that I didn't caution anyone or send anybody off. I was behind play most of the time. Along with all twenty-two players I chased the ball around the park, and there were several times when I found myself in the wrong half of the field when a player was running with the ball into the other penalty area. At that level, there were no linesmen to give offsides, just the team secretary or a substitute waving a flag when the ball went out of play. So I had to make offside decisions when I was sixty or seventy yards behind play, and with no idea of whether the player involved was offside or not. But there were no big arguments over any of my decisions, and I felt that my refereeing debut had been a good one.

I ambled through another five games in the Middlesbrough and District Sunday Morning League without a booking. Harry's notebook remained unopened. Some of my decisions were disputed though, especially those regarding offside. My positioning was poor, but I managed to stand my ground. "He was at least two yards off," I used to say as I ran away from the incident, which from fifty yards away was taking keen observation to the extreme.

I pulled my notebook out of my pocket for the first time in the sixth game I refereed, Grangefield Youth Club versus Yarm FC, when two players had a punch-up in the middle of the pitch. In the next game, I sent off a chap called Malcolm Lambert of St Alphonsus for persistent misconduct – he was later to become a senior referee in the Northern League.

By the end of the season, I'd refereed thirty games, cautioned thirteen players and dismissed five. I mixed with a lot of other referees, especially at Prissick Base ground in Middlesbrough, where there were ten pitches, all of them in use on Sunday mornings. It was here that I met more senior referees, who officiated in the Northern League and Central League, as well as Bernard Eland and Stuart Loudon, both Football League linesmen. Bernard took me under his wing and persuaded me to attend a Middlesbrough Referees' Society meeting, where I was made to feel part of the refereeing fraternity, even though I was a first-year novice. That helped my career, and I was given my first cup final appointment at the end of that season, the Teesside and Cleveland Junior League Under-18 section final, at Smiths Dock Park.

Much to my surprise, I was given the luxury of two linesmen. But I forgot to use them because I was so accustomed to making offside decisions on my own. It was only after I had made a couple of decisions, probably dodgy ones, that I noticed the quizzical look on the face of the linesman on the far side. His face betrayed his feelings: "Why is he ignoring me? What's the point of me being here?" It was at that point that I realised we should be a team of three. I sheepishly apologised to them at half-time.

I was also appointed linesman for a cup semi-final at the Dorman Long ground. The pitch was adjacent to the clubhouse, which gave the drinkers an excuse to take their glasses out of the club and stand next to the pitch, watching the game. The pitch was roped off in order to stop spectators encroaching on to the field, but there were so many of them that they climbed over the rope and stood three deep all the way along the touchline. So as well as watching for offsides, I had to ask the crowd to stand back so I could see when the ball had gone out of play. However, the crowd slowly edged towards the pitch again, and I had to watch where I was going.

I knocked one chap out of the way "accidentally" and he fell over, spilling his drink and prompting a few laughs from his mates. On the next occasion I ran towards him, he took a swipe at me, and knocked me over. There were more laughs. And on the third occasion, I timed my run perfectly and knocked him flat with a shoulder charge! It was just like being part of the Boro travelling hordes when we were taking over the home end. I can't remember who was refereeing, but the man in charge made a point of asking club officials to make sure that the spectators stood well back from the touchline for their own safety – which was just as well, because my assailant could have ended up with a couple of broken bones if he'd continued to block my way.

I accepted a couple of Saturday games, when Boro were at the opposite end of the country, but clearly if I wanted to progress, then I would have to sacrifice more Saturdays to refereeing, which put me in a dilemma. Would I have to give up my place on the Ayresome Park terraces and on the bus to away matches? After some soul-searching I did, and in August 1980, I accepted a game at ICI Wilton in the Teesside Junior Alliance, the same day as a Boro home game. I lived in Acklam – which is to the south of Middlesbrough – at the time, and to reach Wilton's ground meant that I would have to drive past Ayresome Park. It was a real test of my ambition and determination to progress as a referee.

The Boro fans were starting to gather around the ground and nearby pubs, and I could see the red and white scarves, the programme sellers, and one or two familiar faces. I slowed down because I could feel the tug on my heartstrings, and was tempted to pull over into one of the side streets, park up and go to the game. But, in a defining moment in my life, I put my foot down, picked up speed and turned my back on the previous fifteen years spent following the Boro – probably the wisest decision I'd ever made. The bond was broken, at least as far as watching them every week was concerned.

I took every opportunity to referee, so much so that I was in charge of four games every weekend. I was involved in a few incidents, one in particular in a stormy game in the Teesside and Cleveland Junior League game. It was a bad-tempered affair from the first whistle, and I sent off a couple of players. I was then verbally abused by another – I think he called me a bastard or something like that – and I called him over to me.

"Name?" I asked.

"Selwyn Froggitt," he replied. Selwyn Froggitt was a character played by Bill Maynard in a television sitcom at the time.

"I don't think that's your real name. What is it?"

"Selwyn Froggitt."

"All right, then, Mr Froggitt, you're in trouble for swearing at me."

So "Selwyn Froggitt" was reported to North Riding FA. He turned out to be the brother of a referee in our branch!

I quickly learnt that being called a "bastard" was one of the nicest things a player could say about a referee. In a perverse way, it showed that they respected my authority.

The walls of some dressing rooms were paper thin, and when players saw me arriving for a game I could hear them say, "Oh no, it's that bastard again," which probably meant they had learnt from their previous misdemeanours.

As a referee, you need a firm, unwavering approach. But on one occasion I changed my mind about taking a player's name.

It was a freezing grey day with a bitter, biting wind, on an exposed pitch in the Cleveland League. But duty dictated that I should book a player in one of the pub teams for persistent misconduct.

"What's your name?" I asked, having explained why I wanted to know.

"Propacawicz." (Or that's how it sounded to me.)

"Sorry, can you repeat that."

"Pro-pa-ca-wicz."

I started writing his name in my notebook.

"No, that's wrong," the player said.

Three attempts later, and only up to the sixth or seventh letter in his surname, I put my notebook away. My hands were turning blue with the cold, and I could hardly grip my pencil.

"Let this be your last warning. No more fouls."

The refereeing fraternity continued to encourage me, and Bernard Eland and Stuart Loudon invited me on a training night with them. Training? What was training? I figured that I was fit enough simply by running around for ninety minutes in four games every weekend. Bernard and Stuart suggested that we did a few laps of Nunthorpe Athletic's pitch to warm up. I quickly lagged behind, and after a couple of laps, I was blowing out of my backside, and stopped. They kept going for at least another six laps, before they started doing some more exercises, while I continued to gasp for breath. I had learnt a valuable lesson. You have to get fit to referee, not referee to get fit. If I was to progress up the ladder, training was paramount, as I was to find out.

Another boost to my career came from George Courtney, who in the early eighties was one of the top refs in the world. He came to one of our Society's meetings, and I was introduced to him. "Keep working hard, and always do what you think is right," he told me. Simple advice, but invaluable. I bet George didn't have the same claim to fame as I did, however, when shortly afterwards, I booked three people from the same family – brothers David and Derek Parry, and their cousin Ronnie Parry. Was it the first time three members of the same family had been booked in a game? It could have earned me a place in the *Guinness Book of Records*.

It's funny how you meet people you know on a football pitch. On one occasion I had a lad at my house to repair the roof. After he had worked on it for a couple of evenings, he said that he wouldn't be there the following night because he was playing football. It suited me, I told him, because I had a game to referee. When I turned up, there was the repairman playing for one of the teams. We exchanged pleasantries. In the second half, there was an incident involving the repairman, and I decided I had no choice but to send him off. I called him over.

"Name?"

"You know my fucking name – and the cost of my fine is going on your repair bill!" he stormed.

He turned up to finish the job the following night, and it's fair to say that there was a bit of an awkward atmosphere. But we shook hands and I remain friends with Geoff Smith to this day – but I checked the roof for leaks for days afterwards.

Under that roof I now had a pregnant wife. Not only was I focused on becoming a successful referee but I was about to become a family man. Who would have thought it? I was working in a bank, and had become an authority figure at weekends, while my wife was employed in a library – though she was a fun-loving girl and not the sort you visualise working in such a hushed atmosphere. The arrival of Emma in January 1981 brought us immense joy. I was on cloud nine as I brought them home, and was thinking only of the two girls in my life.

Elaine was happy that I was out of the house refereeing at weekends, and not travelling with the Boro to away games, with the risk that I might get up to my bad old ways. Refereeing was time-consuming, and gardening, washing the car and the chores of weekend suburban life were not for me. These jobs were squeezed in only when absolutely necessary and when I couldn't get out of them. Elaine supported me as I chased my dreams. She accepted that I had to train, and even encouraged me to do so. She was equally enthusiastic that I should attend meetings as well as throw my heart and soul into match day duties. With hindsight, I can see it must have been tough for her, with me so focused on my career.

Without the support of Elaine, and her willingness to run the family, I would never have progressed as far as I did. With Emma just a few months old, I achieved a major ambition, when on 12 April 1981 I officiated at my spiritual home of Ayresome Park.

The ground had been chosen for the North Riding Junior Cup

final between Nunthorpe and Whinney Banks. I think I was even more cock-a-hoop than the star-struck young players.

With an immense feeling of pride I walked up the tunnel and on to the pitch. I could see the places where I used to stand with my mates. I imagined I was taking a penalty in front of the Holgate End. I sat in the manager's seat in the dugout – I was just like a kid, wide-eyed and revelling in every second. Nunthorpe won 1–0, and my concentration on the line was 100 per cent. Well, almost.

In September 1981, the door to a higher level opened when I was appointed as a linesman in the Northern Intermediate League, in which the youth sides of the professional clubs played. Sometimes games were staged on training grounds, but on other occasions, such as the derby games involving Sunderland, Newcastle and Middlesbrough, the first-team ground was used. York City staged their games at Clifton Hospital, a home for the mentally handicapped, and one day when I was on linesman duty, Leeds United were the visitors.

Spectators and residents under supervision were allowed to watch games, which nobody minded, especially when a big club like Leeds was involved. During the first half, I could see out of the corner of my eye that one of the residents was watching me closely, particularly when I raised my flag for offside, and laughing loudly. Obviously I was a great source of amusement for him. In the second half, the same chap decided to imitate me. I heard a huge shriek behind me – and there he was, trousers down, holding up his own version of a linesman's flag. The game suddenly stopped, and a nurse escorted him away.

I once committed the unforgivable sin of forgetting an item of kit, my referee's socks. It was too late to dash back home and find them, so I had to wear a pair of old red Boro socks that I always wore underneath my refereeing pair. George Courtney had told me to wear two pairs to make my boots feel more comfortable and limit the risk of blisters. But as I had only my Boro socks, it eroded my authority. I couldn't caution or send anybody off, because spectators and players were saying after each decision: "Are you sure ref? You couldn't even remember your socks!" That was a lesson to me. It is important for a referee to command respect.

Sometimes Sunday morning matches could not start on time, because some players were still recovering from the night before, and teams arrived late. That was the case for a game at Head Wrightsons, who were a big local firm with their own football team, run by Tommy Osborne and Dave English, two committed lads. Tommy's son Wayne went on to play in the Football League for York City. I arrived at the ground at about 10 o'clock for a 10.30 kick-off, and started to get changed. I noticed there were a few balls in the corner of the room. I popped outside to have a chat with someone, and then close to kick-off time, there was only one thing missing – the match ball. I asked Tommy where it was. He shrugged:

"I don't know, ref. Can't lay my hands on it."

"Have you got a spare one? I thought I saw one in my changing room when I got here."

"No, I can't find any at all," came the reply.

There were a couple of practice balls, but the plastic coverings were peeling away, and they clearly weren't suitable.

"Come on, Tommy, you must have a good one somewhere."

Kick-off was by now ten minutes overdue, and one team was very keen to get under way. A few minutes later, Dave English arrived in his car. Out jumped two of his star players – who were clearly the worse for wear – and then he opened his car boot and threw me a ball. "Sorry, ref, must have picked it up by mistake." I couldn't prove that he hadn't done it deliberately to ensure that he had a full complement of players in his side. But I had no doubt that he was guilty.

By now I was gaining increasing respect with the football authorities, either for my dedication in doing four games every weekend, or because I was officiating well. Maybe it was a combination of both. The 1980–1 season ended with another cup final, the North Riding Junior Cup final, Whinney Banks versus Billingham Social, again at Ayresome Park. One of the players was Mark Hine, who went on to play professionally for Darlington, Grimsby and Peterborough. Little was I to know that I would be following in his footsteps into the Football League a few years later.

In the summer of 1982, I was given my first appointment in the Northern League, the most senior league in the North East. I was linesman for the Tow Law against Evenwood fixture. I hadn't been to Tow Law before, but the ground is said to be one of the highest in England at around eleven hundred feet. I didn't know the Tow Law weather was legendary. There had been many occasions when a player had to be treated for exposure in the icy winds, and Mansfield Town found out to their cost that you can't automatically expect to beat a non-league team on their own pitch in the wind and snow when they visited Tow Law in the sixties. They lost 5–1 in an FA Cup tie.

It was a warm sunny day when I set off from Middlesbrough, and the drive up the Pennines to Tow Law – which is about a dozen miles north-east of Bishop Auckland in County Durham – was quite pleasant. However, when I arrived in the hilltop town, there was a marked drop in temperature. There were one or two knowing looks among the fans as they stood on the terraces gazing across the valley. Twenty minutes into the game, the fog came down, and what had started as a nice sunny afternoon became a pea-souper. We could hardly see, but managed to finish the game. "Just wait till you come back up here in December, lad," said one of the locals. "Bring your woollies."

Chris Waddle, later to play for Newcastle, Spurs, Marseilles and England, started his career on the sloping pitch at Ironworks Road, Tow Law, and maybe those freezing conditions toughened him up for so many years in the professional game. I certainly went prepared for future games there.

A few weeks after that, I fell foul of the footballing authorities when I abandoned a Sunday game out of sympathy. The match was between Ossie's Bar and Lindin, and after seventy-seven minutes, with the score 14–0 to Ossie's Bar and some of the Lindin players on the verge of walking off out of sheer frustration, I abandoned the game, much to the annoyance of the Ossie's Bar players. I was carpeted by North Riding FA, and even though I protested that if I hadn't abandoned the game when the fourteenth goal went in then I might have had to call a halt anyway if the

Lindin players had walked off, I was given a rollicking. Rules have to be applied whatever the circumstances.

In November 1982, I was asked to run the line in another game at Ayresome Park, this time for John Craggs's testimonial. John was one of my heroes, a solid, tough-tackling full back who never gave anything away, and was a member of the promotion-winning side under Jack Charlton. There was a big crowd for the game between Boro and an all-stars eleven, and even though David Hodgson, who had just been transferred to Liverpool, scored a hat trick on his return to Ayresome Park, the game was more remembered for an eye injury to Kevin Keegan after a collision with Boro's Darren Wood. Keegan was worried for a few days afterwards that he might lose his sight, and the story made national headlines.

I was soon back at Ayresome, but I took my life in my hands with my timing. The football fan in me still ran deep, and resurfaced when my first son, Craig, was born. It was New Year's Day 1983 when I proudly brought Elaine and Craig home from Middlesbrough Maternity Unit at around noon. As soon as they settled into the house, I rushed off to watch Boro at home to Leeds, as I had no refereeing duties. We lived in a three-bedroomed semi-detached house, within walking distance of Ayresome Park. I remember the score – a dire 0–0 draw – but I don't recall Elaine's reaction to my hasty exit.

At the start of the 1983–4 season I was appointed as a referee to the Northern Intermediate League. The league was very strong in those days. Middlesbrough had youngsters Tony Mowbray and Gary Pallister in defence, while Leeds had Denis Irwin and Scott

Sellars, who was the best player I had ever refereed at the time, because of his speed and wonderful left foot. These games were easier to control than those in the local Middlesbrough leagues. The professional lads didn't play kick and rush. Instead, they allowed the ball to do the work, so it was easier to position myself, unlike with the part-time games, in which players were mainly happy to thump the ball forward and chase after it.

Another promotion followed in season 1984–5, this time into the Northern League middle. My first game was a 2–0 home defeat for Ferryhill against North Shields, but my second was between two of the top teams in the league, Spennymoor and Blyth. The two teams enjoyed a keen rivalry – between them they had won the Northern League regularly in previous years. Maybe being given the game was a test of my character from Northern League secretary Gordon Nicholson, who was no shrinking violet. I received many similar appointments from him and we developed a lasting friendship.

Big crowds followed Northern League football, because clubs included several ex-professionals, like former Leeds and Burnley striker Ray Hankin, and hardened Northern League veterans in their line-ups. Play was therefore of a good standard, and offered a steep learning curve for me. They were tough men, playing with passion, and the referee was under a lot of pressure to get decisions right, then hold his nerve after he had made them.

Referees don't like to send players off in pre-season friendlies, but I was left with no option in August 1984 at a game between Stockton and a Middlesbrough select eleven. Boro sent some first-team players, but I had to dismiss one of them, Steve Corden, for spitting. I had no alternative because spitting is a sending-off offence no matter how minor the game. Afterwards, representatives of both clubs tried to persuade me not to submit the paperwork to North Riding FA, but I was adamant. I had seen the incident, as had plenty of spectators, so had to apply the laws of the game. Poor Steve had a bad week, because days later he suffered an awful injury against Wimbledon that eventually ended his professional career.

It was around this time, as I was making my early tentative steps through the ranks, that I first became aware that the game was not always as well run by the authorities as it should have been. I refereed a county cup final, sponsored by Guinness, who provided sufficient funds for the event to be run well. But in the post-match presentations, it suddenly dawned on organisers that they hadn't ordered trophies for the referee and linesmen. So for appearances' sake, we stepped up, shook hands, and were each handed one of the medals for the losing team. We received them in one hand, and gave them back with the other, so that each could be presented to a player. Along with my linesmen, I was only too happy to help disguise this particular cock-up. But it was eighteen months before we finally got our mementos. While I can live with shoddy organisation, of which this was an example, I can't accept rules being twisted or overlooked to suit those in the corridors of power. At an inter-county youth match between the East Riding of Yorkshire and County Durham at North Ferriby I got my first real experience of the latter.

The Durham team turned up late, though it was not the fault of the players. These impressionable young lads were joined on the team bus by the county officials, who in those days formed the controlling bodies of the County Football Associations, and were basically a law unto themselves. It was evident that the alcohol had been flowing, because when the team sheet arrived late, it was handed to me by a chap in a suit, whose red face was caused by more than embarrassment. The team sheet was meant to be in an hour before kick-off, but by the time the team arrived there was barely time for the players to get changed. And when they did take the field, their shirt numbers did not correspond to the team sheet.

It was clear that this was more a day out for the big-wigs within the county FA than it was for the young players. The players conducted themselves properly, their bosses less so. After returning home I brought the matter to the attention of the county secretary, who had to deal with breaches of rules and discipline. He thanked me and said he would call me back. A few minutes later he did. He again thanked me, but asked me not to take it any further and said he had sorted it out. The matter was swiftly dropped. Yet if a pub team, struggling financially, had turned up late, they would have been handed a heavy fine for breaking the rules. I said no more about it, and as appointments kept coming my way, I knuckled down to doing the job as well as I possibly could.

Football is at the centre of many communities, and that was brought home to me when I was linesman for Frickley against Boston in the FA Cup in 1985. Frickley was a mining town in South Yorkshire and, at the time, the miners in that area were on strike. As I drove into the area, I could feel the tension. There was an air of uncertainty, maybe even fear, as to what the future held.

For these were people who might lose not only their jobs, but also their whole way of life.

I could identify with them, for the residents of the mining towns of South Yorkshire shared a lifestyle with the steelworkers of Teesside, of which my dad was a part. There was pride in their work and way of life. To have that ripped away by government policy was bound to cause resentment that ran deep. Against that backdrop, a non-league football match seemed insignificant, though it wasn't. It was the sort of occasion where, for a couple of hours, other problems could be put to the back of the mind. Or so I thought.

As feelings were running so high at the time, it was decided that there should be no police presence at the game, because the police had borne the brunt of much of the anger for protecting strike-breakers as they made their way to work. The atmosphere was tense during the first half, and at half-time a fight broke out in the main stand between those who were supporting the strike and those who weren't. The police had to be called, and the fighting intensified, though the game continued. Those incidents brought home to me how deep-rooted the social problems were in that era.

I was learning all the time, and my climb up the ladder was set to continue – assuming I could satisfy the dreaded assessor in the stand, a figure held in awe by even the most senior referees, whether they admit it or not.

3

CUPS, KIPPERS
AND BAKED BEANS

As I never wished to be far from sporting activities, I ambled up the road the few hundred yards from my house to the cricket ground at Acklam Park. It was a warm summer's afternoon, the gentle breeze stirring the garden plants, creating just enough movement to test the agility of the bees as they attempted to land on the nodding flowers. This area of Middlesbrough, with its tidy semi-detached houses, most with neatly edged lawns and lush herbaceous borders, is a far cry from the image that southerners have of our town. In Acklam there is no glint of the sun off the steelworks, nor, today at least, did the sulphurous smell of the chemical works mingle with the scent of the flowers.

Despite moving upmarket from Jedburgh Street, I had no desire to forget my roots, or turn my back on friends I had grown up with. I was in fine spirits, and all seemed well with the world. In my world all was indeed well – a few days before-hand I had received the letter informing me that I had been promoted to become a Football League linesman. It was the summer of 1986.

The perfect way to relax in the knowledge that I was on the up, was to soak up the sun from the terraces of the cricket ground, watching Yorkshire in action in their annual visit to Middlesbrough for a county match. The sound of willow on leather was broken by a familiar voice. "Hello Jeff," it said. "Congratulations, you bugger. I knew you'd make it."

Shielding my eyes from the sun, I put a face to the name. It was Geoff Lilley, a typically robust local league footballer, who had given me loads of trouble over the years. But he was also an excellent player, who had once been on Nottingham Forest's books. I wonder what legendary Forest manager Brian Clough, a fellow Smoggy, made of him. Geoff's name had appeared in my notebook many times, and arguments between us, during and after games, had been frequent. Because of that I thought his cheery blessing at my promotion might have been tongue-in-cheek. On more than one occasion he had called me a "useless bastard" yet here he was showering me with praise.

He was genuine, though, his good wishes being an indication of the warmth that people had for me in the area. Middlesbrough, despite being a big town, is a close-knit community, and the people are good-hearted. They love to see one of their own prosper. No doubt Geoff would watch me on the television in future years, turn to his friends and take some of the credit for me being at the top of the refereeing tree. And I wouldn't begrudge him that view, because it is partially true. Dealing with tough, uncompromising North East lads who played hard was a harsh lesson, and one I had to pass if I was to head onward and upward.

The reaction of Geoff made me realise that I had served my apprenticeship, part of which was being verbally abused and laughed at. But that's all in the game for a referee and, for the most part, I had brushed it off without a second thought. Just as well, for there was plenty more of the same awaiting me. Coping with the hostility of places in the lower leagues and at regional level is a vital part of a ref's education, because it gets a whole lot more intimidating at the top.

The professional game was now opening up in front of me. Three of us were promoted from the North Riding FA at the same time, the other two being Terry Lynch and Paul Henderson. We had been picked out on the basis of our match markings from clubs, and occasional visits from assessors. At local league level, assessors didn't go to every game, but you were still under the spotlight. Each league and the county football association compiled the marks, based on what clubs put on the match report forms that they all had to fill in. Sometimes, marks would be quite good from both clubs, but if one of them felt aggrieved that I'd sent somebody off, or made a bad decision, I risked the dreaded zero. Fortunately that didn't happen to me many times.

The assessor is invariably an ex-referee. Assessors exist at all levels of football and are charged with monitoring each referee's performance by writing a brief report on the ref's fitness, positioning, management of players and application of the law. While each club also writes a brief report, or gives the ref a mark (out of 10) for his performance, their comments are often influenced by the result. The assessor, by contrast, is supposed to provide an independent, informed view.

The County FA usually asked a club why it had given a referee a zero mark, and that would prompt them to reconsider – and to save them having to file a long report they would usually give the referee a mark of one or two instead, but begrudgingly. Whichever team won tended to award a far higher mark than that given by officials of the losing side. That's hardly surprising. If you lose, you scratch around for excuses, and the man in the middle is an easy target. Blame him, and you don't have to look at the deficiencies of your own team. Of course I had done it countless times myself when I was young, and the Boro lost. I would often storm back into the house, and mutter, "Bloody referee." Mum and Dad would glance up at me, knowing there was no need to ask what the result was. But football is a matter of opinion, and it would be poorer if this weren't the case. If every issue were black and white, there wouldn't be half as much banter and passion in the game. It did occasionally occur to me that a high mark from the local league side might not in fact be a reflection of how well I had performed. Some clubs no doubt wanted me promoted, so that they didn't have to put up with me again.

Whatever the whys and wherefores, things were going well for me. When the news broke about my promotion, many people congratulated me, and there was an article about Terry, Paul and me in the *Evening Gazette*, our local newspaper. Maybe that's where Geoff Lilley read about it. When the media takes an interest in your early career, all is sweetness and light. But as many a footballer and celebrity has found, if you stay in the spotlight you're there to be knocked down. However, at that stage of my career, the spotlight was a wonderful place to be. My ambitions were starting to change and grow. Not only did I feel that I could do a good job running the line in the Football League, I wanted to go higher, and be the man in the middle. I knew that I would have to be patient but I still wanted to reach the top as quickly as possible.

My first Football League appointment as a linesman was on Sunday 14 September 1986 at Belle Vue, Doncaster, where Blackpool were the visitors. It was an old, homely ground, a throwback to the "cloth cap" era. The facilities did not give the impression that I was making a step up at all. Even though I was floating on air, and a little nervous at the prospect of entering the big league, I couldn't help but notice the rutted and worn surface of the car park, which was full of holes. The changing room was similarly run down and in need of repair, but money was, and still is, tight at the bottom end of the Football League, so a refurbishment of the cramped officials' changing room wasn't top priority.

The Doncaster set-up was just like some of the older Northern League grounds, such as Willington in County Durham and South Bank in one of the most impoverished parts of industrial Teesside. On the other hand, to walk out in front of what I thought was a huge crowd of 3,335 with a good friend of mine, Stockton referee Ken Lupton, was nerve-racking. I'd never officiated in front of such huge numbers, even in those junior finals at Ayresome Park. I felt that the eyes of every one of those spectators were upon me, waiting to examine every decision I made. I prayed for an easy one to come my way, so that I could relax, pretty much in the same way that a player relaxes after he has had his first touch of the ball. But for ten minutes the ball didn't go out of play on my side of the pitch, nor was there an offside decision to make.

I stayed focused and ran up and down the line keeping up with play. When the ball finally went out, I raised my flag with gusto and a huge feeling of relief. Ken, knowing how I was feeling, acknowledged me with a smile. Thereafter it was plain sailing. The game flew by in such a blur that it seemed the remaining eighty minutes passed more quickly than the opening ten. I was on my way, and felt elated in the changing room afterwards. Suddenly the cramped room, rough floor and peeling paintwork didn't matter at all.

There were no problems in that particular game, but before long I learnt that it isn't always the referee who takes the flak. And when the linesman gets it wrong, it is even worse for him, because irate fans are breathing down his neck. You can't turn and look at them, because that is an indication that you are intimidated. You have to try and shut them out. But for a linesman who is new to it, that task is not easy.

One of my biggest clangers came when I badly lost concentration in an FA Cup tie between Darlington and Mansfield in November 1986. The Darlington keeper was about to take a goal kick to my left, and I looked up and saw George Foster, the Mansfield defender, pushing up-field to try and take the

Darlington forwards away from goal. I was keeping my eye on them, when all of a sudden the ball was launched forward for Darlington's former Boro striker David Currie, who I'd refereed in junior football on Teesside. Currie was about ten yards clear of everybody else, and with just the keeper to beat.

"Kid" Currie, as he was known, rarely missed, and his eye for goal led to Brian Clough signing him for Nottingham Forest. But on this occasion, fortunately for me, Currie fired well wide. Even so, the Mansfield players went ballistic, Foster leading the way by running furiously over to confront me. He demanded to know why I hadn't flagged for offside. I smugly replied, "You can't be offside from a goal kick, everyone knows that." But George retorted, "It wasn't a goal kick." The referee, Tom Fitzharris, came over, waved George away and gave me a quizzical look. He then asked the same question that George had posed. I was a little less cocky this time. "It was a goal kick," I ventured timidly. "No, it wasn't," he said, "the keeper played the ball quickly to his full back, got it back, and punted it up-field." (In those days, a keeper could receive a back pass and legitimately pick the ball up.) I hadn't spotted him doing that, so had made a basic error. Darlington's former home at Feethams, among the most quaint in the league, with its adjacent river and cricket ground, may have been a far cry from Anfield or Old Trafford, but even so mistakes made there infuriated the crowd and were highlighted by the media.

The next edition of the *Northern Echo* reported, "Darlington should have scored when David Currie, who couldn't have been more offside if he was standing on the adjoining cricket pitch, ran through but missed." As that newspaper circulates in

Middlesbrough, I was exposed to my mates. On the Monday morning I hid the copy delivered to the bank, but couldn't collect them from the whole of Teesside. In the days that followed I thought I'd blown my career, but the appointments kept on coming. If there was an assessor in the crowd at Feethams, I didn't hear anything about it.

Nevertheless, I'd learnt another valuable lesson – be aware of every touch of the ball, and don't be complacent. The Feethams incident was a kick up the backside. I apologised to the referee at the end of the game and, thankfully, he didn't make an issue about it. He probably felt that I wouldn't make the same mistake again. And he learnt what it was like to be on the receiving end at Darlington, for it was there that he once had an apple thrown at him. I can't condone that sort of behaviour, but I have to admire the Darlington fan for the accuracy of his shooting. I'm told the apple hit Tom smack on the head despite being thrown from many yards away.

You need friends at times like that, and I had excellent ones to turn to. The North East had an abundance of referees, among them Robbie Hart, George Courtney and Peter Willis, who had been there, done it, and could lend a sympathetic ear. Around this time I began to realise that I had to think about putting quality before quantity. I didn't want to seem like a "Big Time Charlie" so didn't at first turn my back on the local leagues, though gradually I cut down the number of matches I was officiating. I'd been doing well over one hundred games each season, but decided that some Sunday commitments had to go. However, I did accept one Sunday appointment that was to give my career a massive boost.

The game was the seemingly low-profile FA Sunday Cup tie between Blackhall CW from County Durham and Croxteth and Gilmoss British Legion from Liverpool.

I'd learnt from my early days that the aggression of players and fans was not watered down on the Sabbath. And this tie was as passionate as they come. Some Sunday clubs can pay good wages to players – even if it's in the guise of expenses – and therefore attract the pick of an area's talent. The match attracted a big crowd, quite a few having travelled from Liverpool. Towards the end of the game it was apparent that Blackhall were going to win. Fighting suddenly broke out on the terraces, and then in the dugouts. I thought that this was an orchestrated attempt to have the match abandoned and replayed. And I was having none of it.

Even though there were just a couple of minutes left, I stopped the game, and with police help – they had been alerted and arrived with sirens blaring – I had the ground cleared. I was determined to finish the game, even if we had to wait all afternoon. To abandon it would possibly have caused even more trouble. And besides I wanted fairness to prevail.

I kept my composure, told the players what I intended to do, and waited. I must have been maturing. I didn't even think about sticking the boot in. I worked in co-operation with the police. I told them I wanted to complete the game, and if they could help me achieve that I would be delighted. Then I let them handle the trouble-makers, and they made a good job of it.

About an hour later, with the ground empty, we played out the final few minutes. I was chuffed: Jeff Winter, the man of authority and calm in a sea of mayhem. How different it would have been a few years earlier, had I been a Croxteth fan! The following day, my first action at the bank was to cancel my appointments, for I spent the whole day compiling my report. I was by now in a management position at the bank, so could hide what I was doing in my own office from my bosses. They may not have been too pleased, though on the other hand my rise up the refereeing ladder brought them good publicity, and probably new customers from the world of local football!

The FA set up an inquiry into the match. The chairman of the commission was the late Bill Fox, chairman of Blackburn Rovers, and also of the FA referees' committee. From my point of view, it was a case of the more witnesses the better. In those circumstances, the referee can usually sit back, and listen to witness after witness contradict what had been said before, leaving his own explanation as the only credible one. That's exactly what happened in this case. The upshot was that Croxteth were suspended from the competition and heavily fined. I was lucky enough to be in the right place at the right time on that day, and it appeared I'd made a good impression on Bill Fox and the commission. It was an impression that wasn't to be forgotten by the powers-that-be. My confidence in my ability to handle trouble-makers was growing, and, before long, I sent off a player for the first time as a Football League linesman.

The more games I got under my belt, and the more big decisions I had to make, the more relaxed and confident I became. Home life was still going well too, and my family was completed in 1987 when our second son Mark arrived.

The biggest crowd I officiated in front of in the 1987–8 season was the old Third Division game between Sunderland and Northampton at Roker Park on 2 May 1988. Sunderland were looking to clinch promotion that day in front of over 30,000 fans, but all the match officials were looking for at the end of the game was the sanctuary of the dressing room, for we knew that the crowd would rush on to the pitch to celebrate if the result went Sunderland's way. I was on the opposite touchline from the tunnel, so was ready to sprint hell for leather. The referee, Jim McAuley, said that he would make the pre-arranged signal just before he was going to blow the final whistle. Sure enough he did – just as I was passing him on the way to the dressing room. As a Boro fan, there was no way that I wanted to be caught up in a Sunderland celebration.

At least when rival fans were fighting behind me they were pre-occupied with each other. When a whole stand of angry fans is breathing down your neck you have to try to blank them out, something that was difficult in a match at Hull, because I had a baseball cap hurled at me by a Hull fan, who claimed he was trying to help me. The sun was setting above the Boothferry Park stand opposite me, and I was blinded by the powerful rays. I spent most of the game running with my flag in one hand, and using my other hand to shield my eyes. The fans laughed at first, but as they felt that my judgement was being impaired and their side was on the receiving end, the cap flew in my direction. I heard words to the effect of "You'll probably still cock it up, but at least you've no excuse now."

Sometimes it was others who were on the receiving end, and human nature being what it is, I found that more funny. One of my early League matches had to be postponed – despite the efforts of one of the managers to influence referee George Tyson. Rochdale was the venue, the visitors being Preston for a Lancashire derby. It was the sort of Manchester weather the locals know well: rain streaking down from a leaden sky, the grey buildings merging into the landscape. Like a Lowry painting, only even more grim. And this was after the rain had eased. The previous night it had lashed down, leaving the pitch clearly unplayable.

Preston manager John McGrath insisted that he wanted the game on, and was gruff, and insistent. George wouldn't back down, pointing out that there were pools of water all over the pitch. McGrath jumped on to an island of green among the puddles, and snarled, "Look, there's nothing wrong with it." The referee remained unmoved, so McGrath swung his foot at a nearby ball, either out of frustration or in a final bid to show that the ball would roll freely enough for the game to take place. Either way, his standing foot gave way and he landed flat on his back on the sodden surface. As he eased himself to his feet, slime running off his suit, he blasted, "Get this fucking game called off and let's get out of here." After our laughter had subsided George could see the disappointment on my face, and said, "Don't worry, Jeff, you'll still get half your match fee now, and the full amount when the game is rearranged. You'll be quids in." Hardly, as the fee at the time was only £25. The game was rearranged for a few months later. Feeling quite satisfied with my performance, I stopped for a beer before heading home. While I was propping up the bar my car was broken into, despite being in the club car park. Two coats were stolen, so my profit was lost.

In the build-up to the following season I refereed a Newcastle United game with a difference. It was a friendly at Whitby Town, around eighty miles down the North East coast from Newcastle, and for me just a short, delightful drive over the North Yorkshire Moors. By this time I was deemed ready to referee a match of this status.

To a non-league club, a pre-season friendly against Football League opposition, especially one as huge as Newcastle, is a fund-raising opportunity to be grasped, for the cash can pay the small club's running costs for several months. Whitby had spent a long time persuading Newcastle United to send a team, so you can imagine their delight when the generous Geordie management promised star names.

However, when the local police found out, they pointed out that because the Whitby Regatta was taking place the same week-end there would be thousands of tourists in the resort. The police didn't want an equally large number of Newcastle fans also making the journey to the seaside and adding to the burden. They insisted that the game be held behind closed doors, and details of who would be in the Newcastle starting eleven were not to be advertised in the media, otherwise police would insist that the match be called off.

Never has a game had so many ball boys, for I'm told that the Whitby officials tipped off lots of fans. So there were a few hundred "ball boys" there, though certainly not the crowd of several thousand that would have turned up in different circumstances.

Newcastle were as good as their word, sending their full first team – including Peter Beardsley, Mirandinha (their Brazilian striker), Dave Beasant and Andy Thorn. It was the first time I'd refereed Beardsley, and he struck me as a shining example of how a professional footballer should be. His attitude and skill were first class, and he also gave lots of encouragement to the Whitby players. I ran the game for the fee I usually got when visiting Whitby – a box of kippers!

By this time, as well as running the line in the Football League, I was refereeing top games in the Central League, and rising up the non-league ladder. But being in charge on the pitch meant that you had to answer for your decisions to the referees' assessor. As a new kid on the block – certainly at Central League level – I had to satisfy the assessors at every game. Being under constant scrutiny was tough, but on the whole, in the absence of any harsh reports, I felt that I was doing well. So it was out of the blue that a very negative report arrived at my home. They were sent personally to each referee, and bad reports became known to me as "baked bean" assessments.

A few days after one particular game I was having my lunch of baked beans when I opened the assessor's report and read something so damning that I spluttered my lunch all over the report. Both clubs had given me good marks, so I was not expecting it. The assessor had crucified me, and there wasn't even a "however" at the end of it. The mark reflected his tone throughout the letter. I thought it had put paid to my chances of a promotion to the Football League middle at least for the time being.

Footballers, managers and fans sometimes think that a referee will occasionally make a decision simply because he knows it will go down well with a watching assessor. It's true. Shortly after the "baked bean" report, I received another of a similar kind, this time from an FA Cup fourth qualifying round game between Frickley and Chorley. The game was drawn, and therefore I was in charge of the replay three days later. After I read the assessor's report, I spoke to one of my refereeing friends, who told me that it was important to give the assessor the impression very early in the game that I was the man in charge.

I took that literally, so on the day of the replay when I walked on to the pitch for the formalities and noticed one of the goalkeepers scratching a mark with his boot across the six-yard line to keep his bearings during the game, I decided to act. I walked over to the keeper, and booked him. He couldn't believe it, and nor could his captain, even when I reminded them that it was against the rules But it seemed that I had done the right thing in somebody's eyes. The subsequent assessment included, "You showed early on that you weren't going to tolerate any misconduct. Well done." Easy really.

Was that the fastest ever booking in an FA Cup tie? Thank goodness the assessor was in his seat and saw me doing it. I don't think I booked a keeper for the same offence ever again. But it ensured that I got no more "baked bean" assessments for a while. I was learning to think on my feet, officiating as fairly as I could, for the good of the game, but at the same time looking after number one.

I loved the job, which is important, because otherwise it would drive you nuts. So despite all the trials and tribulations of trying to climb the greasy pole, I always grabbed the chance of a laugh. I was thrilled to be running the line at Newcastle when former Magpie Paul Gascoigne returned for the first time to St James's

Park with his new club, Spurs, in the autumn of 1988. Gazza was adored by the Geordie masses and while they were disappointed that he had headed for the bright lights of London, there was little or no animosity towards him. How can you get angry with a man who is not only such an entertainer but can burst into tears, or the widest grin, for the slightest reason?

The Newcastle fans were determined to have a laugh with him, and as he had recently declared his love of chocolate bars, they made sure to bring along the perfect prop. The Tyneside shop-keepers must have made a fortune from the sale of Mars bars as fans made their way to the game. When Gazza ran on to the pitch, there were dozens of bars thrown towards him. Ever the clown, he took it all in good part, and ate a couple before the match started. No wonder he had club dieticians, physiotherapists and managers tearing their hair out. Several of the bars hit me – perhaps, with my Middlesbrough roots, they were deliberately aimed. But Gazza had set the standard, so I followed suit and took a bite or too as well. The fans laughed, and I almost forgot myself. Just for a second I loved them. Newcastle games invariably had an amusing twist to them, perhaps a reflection of how fun-loving the Tyneside people are.

Back at Newcastle a few weeks later, I was definitely the crowd's target. The match programme always printed the names of the officials. My entry was 'JT Winter, Middlesbrough' (at that time the ref's home town was printed in the programme, unlike today). There was one voice in the throng that boomed above the rest. "You'd better not give Mirandinha offside today, linesman," it said. As the game progressed, the banter increased.

"What does the T stand for, lino?"

"Is it Trevor?"

"Is it Thomas?"

"Is it Timothy?"

A few minutes later, Mirandinha was caught offside, and I flagged. "I know what it is now," yelled a wag in the crowd. "It's Twat." (It's Thomas actually.)

On another visit to St James's Park, I was on the receiving end of some physical abuse from Newcastle full back Neil McDonald, though it was accidental. Aston Villa winger Tony Daley broke down the flank in front of me. McDonald made a perfectly executed sliding tackle which took the ball, then Daley, then me in rapid succession. I may be big and strong but was flipped up in the air in an instant and landed on my backside – to huge laughter from the crowd. Not wanting to be ridiculed any longer than necessary, I was on my feet almost as quickly as I went down. In a flash I picked up my flag and gave a throw in. The right way, of course. The shock of the incident masked the pain. When I glanced down I saw blood pumping from my knee, and so did some of the fans. I was able to continue, but the crowd had no sympathy. "Just wait until he gets the other leg," they shouted.

I was feeling increasingly confident after games, believing that my standards were improving, and that I would earn my just reward. But of course tangible evidence that I was pleasing the authorities too was always welcome. And on Monday 3 April 1989 it arrived. I was talking to Peter Mulcaster, a local non-league manager, in my office at the bank. It's not for me to divulge why Peter was there. A man's finances are his own business. But for the rest of his visit we were talking football. We were interrupted by a phone call from the FA referees' department. That was unusual on a Monday. "Jeff, it's the FA here." I knew it was a genuine call, because I recognised the voice of that particular member of staff. "We would like to advise you that you have been appointed as fourth official for the FA Cup final next month. Will you be able to accept it?" After a moment of stunned silence at my end, which probably seemed an eternity at the other, I stammered, "Of course, I will. It will be a pleasure." Their reply was instant, because they knew I wouldn't say no. "Good. Now, because the news won't be released until tomorrow, we want you to tell only your close family. You must not let it go any further."

Peter had noticed that my face showing a mixture of surprise and delight, and as soon as I replaced the receiver, he asked, "What's up?" I blurted, "I've just been appointed fourth official for the FA Cup final." So the secret was out within five seconds, everybody in the bank knew within five minutes, and most of Teesside knew by the end of the day. Whatever Peter asked for that day, he got it. I was on cloud nine. Bill Fox had remembered me!

It was a tremendous feeling to be handed such an honour. The role of fourth official may seem menial to some, but it shouldn't. And certainly not at Wembley. It had long been an ambition to officiate at the home of English football but I didn't expect the opportunity to arrive so soon, if at all. I'd been to Wembley a few times for England games and Cup Finals, courtesy of Tommy Harper, and thought to myself every time, "This is where I want to be." I was on cloud nine for rather too long, and as is often the case – the journey back from dreamland had a crash landing. That very night, I was refereeing the Banks Group Northern Youth League cup semi-final between Guisborough and Shildon. I was floating on air, and everything seemed to be going well. That was until a player was hurt in an accidental collision. I allowed the game to carry on, despite protests from the home side that I should let the stricken player get treatment. But I was in charge of the game, and I had been deemed worthy of a Wembley appointment! I was not going to allow myself to be influenced. When the ball finally went out of play, the player was attended to. It turned out that he had swallowed his tongue. Fortunately – very fortunately – the delay did not prevent him from receiving the necessary treatment, and he made a full recovery.

As with my error at Darlington, this latest lapse could not be brushed under the carpet. But first came more Wembley adulation. The Cup Final appointment delighted the local media, and there was a big spread about me in the *Evening Gazette*, featuring my refereeing career and banking background. But the paper heard about my handling of the Guisborough game, and that put me in a very different light. I was castigated.

It was a perfect example of the media building you up, then knocking you down. In this case both stories were justified – and the public will view you as they see fit. Some will focus on the Middlesbrough lad made good, others will reflect on how my mistake could have led to a player dying. And those who linked both stories no doubt thought, "Fancy letting an idiot like that into Wembley!"

The down-to-earth outlook of the locals was brought home to me in my next game, a Central League match at Huddersfield in which I booked Middlesbrough lad Steve Livingstone, a striker who was playing for Coventry. He threatened to make sure that word reached his friends back home. "You'd better not go to Madison's night club tonight," he said. I didn't – though I wasn't going to anyway.

I didn't feel I refereed that game particularly well, but the assessor gave me a good report. Maybe he didn't want to earn a black mark himself for criticising a referee who had just been appointed to the Cup Final. I was now counting down the days to the final, unaware that tragedy was to strike.

Spring was in the air, when, on 15 April 1989, I was the referee for a Northern League game at Northallerton. It was FA Cup semi-final day, with Liverpool facing Nottingham Forest, and Everton playing Norwich City. By five o'clock that afternoon, unless either game was drawn, I expected to know who would be in the final. I didn't need to know, but I wanted to, so that it would add to my anticipation of the big day. I would know throughout the afternoon from the radios among the supporters at Northallerton how the semi-finals were progressing.

Yet I could sense that something was wrong. After I had blown the half-time whistle, I heard people talking only about an incident at Hillsborough, caused by a problem in the crowd. There was a television in the bar, and a newsflash was broadcast. Northallerton manager Ray Hankin told me that some people had been killed behind the goal. Everyone was stunned. Most had seen the television pictures of the terrible fire at Bradford four years earlier, when scores of people died, and those images returned immediately when we heard what had happened at Hillsborough.

Nobody at Northallerton had the motivation for the second half, but we managed to finish the game. There was no banter at the end as there usually was. Everybody's thoughts were on events unfolding at the other end of Yorkshire. We crowded around the television as the horrific details emerged. The news affected me badly. I didn't care about myself; football didn't matter; the FA Cup final didn't matter. Nearly a hundred people who went to a football match didn't return home.

I was due at Hillsborough the following Tuesday for a Central League game, but it was postponed, much to my relief. I would have struggled emotionally upon seeing the buckled and twisted barriers at the Leppings Lane End. The disaster led to my next involvement with the media, for a local journalist phoned me and asked what my reaction would be if the Final didn't go ahead because of the tragedy. My reaction was simple. I told him in no uncertain terms that it didn't matter what I thought. "Ninety-six people have lost their lives," I said. "My Cup Final appointment means nothing."

A long period of mourning followed, and before it had properly elapsed, slowly football returned to some degree of normality. The FA consulted the clubs, and the competition restarted, although I had mixed feelings about it. I was delighted that my big day was still going to happen, but I felt deep sorrow for those who had perished, and my thoughts were with their families. I was a parent by now, so had some understanding of what it must have meant to lose a loved one.

It also made me reflect with some regret on my past as a terrace boot boy. It troubled me that I had been involved in the swaying when a large number of fans were together. There had been many times when I'd been in a gang of fans going to an away ground and we'd piled on to the terraces, just as the Liverpool fans had on that fateful day. Surging forward was a way of football life. You went with the crowd. Maybe you got some bumps and bruises, and on the occasions when you tripped, somebody always managed to pick you up before you were trampled upon. But I'd never thought that my life was in jeopardy, nor did it occur to me that my actions could lead to such an outcome. What plagued me after Hillsborough was that it was the behaviour of fans of my generation that led to fencing being erected between spectators and the pitch.

Liverpool eventually beat Nottingham Forest a few weeks later and set up an all-Merseyside final against Everton, probably the most emotional final of all time. Fences had indirectly caused the deaths at Hillsborough, and before the final, the fencing at Wembley was dismantled. Maybe that helped the atmosphere slightly, but there were a lot of tears when "You'll Never Walk Alone" was sung.

The Wembley experience was tremendous, but the disaster was in the back of my mind, despite my pride in arriving at the magnificent stadium, the Twin Towers gleaming. I was pleased to be able to take Elaine with me. Appointments such as the Cup Final were seen as a reward for the family as well as the match officials. That was quite right, because the wife of any football official makes huge sacrifices.

I'm pleased she was there because the whole weekend was un-believable. Players are told to make sure that they savour every moment and it's the same for a match official. There was some-thing of a surreal atmosphere because of the togetherness everyone felt following Hillsborough, even though this was a Merseyside derby, with the most famous trophy in football at stake. Maybe if I had been a regular official at Wembley I could have compared the atmosphere with that of other occasions there. But there was no precedent, and once I stepped out of the famous tunnel, I experi-enced the awe that everyone else feels when they first sample it.

It was a great game as well, with Liverpool winning 3–2 in extra time. Maybe they were destined to win the Cup after the disaster. I didn't have much to do. Maybe I didn't control the substitutes and others on the bench as well as I could have done but I think that there was a deep feeling among everybody there that we had to make sure that the day went well out of respect for those who had perished. I can't remember there being one contro-versial incident.

Afterwards I reflected on how far I had come since that day when I walked to see the cricket at Acklam Park. A long way. Yet I still felt that inevitable deflated feeling you do when a momen-tous occasion has been and gone. I needed a reality check. Mine came in the form of a testimonial for a non-league player at a run-down North East ground which was a far cry from Wembley. I took it very seriously indeed – after all, there might have been an assessor watching.

A few weeks after the Cup Final my private life changed in a way that went against the advice of my refereeing mentor Harry Bage.

He had told me that to be a successful referee you must always win your home games. He meant that you needed a strong home life, with the support of a loving family. He was right, but I was proving more effective away from home.

It was a chance meeting with Lynette which was to set in motion the road to divorce. We met in the Tall Trees nightclub in Yarm on Teesside. I was on a night out with a couple of mates and Elaine's brother. Against that backdrop of a new love, and what was becoming an increasingly difficult home life, my refereeing career continued, and offered some relief from domestic tensions.

4

THE PUSH FOR PROMOTION

The marriage break-up was my fault. I had fallen for Lynette. There was much bitterness, which, happily, time has healed to a large extent. By the time I left to move in with Lynette, Emma was around ten, an impressionable age, and the boys were old enough to know what was going on, if not exactly why.

But I know the split was for the best. Couples in these circumstances think that they can keep it from the children, but the strained home atmosphere is obvious, even to the youngest. Emma said that she had been able to tell, for a long time before I left home, that something was wrong. We all went through the problems that all break-ups cause. The children had to try and accept Lynette while coming to terms with the fact that their dad no longer lived with them, while Lynette had to accept that I not only had to devote a lot of time to my children, but very much wanted to.

Everybody appeared to cope well in the difficult circumstances, and during the years that followed I tried to be the perfect absent father. My three children were, and are, the loves of my life. I had always wanted the warmth of a large family, perhaps because I didn't have it as a child. My father and I were never close. Whether I was a good dad is for the children to judge. But I did try, to the extent of taking them on holiday together, with me in sole charge. I remember clearly one detail of a trip to Malta.

The bath was deep and warm, and my feeling of relaxation was heightened by the knowledge that these precious few minutes of peace and solitude had been hard earned. Two things stirred me into easing myself out of the calming water, however. One was a pang of hunger, the other was a parental instinct that told me all was not well on the other side of the bathroom door.

"Where's Mark?" I asked my elder son Craig as, wrapped in a towel, I emerged into the hallway, dripping water on to the marble floor of the apartment. Boys being boys, nine-year-old Craig and his brother Mark, five years his junior, had been fighting, though the noise of them doing so had washed over me like the bubbles in the bath.

Craig, to his credit, did not hold back with the answer. "I've locked him in the bedroom." I grabbed the key and entered the room just in time to see Mark make his escape by jumping from one balcony to another. We were on the third floor, and had he failed to make the distance – which nearly happened – he would probably have been killed, and certainly seriously injured. The rollicking handed out to the pair of them was born of anger, blame at myself for leaving them unattended, and, perversely, relief when I thought about how close I had come to losing a child.

By now I had lost my father, and while I was saddened by his death I recognised it was a blessing for my mother. Once she had come to terms with losing him, she was able to enjoy a freedom previously unknown, and I grew much closer to her. She was free to share family holidays with us and made the most of them.

While my commitment to my family remained very strong, I was also focused on my refereeing career. With my growing experience on the Football League panel, and having been involved in the FA Cup final, I felt good about my prospects. And whenever I reined in my optimism, and told myself not to take anything for-granted, friends would tell me that I would soon be in the middle, refereeing League games.

That's what friends are for, of course, and I was right to take a more cautious view. I was not exactly being fast-tracked; I faced another three seasons as a Football League linesman, while refereeing Northern League and Pontins Central League games. In those seasons I covered a lot of miles in cold, windswept and unglamorous locations. To put it in motoring terms, I began to wonder whether I would be a clapped-out model by the time I got to drive in the fast lane of refereeing, if I was to get there at all.

By the end of that spell the frustration was beginning to grate. I wouldn't say that I was close to calling it a day, and going back to my beloved Boro on Saturday afternoons, but I was beginning to wonder whether all the effort that had gone into getting me this far was to take me no further. Refereeing is like other careers in that respect, not least that of a footballer. I guess that manufacturing assembly lines and offices up and down the country contain many a man who made the ranks as a professional footballer, only to progress no further than the Rochdale substitutes' bench, many of them no doubt while I was running the line at Spotland.

Nevertheless, I decided to soldier on. Referees are always deemed to be ready to take any appointment asked of them, unless they have given a date when they are unavailable. And I was delighted when, at short notice, I was asked to referee a New Year's Day GM Vauxhall Conference game at Runcorn. I raised a glass to Wally Nattrass, who had pulled out of refereeing the game because he was unwell. Whether it had anything to do with it being his birthday on New Year's Eve, I don't know! But whatever his ailment, it provided me with the chance to referee another game just one step below the Football League.

This told me how close I was to making the grade. It lifted my spirits and gave me the will to carry on. A non-league game at Runcorn on a cold, grey winter's day, with the mist coming in off the River Mersey, may not sound that appealing to many, and there are those who may feel – with due respect to the locals – that Runcorn is not the most salubrious part of the country. But I won't hear a word said against it. I'm sure it has a lot to offer. One thing's for sure: it's a hotbed of football, with passionate supporters, though on that particular day there was no one in the ground feeling more up for it than I did.

I saw that game as a key part of my education if I was going to reach the top. It went well, but the next time I went to Runcorn as a referee, I made a bad mistake. I booked a Wycombe Wanderers player without asking his name. I took a note of his shirt number, deciding to add his name later. I duly reported Simon Stapleton, only to realise later that there had been a mistake with the shirt numbers, and the real culprit was Dave Carroll, who went on to become a Wycombe legend by playing for them in the Football League following their promotion.

My misjudgement got me into trouble with the authorities, gaining a black mark I could well have done without. It's an easy mistake to make, but while the shirt numbering should not have been wrong in the first place, I fully accept that it is the referee's responsibility to get the name right. It would hardly happen in the Premiership, where almost all of the players are household names. You don't have to check to make sure you've got the right name when Paul Ince or Roy Keane transgresses.

Shortly afterwards I was in the middle at St James's Park for a Newcastle versus Sunderland derby. No, I hadn't progressed that quickly. It was a Pontins League match. Even so, I felt proud. And not just because I had been chosen to referee another derby. For here I was in the heart of enemy territory again. What a transformation from the times I'd been there as a Boro fan, spitting venom at the Newcastle fans, players – and of course the referee. I was welcomed into the ground and shown the dressing room. I had been there before as a linesman but this time I was in charge. Had I ever got the chance to enter the business area of St James's Park when I had been in the Boro gang, I would have written "Up the Boro" and something suitably derogatory about Newcastle on the wall.

I booked six players. The assessor asked me if I had felt it was a game worthy of six cautions. I gave him an honest answer, "No, but there were six offences that warranted a booking." That's the nature of refereeing. Sometimes you can get a niggly game where there is an undercurrent of hostility between the teams yet nobody quite oversteps the mark sufficiently to get booked. And then there are games that flow, are open and largely honest, yet bookable offences crop up regularly even though there may be no malice. That's very much what this game was like. You have to go by the rule book if you want to get noticed and move up the ladder. I was setting my stall out to make the final push.

On one of my many visits to St James's I ran the line for referee Peter Tyldesley in a first-team match in front of the usual enthusiastic Newcastle crowd. Although I felt that Peter controlled the game very well, I did form the impression that he was rather lenient to bustling Newcastle striker Micky Quinn who had a typically robust game. We could tell by the comments of the match assessor after the game that he agreed with me. However, Quinny was very knowledgeable on horse racing – and is now a trainer – while Peter is a big racing fan. So maybe the couple of useful tips Quinny gave him made up for the assessor's report. These things happen.

In early January 1991 I received notification that I had been earmarked to run the line in an FA Cup replay, should Barnsley and Leeds United draw. They did, referee George Courtney allowing a controversial Barnsley equaliser to stand. The Leeds fans were sure to give him a hard time in the replay four days later. Much as I respected George and found it an honour to officiate with him, fellow linesman Doug Charnley and I realised that we could have a bit of fun at his expense on this occasion. "OK, here we go," said George as we left the sanctuary of the dressing room. I replied, barely able to suppress a giggle, "We're either side of you."

George then stepped from the tunnel to a deafening chorus of boos and jeers from the Leeds supporters. He had heard it all before, yet he glanced over his shoulder for reassurance from us. But we had deliberately lagged ten yards behind to let him take the flak on his own. George looked bemused, and I knew him well enough to shout, "Nothing to do with us, mate, you can take it yourself." George took our prank in good heart – eventually.

That game was memorable for another reason. It introduced me to a gentleman that I would fall out with in later years, and I don't think I was alone in that. Fiery, flame-haired Scot Gordon Strachan is, and was, a colourful character, full of strong opinions. During the second half I signalled for a throw-in to Barnsley. Gordon, who was playing for Leeds, turned to the camera at ground level behind the touchline, his face red with rage, and screamed into the lens exactly what he thought of the decision.

The camera panned straight on to me, and the match commentator passed comment on Gordon's views and choice of language. That created two problems for me. The first was that it appeared that I had let a player escape punishment even though he had sworn at me, which is a red-card offence. In fact I hadn't let him off, because I hadn't heard it. I was forty yards away, though the camera switching from him to me gave the impression that I was next to him. I know that Gordon can shriek at some volume, but even his high-pitched voice does not travel that far through the passionate crowd at a derby. And the second problem? If he had only been two yards away I still wouldn't have been able to understand what he'd said.

Shortly afterwards I had a brief respite from the pressures of the job when the unthinkable happened. Boro reached Wembley. Even though it was in the final of the much-maligned Zenith

Data Systems Trophy, it was a joyous time. Boro won 1–0 at Aston Villa in the first leg of the semi-final, but Villa struck first in the return leg at a packed Ayresome Park. Typical Boro. They never made it easy for themselves or the fans. Then Paul Kerr and the prolific Bernie Slaven scored to send Boro to the Twin Towers. The fans danced home through the terraced streets that night. But we lost to Chelsea in the final when Tony Dorigo scored the only goal.

I had little time to reflect on that excitement for, as the season progressed, my fixtures came thick and fast. My fitness was tested to the limit, but unlike some top footballers who reckon two games a week is too many, I was not going to cry off. At local league level there was no organised training for refs. Technical training (rules of the game, updates, etc.) was carried out by the referees' association but fitness training was left entirely to each ref's discretion. I trained as best I could but it's hard to put quality before quantity when you are faced with game after game.

One typical itinerary from 1991 was: Thursday – Huddersfield versus Aston Villa in the Pontins League; Saturday – back to Runcorn to referee a Conference game; Monday – the return Pontins League fixture, Sunderland versus Newcastle; Tuesday – linesman for Huddersfield versus Rotherham. Even during the first few minutes at Huddersfield I was feeling pretty jaded. With ninety minutes to get through I hoped that I would get a second wind as the game progressed.

Shortly into the first half it became clear that I would have to, for referee Alan Wilkie was clearly not moving freely, and it dawned on me that my debut as a Football League referee, albeit as a substitute, could be imminent. Two minutes later he came over to me, as senior linesman, and said he couldn't continue. But despite the pain from a damaged leg muscle, he carried on refereeing for a couple of minutes to give me time to compose myself. I appreciated that. It showed that the ref and linesman are a team who look after each other just as players do.

So this was it. The back door had unexpectedly opened, and I was about to step into the spotlight. Suitably composed, and having forgotten the tiredness, I handed over my flag and ran out for seventy minutes of refereeing in the Football League in front of 4,578 fans. It's worse than starting a game, because while fans will take any opportunity to blame the referee, a substitute ref is even more of a legitimate target. For a start, nobody laughs when a player suffers an injury, but when the ref does it is a source of amusement. For the first few minutes it was like being back on duty for the first time in the Yarm versus Cleveland Nomads match. I found myself running around on adrenalin, chasing the ball. The headless chicken syndrome had struck again.

But I settled down, and started to enjoy the game. I dished out three yellow cards, all to Rotherham players. The assessor's report suggested that I had the ability to take charge at this level. It was hardly the highest praise, but I knew that it meant that the door, which had been tantalisingly ajar for some time, would soon swing wide open and I would be welcomed in.

It was around this time that I left the bank. I knew that being self-employed would give me more flexibility to climb the refereeing ladder so I set myself up as a financial adviser. A full day's work for an employed ref, followed by training, and maybe two games a week was very demanding, whereas a self-employed ref could maybe go for a midday run, and work in the evening.

The Rotherham match had given me a real taste. Thereafter, my viewpoint changed. Wherever I went as a linesman, I envied the man in the middle and tried to see everything through his eyes. Even though the next game was a thrilling 4–4 draw between Scunthorpe and Halifax, all I did was analyse every decision to see whether I would have come to the same conclusion as referee Ian Hemley. And so it was until the end of the season, though in one of the last games, I had an insight into a way of being promoted. As I was driving away from the Doncaster Rovers ground after linesman duty, I spotted the match referee, sleeves rolled up under the bonnet of a car. It turned out to be the match assessor's car, which had broken down. The things you have to do to earn a good report! I'm no mechanic, so that avenue of progress was closed. I would have to earn promotion in a more traditional way.

Refereeing duties for the next season continued to be in reserve games only and it was in one of these that I had the opportunity to meet Brian Clough, when I refereed Nottingham Forest's reserves against Manchester City. He was known as much for the discipline he instilled in his sides as the footballing quality. In that respect it was a strange game to officiate, because there was not a hint of dissent, or even a raised eyebrow, from any of the Forest players, even when decisions were a close call. I had only a brief word with Cloughie, no more than wishing each other well. But when he shook hands with you, you felt as if he meant it. He was known for his controversial views, and the manner in which he put them across. But he set a standard, yet to be matched, in moulding quality, disciplined teams.

The next time I officiated a Forest game, it was a first-team affair, and I saw an example of arrogant behaviour from a senior referee that disappointed me. At the end of the game, the other linesman Paul Rejer and I were chatting, when it dawned on us that Roger was not there. It is normal for the officials to stick together for at least a little while after games. As linesmen we expect the referee, who is senior to us, to offer encouragement, and make a few constructive comments about our performance. After all, we are a team. The referee, however, had gone off to hold his own counsel with his friends and the media, without giving us a second glance. He was a good referee, but not a good colleague. At least not on that occasion. Paul and I bought our own drinks, and talked of the lessons of the day. The main one was never to be the big "I am", no matter how far we progressed.

Lower division games improved our fitness no end. The sides lumped the ball from one end to the other, and you had to be fit to keep up with play. As simple as that. The referee who sticks out in my mind as handling that style of play better than any other is Steve Lodge. I ran the line for him at Rochdale once, and his positioning and anticipation of play was exemplary. He remained in control yet hardly broke sweat. It occurred to me that perhaps I was handed that game to learn from him because I would soon be following his footsteps. Equally it was possible that he had been asked to work with me so that he could monitor my progress.

I went through a spell of working with the top referees, but my cause was probably not helped when I assisted David Elleray in an FA Cup fourth-round replay at Old Trafford. The game went to extra time, and even that didn't separate the teams. I've heard many a fan moan that the opposition never get a penalty at Old Trafford, but credit where it's due, David Elleray handed Southampton five spot kicks!

It was my job to apply the rules by making sure that the players taking penalties in the shoot-out, and nobody else, be allowed in the centre circle. But I failed miserably. Keeping Sir Alex Ferguson and Co. in check proved impossible. Neither David nor I received another FA Cup appointment that season, though if it was because of that match, it wasn't his fault. Even so, rumours were rife that I was set to make the grade as a Football League referee, and when I was given an FA Vase fifth-round tie to referee I had more grounds for optimism.

The tie went well, and shortly afterwards I got another sign that I was being closely watched, on the occasion of a Conference match at Northwich Victoria. I noticed that the assessor was Dennis Turner, the chap who co-ordinated the assessments for the Football League. They had sent their top man to run the rule over me. I had a good game – until just before half-time, when a searing pain in my calf brought me to an abrupt standstill. There was no way I could carry on. It was the 1,184th game I had officiated in, and for the first and last time in my career I was unable to complete a match.

I sat in the dressing room a disconsolate figure. I'd have stood up and booted the ball had the pain from my calf not been so bad. It was a long and painful drive home. But as the journey progressed I started to feel a little better about my prospects. After all, they couldn't turn me down just because of one strained calf. Fitness-wise I felt I could compete with any referee in the country, and was not exactly injury prone just because of a single setback. And I was right. I had already done enough to earn the big step-up.

When eventually the confirmation of my promotion clattered through the letterbox, it came as a surprise, because I had convinced myself that it wasn't coming. I had built myself up so much that it would have been hard to motivate myself for another season. It's funny how the mind reacts once a situation has resolved itself favourably. For months you've cursed the ones who hold your fate in their hands, then when you are chosen, you turn all philosophical. "Well," I thought to myself. "I suppose that when there are 30,000 referees in the country, the authorities have to choose carefully when selecting the elite group. It's not a decision to be rushed."

There are nineteen top referees for the Premiership, and only around forty-five in the professional game. For the vast majority the letter never comes.

Once I had been chosen I began to look back with fondness at the six seasons that had elapsed since I became a Football League linesman. One of the highlights of my apprenticeship, as I liked to think of it, was in October 1989 when I ran the line for George Courtney in a Littlewoods Cup tie between Aston Villa and West Ham United. George went to the World Cup in 1990 and was clearly the number one referee in this country and, in many people's eyes, the world. He had always been an inspiration to me but to see him in this game at first hand was a lesson in exactly how the job should be done. From the moment he arrived at Villa Park to the second he left the stadium he was held in high esteem and respected by everybody. He's a great referee, and a man who can combine authority with a human touch. He earned his respect over the years and when I looked at him that day my one ambition was to earn the standing in the game that he enjoyed.

I had grown up. And I realised at this point the extent to which refereeing had been responsible for my maturity. My first taste of football had been as an aggressive young fan on the terraces at Ayresome Park. Rival fans apart, the most hated figure in the ground was the referee. As a young supporter I had an inbuilt dislike of refs, because I was a rebel. And like the rest of my gang, I rebelled against authority. Yet George Courtney was the example I now aspired to. Quite a transformation.

I was well on the way to becoming poacher turned gamekeeper. My desire to step into the middle, whistle in hand, was greater than ever. And my chance was imminent. My last game as a Football League linesman came on my thirty-seventh birthday. Fittingly, it was in the North East – at Newcastle. I think that was the first time ever that Middlesbrough (in this case me) had clinched promotion out on the pitch at St James's Park. And nobody booed me, though they probably would have done had they known.

5

THE FUTURE AT STAKE – MINE AND HALIFAX TOWN'S

Summer always seems to fly by, but the summer of 1992 dragged on, as I was impatient for the football season to begin. The fixtures came out at the end of June and I studied them to try to guess where my first appointment might be. To get in the groove I accepted a couple of pre-season friendlies. The first was at Darlington, where their former manager Brian Little, a hero after leading Darlington to successive promotions for the only time in their history, had brought his new club, Leicester.

You'd have thought that the chance to impress the old boss and earn a move to a higher league would have focused the Darlington players' minds. But anyone who has come across Kevan Smith will know that the former Darlington skipper's eye for a laugh is sometimes rather better than his eye for a good pass. I had decided to give my new bright-yellow refereeing shirt an airing, while still sporting the traditional black shorts and socks. During the first half Kev kept making a buzzing noise every time I went near him.

"What are you doing?" I asked him.

"Nothing, buzzer," he replied.

"Why buzzer?"

"Because you look like a fucking bee with that yellow shirt on."

At Hartlepool a few days later, when Leicester were again the opposition, the banter was similar. "Jeff, there are flies all over your shirt," said one Pool player, referring to the black specks on the shirt. "I know, I can't get rid of them," I said trying to rise to the challenge. "Well, you know what they say about flies and shit," he said. There was no answer to that!

However, despite the banter, my nerves almost got the better of me when my League debut arrived. The drive over to Carlisle had, as always, been a pleasant one. From Middlesbrough almost every game necessitates a drive down the A19, then the A1 – the same familiar route. Carlisle is different. The A66 climbs up high over the wild, windswept Pennines, where the hardy sheep eke out a living on the bleak moorland. Even in August (it was the 13th) it can be cold up there. A bit like Tow Law without the buildings.

But the road then winds down the Eden valley and into Cumbria, the Lake District mountains forming a dramatic backdrop. I love that view, and, inevitable nerves apart, I was looking forward to my big day – until the match-day programme struck. Ever tried reading a magazine while you are sitting waiting for the call from the dentist to have a tooth pulled? It isn't easy to concentrate on trivia when your nerves are frayed. That's how I felt sitting at Brunton Park a couple of hours before kick-off. I picked up the programme, read a few lines, put it down, paced up and down the room, picked it up again and generally didn't know what to do with myself. Having just started to compose myself and settle my nerves, I was hit by a bombshell. There it was in black and white. The programme stated that it was my first game in charge. There was no escaping the fact. If I had seen it, so would the fans, and players. So much for my hopes of quietly letting my first game slip by without anyone noticing. It was like the kids at school realising it was your birthday when you had desperately tried to keep it quiet to avoid being given a hard time.

In hindsight it did me a favour though, because after that point I managed to clear my head and ease my mind sufficiently to be ready for the big moment. While I was in the tunnel with the two teams – Walsall being the visitors – Carlisle's keeper Kelham O'Hanlon turned to me and grinned. "It's your first game, isn't it, ref?" He was just trying to poke some fun, and that relieved some of the tension. If I hadn't read the programme, his light-hearted quip would have affected me badly. There would have been no time to get my composure. But I was ready for any digs. I was now prepared for the action, just like an actor on the first night of a new play, when he steps from the wings. The game went well, and I didn't have to brandish a card until deep into stoppage time, when Walsall's Wayne Clarke deliberately wasted time after Carlisle pulled the score back to 3–4. I flashed the yellow.

I felt I'd made a decent debut. As a new kid on the block at this level, I thought I had adapted well, but knew that the "rookie" tag would stick until I had a few games under my belt and had gained respect from the players.

Yet already I saw the Football League as a stepping stone. The Premiership had just been formed from the old First Division, and stood proud and aloof above the cluster of leagues below it. Television and sponsors were falling over themselves to grab their slice of the Premiership spotlight. They smelt money, and so did the players, the scent of it drifting to Europe and the world beyond, drawing the best players to the English game. Crowds and television viewing figures were rocketing. Suddenly England was the centre of world football again. It was the place to be, for the top players, and for me. But while it called me, like a lamp attracts a moth, first I had to prove my worth in more lowly places.

With Carlisle under my belt, I was ready to fully exercise my newly given authority. The chance soon came, for my second game was a stormy affair – Hull City and Rotherham were each hell-bent on trying to reach the next round of the Coca-Cola Cup. The tackles flew in, and there was plenty of not so light-hearted banter between the players.

The yellow card was out of my pocket six times, with three bookings to each side. Whether the players tried to take advantage of me as a newcomer, or whether it was a typical blood and thunder night match between two geographical rivals regardless of who was refereeing, I don't know. But it didn't concern me. I gave what I saw. Dean Windass, as committed as ever, was one of those booked and Mike Riley, later to become a Premiership referee, was one of the linesmen. He was already highly capable, and I'm not surprised he has gone on to be recognised as one of the best.

Later in the season, one linesman made the most basic mistake possible – he didn't turn up for a game that I was refereeing at York City. I gave him as long as possible, but there was no sign of him. The fourth official, a local referee, had to run the line. I didn't know at the time what had happened to the original lines-man. I checked with the club to make sure he hadn't left a message. He hadn't. So I rang him after the match. As soon as he answered the phone, he knew it was me, and what I was going to say. He explained rather sheepishly that he had refereed a game between two local teams, and it was only when he was in the club-house having a drink after the game and saw the York result on the television that he realised he should have been at Bootham Crescent. He thought the York game was the following week. He'd put the wrong date in his diary. I accepted that explanation. I didn't have much choice. But that wasn't the end of the matter. He had to explain to the Football League how he'd managed to forget about the game, but they quickly forgave him. The govern-ing bodies were much more understanding then, even though it was only a few years ago. They had a human touch which has since, in my opinion, gone, unless your face fits. I've found that it depends on who you are. There was, in the past, a degree of flex-ibility towards everyone. To my mind, that no longer exists. If a linesman made the same mistake these days, he might be taken off the list. However, this particular individual had a quick opportu-nity to make amends, for within days he was drafted in as a late replacement for Newcastle's game with Middlesbrough at St James's Park.

Failing to show is a mistake that, happily, I have never made. It's the sort of thing you would struggle to live down now. Still, the York incident was a reminder to double-check the details of each appointment, and keep the diary up to date. Basic stuff, maybe, but when games come thick and fast, it's too easy to get complacent.

While a referee has to be decisive during games, and not swayed by squabbling players or screaming fans, he still has to listen to advice and learn. That's something I have always tried to do – especially when it comes from the likes of Jim Finney. He is a former FIFA referee, who was working with Cardiff City when I was appointed to one of their games at Doncaster on a Friday night. I arrived early, as usual, to inspect a pitch that was left sodden by torrential rain. It was playable a couple of hours before kick-off time, but I decided to reinspect shortly before the game.

As I went out to do so, I heard a voice from the Cardiff City changing room.

"If the ref's got any sense, he should send one of the young players out to kick a ball around."

I turned round, and there was Jim, though I don't think he intended me to hear him. However, I acted upon his words of wisdom and duly asked one of the Doncaster youth team players to run with the ball around the field until I was satisfied I should give the match the go-ahead. Not knowing that I had heard him, he was probably impressed with my actions.

The next time I saw Jim was just before the FA Cup final in 2004, and I levelled with him about the Doncaster incident. It is often said that the corridors of the FA headquarters are filled with "old farts" in grey suits. There's nothing wrong with being old; it's about getting the right people to influence the game. Jim Finney is one such character. He may be a low-profile figure in football but the sort of knowledge and experience that he possesses is invaluable. Isolated incidents like meeting him are etched on my memory. However, the job in hand was applying the laws of the game. It began to look as if I would complete my first season without brandishing a single red card.

In February 1993, however, I was forced into dishing out my first sending off. Burnley were thrashing Chester 5–1 when, midway through the second half, a Burnley player broke from the halfway line, and was hauled down by Chester defender Chris Lightfoot. It was a blatant professional foul, but players from both sides wanted me to keep the card in my pocket. "There's no need to send him off, the game's over," they said. But I was adamant. What was the point of having laws of the game if I wasn't going to apply them properly? It was easy for all the "referees" in the crowd at Turf Moor to leave the player on, but I had to make sure I protected my integrity. What would happen the next time at Turf Moor if the scores were level and there was a similar incident? Fans have long memories. And I knew there was an assessor in the stand. It was probably the first and last time I took satisfaction in sending a player off. I knew I'd done the right thing, and the assessor felt the same.

A referee's troubles are not always over when the game has ended. At Rochdale that season I booked the manager and several of his players. One of the directors didn't take kindly to my performance and a loud, verbal exchange took place in the packed lounge. He told me, my family and guests exactly what he thought about me. I handled it with as much dignity as I could. When we met at the subsequent disciplinary hearing, the club was fined and warned about its future conduct. You can't beat the ref.

I ended my first season with a game at Halifax Town. It was a never-to-be-forgotten day for the diehard fans of the gritty

Yorkshire club. But this was no ordinary end of season fixture. If Halifax lost to Hereford they would be relegated from the Football League and cast into despair. The town is proud of its club. It is in the heart of a hotbed of football even though dwarfed alongside the relative giants of Leeds United and Bradford City to the east and Huddersfield to the south.

The town is self-contained and has its own character, even though outsiders see it as no more than part of the industrial belt of Yorkshire. The importance of this game to the locals was reflected in the crowd figure of 7,000, around three and a half times the average gate for that season. Such was the occasion that a part of me expected to be taken off the game. There were far more experienced refs who could have been handed it. A few years earlier George Courtney had, for example, replaced the match referee who was originally given the game that would decide whether Burnley stayed in the League.

However, even though it was my first year, the Football League must have had confidence in me, because the call to cancel didn't come. As I sat at home the evening before the game I was aware of its significance, even though to me it was simply another occasion at which I had to apply the laws without fear or favour.

The tone of the ringing phone seemed more piercing than normal – and I was left dumbfounded by what the voice at the other end said to me. It was a Halifax-based referees' assessor. He was a staunch Halifax fan, and spent around ten minutes explaining to me – as if that were necessary – the importance of the following day's game to the club. I wondered as to the real motive of the call. Was it a clumsy and thinly disguised attempt to influence me, or was it genuine, explaining the plight of the club and the consequences should they be relegated? I assured him that I fully understood the magnitude of the occasion, but that apart I said little. I thought it best not to, but I let him have his say, and listened intently. When I had put the phone down, I spent a considerable time wondering whether to report the incident to the FA. I had been placed in an extremely difficult position, was damned if I did and damned if I didn't. In the end I decided not to. The night before a game is the most nerve-racking time for all concerned, and I decided that he simply wanted to share his thoughts with someone involved, who would understand. After all he hadn't offered any inducement, so there was no suggestion of bribery. I put it down to naivety. When a football club's future is at stake, people do uncharacteristic things, sometimes regretting them later. Besides I knew all about a club fighting for its future.

In 1986, Boro faced extinction, because of mounting debts. Rescue talks collapsed, then were revived, several times, and as the deadline set by the Football League to resolve the problems drew closer, the gates to the ground were locked. Liquidation was imminent.

It seemed as if a lifetime of memories for many thousands of people were about to be destroyed. The club was saved from extinction just thirty minutes before the deadline, a wave of relief, then euphoria spreading over Teesside. So I knew how the people of Halifax felt as they prepared for one of the biggest games in their history. I packed my kit thinking that if Halifax were to retain their League status it would be down to them, not me.

The drive to the game was not difficult. Summer was almost here and I had enjoyed an enthralling season. I didn't dwell on the importance of the game again until I reached the car park. I had been to the Shay several times before and the spirit around the old ground was always good. This time there was an almost tangible sense of anxiety, however. The stewards and staff were not their usual cheery selves, which was hardly surprising. The club's financial situation wasn't very good, and there was a risk the club might even cease to exist. Players and staff could lose their jobs. In its own way, this game was bigger than any Premiership match I would later referee, bigger even than the FA Cup final.

There's still a club to support if your team loses in the Cup Final or a big game in the Premiership – Halifax fans were faced with the possibility of oblivion. Anyone who says, "Ah, well. You can always go and watch Bradford City," doesn't understand football. I pushed all emotions to the back of my mind, though it didn't help that the police asked me to delay kick-off by several minutes to allow the crowd to flock into the stadium. Some were lifelong fans, some were there out of a sense of duty, while others were simply curious, like those who lurk outside a church at a funeral.

The Halifax players tried not to allow the importance of the occasion to get to them, but I could see in the warm-up that they were tense. That tension rebounded among fans and players and grew in intensity. The game was frantic. Not the best I had taken charge of by a long way, but packed with emotion, especially fear. Towards the end the fans appealed for all sorts whenever the ball went in the Hereford box.

Halifax proved themselves unable to pull it off. They lost 1–0 to a second-half goal. A draw would not have been enough but results elsewhere meant that victory would have hauled them off the bottom of the table in the nick of time, and left some other town in mourning. At the final whistle, some of the Halifax players collapsed in tears on the pitch. Others stood looking around in a state of shock. They had given their all, but it wasn't enough to save their jobs. I could see some fans crying, and being comforted by their friends. Some came on the pitch, not with any malicious intent, but with a need to console and be consoled. There was some applause out of sympathy and appreciation for the team's effort, but most fans stood and reflected. Some even stayed long after the whistle, with soulmates, and memories of better days on the same terraces.

I showered, changed, and went into the lounge for a drink, as I did after most matches. A Halifax director approached me, shook my hand and offered me a drink. I accepted. "We didn't play well enough today," he said. "Or for most of the season. It was too much for some of our players. It's a shame, but with luck we'll bounce back." What good grace he showed. It would have been easy for him to look for a scapegoat and criticise some of my decisions, but he didn't. The same could be said for everybody connected with Halifax in that room. They were a credit to their club, football, and life. What a difference from the attitude of some of the people at the top of the game. Time after time we witness, either live or on television, the ranting of Premiership players and staff, who have lost one game. The referee is invariably the source of their complaint. I've yet to see a referee miss a penalty, or score an own goal. At Halifax, by contrast, I witnessed great dignity, as well as a lot of passion. I can think of a long list of people who could have benefited from being with me at Halifax that day. As I drove off, I left behind an air of depression that was hanging like a shadow over the town. I'd detached myself from the emotions of it for ninety minutes. I could travel home, looking forward to my next Football League season. Behind me, it seemed as if a whole town was in tears, wondering whether it would have a football club in the morning.

As Halifax came to terms with life in the Conference League, I was involved in a real tragedy outside football. It was one that could have destroyed my family. The day is etched on my memory – Monday 28 March 1994. It was one of those early spring days that can't decide whether it wants to hang on to winter or race ahead to summer, being cold and blustery one minute, then warm the next as the sun burst out.

Two days earlier my recurring calf problem had come back to haunt me when refereeing at Grimsby, so I needed a massage as I was due to referee at York City the following evening. I had an arrangement with Boro that I could have treatment whenever I needed it at Ayresome Park. John Hendrie, a popular attacking midfielder with the club, was also recovering from injury, and as we lay on adjacent treatment beds I was, as usual, the butt of his jokes. Quick-witted on and off the field, he was a lively character, who always wore a broad smile. We were not allowed to have mobiles switched on in the treatment room. Once my treatment was completed, I drove to an appointment at an estate agent's office, where I took a call from a reporter from the *Evening Gazette*. This was not unusual, as since the 1989 Cup Final the *Gazette* often rang for my thoughts on football issues.

But this time the call was not from chief sports writer Eric Paylor, or any of his team. Instead it was from the news desk. I was asked if I had any information about the incident at Hall Garth School. I told the reporter that I didn't know what he was talking about, but rather than explain, he hung up. This was the school where two of my children, Emma and Craig, were pupils. At this point I was not worried, but curious enough to ask the girls in the estate agent's if they knew anything.

One of them said, "There's been an incident reported on the news." I was out of the office like a shot, in the car and driving towards the school, when my phone rang again, the call being from the same young reporter. He said, "I've found out a bit more. There has been a stabbing, and we understand that your daughter is involved. One girl has been killed and we don't know whether it's your daughter." How I kept the car on the road I don't know. A reporter should never deliver news like that. I frantically made a couple of calls and found out that Emma had been rushed to hospital, and was alive. I hastily rang Lynette, who knew what had happened, to say that we would meet at the hospital.

A thousand questions flashed through my head. And there were no answers. What had happened? Why? How? Was Emma badly hurt? Had anyone really been killed? If so, had the reporter thought that it was Emma, but didn't want to say? It's never a good time for your estranged wife to meet your new girlfriend, but there can't be much worse circumstances than this. Fortunately, that was the least of my worries. The shock that the news had brought overrode everything else. Lynette, who worked close to the hospital, waited for me outside, and we rushed in together.

Elaine had heard of the incident before I had and was already by Emma's bedside. And when Elaine and Lynette met for the first time, both were courteous and concerned only about Emma. It was clear that Emma was not badly hurt and the relief was immense. There was a moment's silence, then an explosion of voices. Elaine explained that she had frantically been trying to get hold of me, but couldn't because my mobile was switched off. And Emma was hysterical as she tried to tell me what had happened. Much of it was high-pitched babble, which couldn't be deciphered. I had already been told by medical staff that her close friend Nikki Conroy had been killed, and it was obvious from Emma's blurted words that she didn't know that.

She was suffering trauma and superficial knife wounds. She managed to say that she didn't know how the other girls were. We tried our best to reassure her, then stepped out of her earshot to speak to staff. They said Emma would be all right as far as her injuries were concerned, but had to be told about Nikki. Elaine was with me as I spoke to the doctor and nurses. It was decided that I should break the news.

If you think that making a penalty decision at Old Trafford is a tough call, it pales into insignificant trivia compared with walking back to your daughter's bedside to tell her that she has lost a dear friend in such an appalling manner. Nikki had been fatally stabbed by a man wielding a knife who had burst into the school.

It seemed to be a random, unprovoked attack. One other pupil had suffered slight injuries, similar to Emma's. The attacker was a former pupil, Stephen Wilkinson, who was twenty-nine when he returned to the school that day, armed with a knife. He stabbed Nikki, and slashed out at other girls, catching Emma, and her friend Michelle, before being tackled and overwhelmed by brave teachers. Considering the state of shock the staff must have been in, they reacted brilliantly. We can never thank them enough, for without their intervention Emma and other pupils would probably have been killed along with poor Nikki. Wilkinson was later sentenced to indefinite detention in a psychiatric hospital. I rarely think of him, but when I do, I hope that, for his own sake, he is never released.

There is nothing that the school could have done to prevent the tragedy, and while it happened in seconds it will never be forgotten. Like Dunblane the following year, these things can, and do, happen. Whenever there is a tragedy on a similar theme, the media contact me to ask me to comment on how the parents feel. They may be well meaning, but I always decline. No parent needs telling how they would feel if it was their child. If there is a good side, it is that tragedy can bring out the best in some people. The way that the school, parents, other pupils and the wider community rallied round bears testimony to the warmth of human nature. The school has since planted a memorial garden in memory of Nikki.

Unfortunately, in other people such incidents can bring out the worst. We were sickened at the time, and remain shocked to this day, at the way some members of the media behaved, with their lust for exclusive angles of the tragedy. Pupils of Hall Garth School were offered money from reporters keen to get photographs of the girls involved. In the days that followed we recognised the blown-up images of Nikki, Michelle, and Emma as those from official school photographs taken the previous year.

Having delivered the awful news to Emma, and spent some time with her at the hospital, we all went back to the family home. The drive there was less frantic than the rush to hospital had been. We were all in reflective mood. But a shock was in store as we turned into the suburban cul-de-sac where I had started married life. The avenue had been taken over by scores of reporters swarming around our car to take photographs through the window.

Nikki lived in an adjoining road, which is why the whole area was under siege. We ran the gauntlet before diving into the house. Even though I had already said "No comment" the doorbell rang incessantly. Other news people came down the side of the house to look in through the back windows. After we had spent some time at Elaine's house, Lynette and I drove to our flat. That evening the phone rang and to this day we don't know who was on the other end of the line. Someone had found our number, even though we were ex-directory. The voice said, "I'm sorry about what happened, but don't get involved. If he [Wilkinson] ever comes on to the streets, it will be sorted." Whoever the voice belonged to, I'm sure he meant what he said. The tragedy gave me a more balanced outlook on life. I was thirty-eight when it happened, and since that time haven't dwelt on minor mistakes, or let problems get on top of me. People say that incidents of that magnitude put your life into perspective. It's a cliché but it's most certainly true.

Twenty-four hours later it was business as usual, at least outwardly, as I refereed York City versus Reading. I sent Reading boss Mark McGhee to the stands. The following day I refereed a Midland Senior League game at Darlington, then on the Saturday, Easter Saturday, was on duty at Cambridge. People may have thought that I was callous to referee again so soon, but it was my way of coping, and I had full support from the family. The back page of the *Sunday People* disappointed us with its headline: "Agony of Match Official" or words to that effect. The story gave the impression that I was putting the job first. I wasn't, and had Emma died, I may never have refereed another game.

That Sunday morning, Leeds United physiotherapist Alan Sutton phoned. He had driven to Elland Road to get my number so that he could pass on his best wishes to Emma. Whenever you read headlines putting football in a bad light, it's worth remembering all the good people in the game, who rally round like one big family. Emma has grown up into a lovely young woman, yet, while very confident, she is still affected by those dreadful memories. However, she copes. Counselling and the resilience of the pupils and teachers, especially the head, were an inspiration. They all drew strength from each other, which helped Emma.

We wouldn't wish tragedy on anybody, but it does strengthen you. Those involved saw life's trauma in a way that no textbook, or teaching, can prepare you for. But Emma came through.

6

ON MY WAY UP

By now I was an experienced Football League referee, and the word on the grapevine from friends at the FA was that if I did well in the coming season, I could be in line for a place on the Premiership list. I was confident that I could officiate at the top level, and the people who held my destiny in their hands were watching my performances, especially when it came to the big matches that were to take place towards the end of the season.

The great unwritten rule of refereeing is to be beyond reproach and do nothing to encourage accusations of bias. However, sometimes (well, a lot of the time) a referee's decision is interpreted wrongly by club officials, players and fans. Different people can have different opinions of the same incident, and react differently.

One extreme example of a fan taking exception to my performance was after Oldham played Portsmouth at Boundary Park. Portsmouth were battling against relegation from the old First Division, and needed to win to ease fears of the drop. I didn't endear myself to Portsmouth – because I gave two penalties to

Oldham in the first half. Both were clear-cut and while the Portsmouth players accepted the decisions without too much fuss, the manager, Jim Smith, launched a barrage of insults at me in the tunnel at half-time. Jim is a fearsome chap when he's riled, and there was no finesse about this exchange. It was face to face, and to his credit he didn't hold back. I appreciate people who say it as they see it, even if I can't agree with them. I kept my cool, but even though I twice asked him to calm down, he continued to bawl, and had to be escorted away by a steward. I had no option but to report him to the FA, because his outburst had been seen by several people, and probably heard by a few more. He was fined.

A few days after the game, a Portsmouth fan announced that he was going to take the Football League to the small claims court to recover the cost of his match ticket and travel expenses. He claimed that the Football League had spoilt his entertainment through my "ineffective and useless performance". Thankfully it never got to court to set a precedent. If it had, every fan in the country would be launching similar claims week in week out and refereeing, rather than being the difficult job it already is, would be virtually impossible. Many a time I'd felt aggrieved with the decisions of a referee too, when I'd travelled away with Boro. We used to moan all the way home on the bus, but by the time the next game came along, it was forgotten about. It is just one of those hard facts of football life – sometimes decisions go against you, and sometimes for you. And human nature being what it is, you always remember the decisions that go against you, even though the laws of probability mean these things even out.

Towards the end of the 1994–5 season I was asked to referee Tranmere against Southend. It was a Friday night game, which would enable me to go to Boro's away game at Barnsley the following day with my son Craig, who by then was thirteen. Tranmere were one of Boro's rivals for promotion and it was a big surprise when they lost the game 2–0. However, some Tranmere fans took defeat badly, and claimed that I'd deliberately given decisions in favour of Southend, in order to help Boro. The Tranmere fans perhaps thought that they were playing against twelve men, but I gave each decision as I saw it. I know that some complaints did reach the Football League and the FA, but nothing came of it. Virtually all referees have a favourite team, as they don't tend to get involved in the game if they are not fans in the first place. I think David Elleray was about the only one who didn't follow a top side. The authorities appreciate that, and have never shown any objection to it. I don't think there has ever been a proven case of bias by a referee.

Ironically, I didn't see the Boro game at Barnsley the following day. On my way to Tranmere, John Goggins of the Football League phoned, asking me to do a game at Burnley instead, because the appointed official had been forced to drop out.

I returned to Tranmere on the final day of the season – as a Boro fan. I didn't have any appointments that day, and so decided to take Craig to the game. If Boro won or drew, they would be promoted to the Premiership, and it was a close race. That was the year that the Premiership was reducing in size from twenty-two to twenty clubs, so there was only one automatic promotion place available. Craig and I both wore our Boro shirts, and it was just like old times when I was cheering the side on, although obviously I stopped short of shouting abuse at the referee. It was great being a fan again but it made me realise there was only thing I really wanted to be now – a Premiership referee. This game was just a nice, pleasant diversion – there was no chance of me being a regular fan again.

Boro drew 1–1, to seal a coveted place in the top flight in player-manager Bryan Robson's first season. But the previous debate was inflamed when I was seen before the game in a pub wearing my Boro shirt. Tranmere fans immediately accused me of being biased against them. I insisted that this was not the case, but quickly downed my drink, and headed for the turnstiles. That still was not the end of the matter, however, as I discovered when I switched on the radio on the way home to hear myself being discussed on a phone-in. Still, my conscience was clear. Fans were always looking for excuses and Tranmere were no different. I'm still reminded about that Friday night whenever I meet a Tranmere supporter.

So Boro would be playing in the Premiership in the 1995–6 season, that much was clear. Whether I would be there as a referee with them was less clear. Just as when I was hoping to become a Football League referee, even though I felt I'd done enough to secure a appointment, I was kept guessing. There were hints dropped by people in high places, and I was being given appointments to big Football League games. It seemed as if I had to prove myself yet again, just to make sure I had the temperament and ability required for the top.

I was appointed to the FA Cup final – not the Wembley Cup final, but the Women's FA Cup final, between Liverpool and

Arsenal, at Tranmere of all places! The women's version of the game is slowly being accepted, and this match was a tremendous advert for their game, and dispelled any myths that women's football isn't to be taken seriously. The game flowed from end to end, there were no histrionics, no feigning of injury, no swearing, no diving – it was a pleasure to referee. Why couldn't players in the Football League and Premiership have the same approach to the game? Certainly a referee's job is made more difficult in those split-second situations when a player claims to be injured by a challenge, or he dives in the penalty area from the slightest touch by a defender. I had none of that to deal with. It's ironic that it takes the ladies' game to display gentlemanly conduct.

The game was a major final appointment for me, but I was there with mixed feelings, because that same day Middlesbrough played their last ever game at Ayresome Park against Luton Town, before the eagerly awaited move to the new Riverside Stadium. I was delighted for John Hendrie, who scored the last ever goal at Ayresome.

I'm told that it was a great day, a carnival but also a funeral, the last chance to pay respects to a place where so many had enjoyed and endured their football. It was a place where I had grown up, and I had plenty of treasured memories. At about ten o'clock that night I managed to get into the ground. It was deserted, the only sound the rustle of a crisp packet picked up by the wind as I stood in my old spot in the Holgate End. I closed my eyes, and remembered my heroes and the great moments of my childhood and adolescence. But it was also a moment to look towards the future of the newly created Premiership – for both of us, I hoped.

After the regular season finished, I was delighted to be given two play-off semi-final matches, another indication that my performances were being scrutinised for one last time.

I took charge of Preston versus Bury in the Third Division play-off, with Eddie Wolstenholme, later to be my room-mate at referees' gatherings, as fourth official, and then Crewe against Bristol Rovers in the Second Division semi-final. Both games went well, so I was hoping to get the First Division play-off final between Reading and Bolton too, but that was given to the retiring Peter Foakes instead. I had received such good assessments that I was statistically considered the top referee of the previous three seasons. And when you know that is the case, you ought to be pretty confident that the bright lights are just around the corner.

Yet I was not at all convinced that I would be plucked from the Football League and put on the Premiership list. I wasn't sure I fitted the image. I was not a figure of authority like Harrow housemaster David Elleray, who was the referee that most of us looked up to. He had the education and training to control youngsters from the higher echelons of society. With my terraced Teesside upbringing, I wouldn't have got anywhere near his school, let alone been a senior teacher there. I know that controlling footballers requires skills of a different kind, but I was nevertheless unsure that my background was suitable in the eyes of those making the decisions.

I had a gut feeling that I would not be chosen. I may well have refereed hundreds of games in a near-perfect way, but you always tend to remember your bad games, and fear that others will remember you for those too. My worries ran deeper than that, however. At some meetings with the top brass I had not been short of confidence and had perhaps opened my mouth at the wrong time and been too opinionated about the game and the job. Also, I had turned up in casual clothes for formal meetings, and in a suit for informal get-togethers. Not often, but possibly enough to cast doubt over my suitability. After all, I was now trying to enter the elite, who not only refereed the top games in this country but who could be relied upon for European games too. Yet here I was, a straight-talking northerner. Nobody had ever tried to mend my ways to my face, but I had the feeling that things were said behind my back on occasions after I had left the room. But my coach – there was one to every ten or twelve referees – had assured me that I was highly thought of, and he must have been right, for my promotion did indeed arrive.

The Premiership appointment system is in some ways rather cruel, in that there is no letter of rejection, only a letter informing of promotion. For those who are not chosen, the first they hear of it is through colleagues revealing that their own letter has arrived. So it gradually dawns on those who have received no letter that they have been overlooked. And there's no confusing the letter. As soon as you pick it up you can tell by the postmark that it's not the gas bill!

My delight was tempered by the feeling that I would be starting all over again. I had to prove myself at a new level where the spotlight and media focus was intense. I was well aware that what awaited me would be light years ahead of anything I had experienced over the last sixteen years. Whenever, in any walk of life, you move to a new level, you have to question whether you are up to it. You have to be honest with yourself, for if you sail headlong into uncharted waters thinking you can deal with it without batting an eyelid, you are almost certainly heading for a fall.

I'm six feet tall, well built, and experienced in the ways of football, but inside I felt like a little boy heading off for the first day at school, wanting to stick to what was familiar rather than venture into the brave new world. Unlike with school, you have a choice. The letter states that you are "invited" to join the Premiership panel and to "please advise us by return, of your acceptance". Despite my doubts, there was no way I was going to say "no thanks". I phoned Lynette, by now my wife, and she was as delighted as I was.

I was a bag of nerves when I arrived at St James's Park for my first Premiership appointment on 19 August 1995. This was the big time, with its atmosphere, hype, media circus and me in the spotlight. Everything that August day was heightened. The sun seemed brighter and the colours of the fans more vibrant. Out of sight under the main stand the build-up seemed fairly normal, despite the butterflies. "All set," said referee Roger Dilks in a cheery tone, aimed at making the new boy feel all right. I was set, but as we led the teams, Coventry being the visitors, out to the strains of "Return of a Local Hero" and heard the roar of 36,000 Geordies welcoming their side for a new campaign, I shouted to Roger, "Blimey, it's not fucking Rochdale is it!" I had arrived.

I had always got a buzz out of the job, but despite all my experience, it hit me that day that I was on a new level, and the self-doubt that I experienced while waiting for my letter was still there. There were cameras everywhere – along the touchlines, behind the goals, in front of the dugouts, as well as in the usual gantry. I was intimidated. There was no hiding place. And I wasn't even the ref. It is policy to hand newcomers fourth official duty on the opening day of the season, to give them the opportunity to acclimatise without too much pressure. It's a key role, and now that there is such a thing, you wonder how we ever got by without one. There's much more to it than raising the electronic board at the end of each half. You are a standby referee or assistant referee; have to keep both benches in check; and are the referee's eyes and ears off the pitch. You are also the butt of questions and accusations from both managers, who often try to put you into difficult and compromising situations.

They ask questions like, "You saw their lad kick my player, why didn't the referee? Aren't you going to do something?" So you need a strong sense of diplomacy, which isn't always easy to put into practice when you're trying to push a manager back into his technical area. It is not the fourth official's role to interfere with any decisions that the referee makes. Fortunately, my first Premiership game on the touchline passed without any incident.

All referees accept that they are not perfect, and I knew that over the season I would make mistakes. Equally, I knew that when I did, I would be savaged by the top managers, players and media. It was inevitable, and it was frightening. There would be no respite. As I gazed around St James's that day, I thought, "This is it. Every week of the season I will be subjected to this. But most of the time I'll be out there where Roger is."

I recall top referee Graham Barber explaining to me a few years later how he felt going into his first Premiership game. He told me that he kept saying to himself in the build-up, "I'm a good ref or I would not be here." But he added, "No matter how often I said it, I couldn't escape the thought that I was as green as grass at this level." His words reflected exactly how I felt. It must be the same for a player who has moved up to a Premiership club. Instead of playing at Cardiff and Grimsby, he's suddenly going to Old Trafford, Anfield and Highbury. He knows his new club has faith in him, or they wouldn't have signed him – but does he believe in himself? Most do, and they make the grade to a greater or lesser degree. But perhaps it explains why some very talented footballers fall by the wayside, leaving fans and coaches baffled. That's what pressure can do to you. I handled it that day at Newcastle, and in doing so passed a huge test.

Newcastle passed a test too, for they beat Coventry 3–0 in what was to be a momentous season for the club under Kevin Keegan. He had led Newcastle back to the Premiership a couple of years earlier with the brand of attacking football that had become his trademark as a player and manager. He was worshipped by the fans, and having established the Magpies back in the top flight he was ready to launch a title assault. That meant taking on the giants of the game, Manchester United. The opening day result was a flying start, especially as Manchester United lost 3–1 at Aston Villa, with new signing Les Ferdinand among the Newcastle goals. I was in the technical area, and believe me, when the club's latest centre forward found the net the roar was deafening.

There was little time for me to reflect on the game for my debut in the Premiership middle was the following Wednesday, when I took charge of Nottingham Forest's home game with Chelsea. The profile wasn't as high as Liverpool or Arsenal, but it was high enough for me. I knew that the whole of my season would be shaped on my performance in this game – my every move would be analysed.

I set off from home feeling confident but the butterflies appeared in my stomach as I approached the centre of Nottingham. Forest's ground is just across the River Trent from that of their neighbours, Notts County, and I could see the two sets of floodlights moving closer. I'd been to the City Ground before as an assistant for a Cup tie, but this was an entirely new experience. I drove past Meadow Lane, Notts County's ground on my left, and then saw the City Ground – or to be more exact the word "FOREST" emblazoned on the seats in the cantilever stand on the far side of the pitch. The letters had the same impression on me that car headlights have on a rabbit.

I eventually prised my gaze away from them and told myself not to be so daft. "It's just another match," I repeated to myself, even though I knew it was more than that. I drove to the main entrance and said to the car park steward, "Match referee, Jeff Winter." "Ah, yes, sir, your place is over there." At least they were expecting me! I drove into my allocated space, took my kit out of the car boot, and walked through the main door. The foyer is packed with photographs and memorabilia, the most eye-catching being a huge photograph of Brian Clough's team celebrating victory after the European Cup final. I could already feel the difference between the Premiership and the Football League, and I could feel the weight of tradition and history at Forest. Frank Clark had taken over as manager from Clough, but I could sense Cloughie, in his green top, still keeping a watchful eye.

The dressing room was immaculate and I carefully laid out my kit – and for one anxious moment I thought I'd forgotten my socks. The club safety officer introduced himself, and we ran though the usual procedures such as what would happen in an emergency and who would escort me off the pitch at half-time and full-time. By then my assistants and fourth official had arrived, and we walked out on to the pitch. The City Ground had been chosen to stage matches in the forthcoming 1996 European Championships, and it was worthy, with a capacity of around 30,000 all seated.

The groundsman was carrying out last-minute jobs on a pristine and perfectly marked pitch. I looked at it in admiration, thinking to myself, "This is what it's all about." He saw me and came over, looking slightly worried. "Is it all right for you, ref?" "Yes, of course it is, no problems at all," I assured him. Back in the dressing room there was time to thumb through the match programme. The teams hadn't been named at that point, but I knew that players such as Ruud Gullit, Stuart Pearce and Dennis Wise would be playing. I had never before been in charge of a game involving so many big stars. I'd only seen them on the television. Pearce and Wise would provide me with an early test of my strength of character at the highest level. Pearce was renowned for his whole-hearted tackles that earned him the nickname

"Psycho", while Wise was a talkative workhorse in midfield. He was from the Wimbledon Crazy Gang and knew a few tricks on how to wind up opponents. Would I be able to control them?

I was relieved when the moment came to lead the teams out in front of the 27,000-odd crowd. Nerves are always higher in the build-up than in the moment when the action starts. The game went smoothly. In fact, I couldn't have asked for a better introduction to the Premiership. I made a couple of decisions against the home side that didn't go down well with the crowd who booed me, but that didn't bother me. Wise also questioned one of my decisions by saying, "You got that one wrong, ref," but I knew he was trying it on.

Pearce launched himself into tackles. I thought I felt the ground shake as he lunged for the ball, drops of sweat flying off his hair as he crunched into his work. He caught a Chelsea player slightly late with one tackle, and a quiet word from me was enough to remind him that another similar challenge would lead to a yellow card. He looked at the ground as I spoke to him, but was clearly taking in what I said. "If they're all like him, this Premiership lark won't be too bad," I thought.

In some ways I found it easier to referee than Football League games because the passing of the ball by players at Premiership level was more precise. There were fewer passes going astray that led to 50-50 challenges and the potential for fouls to be committed. However, it immediately struck me that while the tackles at this level are generally cleaner, they are even stronger than at lower levels. Premiership players are not only technically better than those in the lower leagues, but are generally bigger, quicker and stronger as well. The game flowed well, and I was able to read play and position myself in the right places. I booked four players: Kevin Campbell and David Phillips of Forest, Mark Hughes and Erland Johnsen of Chelsea, all for fouls, if I remember correctly. You feel much better for getting a name in the book, because it reaffirms your authority and lets the players know that just because you're a rookie, they can't get away with things. I didn't have much dialogue with Mark Hughes in any of our matches. He was a rugged and intense player who didn't say much on the pitch because of his total concentration – except when he questioned a free-kick decision against him, but even then he was quietly spoken.

The game finished goalless. Frank Clark thanked me and shook my hand as I walked off the field. I thought that maybe that was his seal of approval, which helped to ease lingering doubts. Just as with a new job, you have your misgivings about whether you've done the right thing by leaving your last job, but you feel a lot better after a couple of good days at work. At last I was now starting to believe that I was ready for the challenges ahead by clearing the first hurdle. On the way out of the ground I felt relaxed and confident, and didn't even glance up at the European Cup winners on the wall. I was in the big league with them now and didn't need to feel inferior.

Nevertheless, before long, the insecurities set in again. My first error of judgement at Premiership level arrived in my next match – Everton versus Southampton – even though it came well before kick-off. The referee always speaks to his linesmen before the game to explain what positions he wants them to take up, and the areas of the laws in which he wants them to be particularly vigilant, so that they can give him a helping hand. This briefing is normally held in the presence of the assessor, who in this instance was David Scott, from Burnley. I tended to conduct my briefings on the pitch where the atmosphere was less stuffy than in the dressing rooms. But while the weather was fine by the time we walked on to the pitch, it had earlier been pouring, and as I glanced down I saw water seeping over the top of David's smart shoes. If he minded, he didn't say, but I did wonder what marks he would give me, even if I played a blinder. Fortunately he didn't let wet socks influence him. Everton won 2–0, and Anders Limpar gained the distinction, if you can call it that, of being the first player to score a goal while I was in charge of a Premiership game.

On my return to Newcastle I was in charge, this time against Manchester City. The yellow card was flashed several times and the red once, as I showed the Newcastle fans that I was not going to take any nonsense. They were delighted, because it was mainly City players that were punished, Richard Edghill being sent off for two clear yellow card offences. If I had not been 100 per cent sure I would not have dismissed him. It was the first red card I had dished out at this level, and had there been any doubt, the player would have got the benefit of it. League leaders Newcastle won 3–1 as they continued their blistering start to the season.

You can't, of course, please all of the people all of the time, and Francis Lee, the Man City chairman, went berserk. He blasted me for the red card and for my general handling of the game. It was heat of the moment stuff, and quickly blew over. I took it in my stride. My only concern was that I had made a fool of myself when trying to dish out the red. I showed Edghill the second yellow, so everyone in the ground knew he would be taking an early bath. However, I couldn't get the red card out, as the button on my pocket had stuck. It was one of those situations where the harder you try to rectify a problem, the longer it takes. I was all thumbs, and eventually had to put the yellow card in my mouth while I tried to release the red.

I don't know how long the incident took – maybe no more than a few seconds – but it felt like an eternity. Fortunately, television was kind, the camera shot they chose being from behind me and towards Edghill. So the viewers didn't see me standing there with a yellow card gripped between my teeth. Some of the fans clearly did, however, because I could hear a few of them laughing nearby. It would have caused me more concern if Lee had told me how well I had controlled the game, but that I looked a right pillock for trying to eat a yellow card. Top managers could learn from that, if they really want to have a go at a ref! Criticism over decisions is water off a duck's back – but belittling a referee for his human foibles is much more effective.

By this era the coverage by Sky was in full swing and managers and players were widely interviewed after games – and the referee was often the subject. Equally, newspaper sports editors had by then decided that the ref should be given a mark. I often looked at my mark in the Sunday papers but didn't take it too seriously. Everybody has an axe to grind except the referee. There are very few neutral people in the stadium. When I walked on to Premiership pitches for the pre-match inspection, I could see all the TV cameras dotted around the ground, even the ones perched next to the goal stanchions. If a player or match official made a mistake, it was spotted by at least one camera, and the mistake could be replayed and magnified. Yet it was only before games that this hype and media scrutiny played on my nerves. Once the game got under way, I forgot about the cameras, and concentrated on the players.

Besides, I was my own biggest critic. I knew when I got decisions right or wrong, so had a base on which to justify myself when others questioned my decisions. And nobody was more adept at that than Alex Ferguson. United are one of the biggest clubs on the planet and all referees jump at the chance to take one of their games. That chance came for me in October 1995, in the second-round second leg of the League Cup tie against York City. That was when Ferguson and I crossed swords for the first time, and I was pleased that by then I was a Premiership ref and more able to handle the pressure.

Fergie had rested some of his stars for the first game at Old Trafford, and with everybody expecting United's reserves to run away with the game, York, then in the Second Division, instead produced one of the biggest shocks of the season, winning 3–0. The defeat hurt United's pride, and in the second leg Fergie fielded most of his stars, including Steve Bruce, Ryan Giggs, Gary Pallister, Eric Cantona and David Beckham, at a packed Bootham Crescent. The eyes of the football world were on little York City to see whether they would humble mighty United.

York held on against a relentless barrage, and even though they lost 3–1, they went through to the next round 4–3 on aggregate. A ranting Fergie wasn't happy, not only with the defeat, but also with the yellow cards I'd shown to Beckham, for a foul, and keeper Peter Schmeichel, for dashing out of his penalty area to protest at one of my decisions, as United got more and more frustrated. I had calmly told Schmeichel to back off and get on with the game. He did as he was told, but with a further shake of his head to stress his disapproval. The greater the intensity with which players protest, the more I stand my ground. And I apply that especially to goalkeepers who come charging out of their area to protest. It's my pet hate.

The United boss let me know his feelings at the end of the game, after waiting for me next to the players' tunnel. "Why didn't you add more time on?" he ranted. I didn't speak, instead simply waving him aside as I walked past. There was no need to stand there while he had his say. The game was over. I didn't even look back to see what he made of me brushing him aside.

The same month I refereed Arsenal for the first time. They won 3–0 at Barnsley in the League Cup, my main error being before the game, when I slipped on the slope between the dressing rooms and the pitch. The tunnel was long and the descent steep. I finished on my arse right in front of the television cameras. But I dusted myself down and got on with it. My main claim to fame where Arsenal are concerned is that I never sent off any of their players in my entire career. So whenever I took charge of Arsenal, there was never an incident that Arsène Wenger didn't see. It's amazing how much better his eyesight is when decisions go his team's way.

My first Premiership appointment with Arsenal was a game at

Aston Villa, in which I booked Ian Wright for diving. He was fuming, and vehemently denied it. I refused to be intimidated just because he was a star name. I looked him in the eye and said I was sticking to my guns. The decision incensed him so much that he even mentioned it years later in his autobiography, and reminded me of it more recently still when he played in a Celebrities versus Legends match on Sky television. I think diving is an awful offence. It's cheating, and angers everybody. If a referee wrongly gives a free-kick for a foul, that team, but nobody else, is angry. But if a player dives, he is not only trying to deceive the ref, but also the opposition players. So as an offence it is really bad because it creates a degree of mistrust missing from other foul play. If a player feels a ref has wrongly accused him of diving, he is more incensed than if he is wrongly accused of a foul. You are branding him a cheat. That's what Wright thought that day.

Wright is a complex character. Off the pitch he is one of the loveliest people you could wish to meet. He combines a wonderfully bubbly personality with being thoughtful and sincere. But once he crossed that white line as a player, he was a different animal. The red mist descended the second things didn't go his way. His language was colourful, and technically he could have been sent off virtually every time he opened his mouth. He came into the professional game late and maybe he felt that he had to make up for lost time, and be a winner whatever it took. I can't knock that, but it was always an eventful ninety minutes when you were out in the middle with him. Arsenal were not quite on a par with Manchester United at that time, but were clearly building a side that would hit the top in seasons to come. They had a steely resolve to go with their undoubted skills and were not an easy side to deal with from a disciplinary point of view.

By this stage of my career I was keen to avoid controversy. Games were now few and far between compared with the previous sixteen years when I had officiated morning, noon and night. I didn't want to be under the spotlight when there was a gap between games because controversy then had time to rumble on, and you couldn't get it out of your system until the next game.

So, in addition to Premiership duty I decided to take several games in the local leagues in order to keep my fitness levels high, and keep in touch with my roots. In a month's break between Premiership appointments, for example, I refereed two games in the Stokesley League, and was fourth official in UEFA Cup ties in Slovenia and Real Zaragoza. These days Premiership referees are given more Football League games to take charge of, whereas in my time, you did only the Premiership and the two main cups – the local league games that I squeezed in around the European trips were my personal choice.

Before long I was back in the thick of the Premiership action. After just twenty minutes of a Goodison Park clash between Everton and Leeds, I sent off Everton central defender Dave Watson for two bookable offences. The home fans made my life hell, singing, "The referee's a bastard." They were baying for my blood and as I came off the pitch at half-time, the booing built into a deafening crescendo. It's difficult to ignore that sort of treatment but I was learning how to.

When I got part way up the tunnel, to the elbow, Everton manager Joe Royle was waiting for me. Joe's a big chap but in the confined space of the tunnel he looked massive. It was impossible to get past him without further confrontation. I braced myself for a one to one which I expected to be more of a problem than the near 40,000 to one I had been experiencing for the previous 25 minutes. To my surprise and relief Joe said "No problem, Jeff. He had to go." It was my first meeting with Joe, a man I found to be one of the most honest people in the game. I can stand on my own two feet, but when you receive that sort of backing it helps. The crowd didn't let up in the second half, but Joe's words had provided an extra buffer between myself and the irate Scousers.

Some fans have long memories, and when I returned to Tranmere for an FA Cup game against QPR, the home supporters quickly turned on me. You rarely start any game afresh. There's always some lingering feeling – good or bad – from locals who remember your last visit. However, this time I was not the main source of controversy because the public address system operator at Tranmere got the sack.

QPR were in big danger of relegation from the Premiership so at the final whistle, in wishing the Rangers fans a safe journey home, he added words to the effect of "We look forward to seeing you again next season in the Football League." I included his comments in my report, but that won't have made any difference to the outcome. He was already in big trouble. You can't have club employees inciting fans like that.

We were midway through the season by now, and I was feeling comfortable and in control. That was driven home to me when I refereed the return game between Chelsea and Forest, my first visit to Stamford Bridge. The ground was in the throes of redevelopment, but just like Forest's ground, you could feel the sense of tradition. This time around I booked seven players, including Dennis Wise, as Chelsea won 1–0.

The quickest booking of my season came just twenty seconds into an FA Trophy tie at Gateshead, when home player Kenny Cramman was guilty, straight from the kick-off, of a typically ill-timed non-league challenge, a sliding tackle that upended his opponent. He looked stunned, using the age-old excuse, "It was my first one." Linesman Eddie Ilderton, who went on to be a Football League referee, was just as surprised. "Got to deal straight away on tackles like that," I explained.

A quiet word was just not part of the repertoire any more. The rules were not made by me. They had been laid down for Premiership referees, and I couldn't change my standards for a lower-level game. It was harsh, but that was the way it had to be. Ken Ridden, who was in charge of Premiership referees, encouraged us to be consistent, not alternative. Referees who are hoping for promotion, or to stay at the top, have to officiate the way they are told. Once you have reached your level, and there's nowhere else to go, your own discretion can come into play at times. My caution count was therefore very high in my first season. In a game between Southampton and Manchester City I booked eight players – four from each side – and red-carded Southampton's Gordon Watson for foul and abusive language. One of the City players cautioned was Gary Flitcroft in one of his last games for the club, and he couldn't believe it shortly afterwards when I sent him off after just two minutes of his Blackburn Rovers debut against Everton. His red card came so early that many of the fans, as well as the assessor, Neil Midgley, missed it because they were still taking their seats. It was Grand National day, and the kick-off had been delayed to allow the fans who had watched the race to make their way along the East Lancs Road. I punished Flitcroft for serious foul play against Duncan Ferguson. To be honest I reckon he got off lightly. If I'd only booked him, he might have had to face retribution from Big Dunc. Not that I had any option, because his tackle left me open-mouthed in amazement. Before the ninety minutes were up, Ferguson had also joined the list of names in my book.

Some refereeing decisions have to be made even before the game. When judging whether a pitch is fit for play, you have to take all sorts of factors into account. I faced a tricky such deci-sion before a Spurs versus West Ham game, which was shown live on Sky television. The pitch was saturated and the game in doubt. Imagine the problems that would be caused if the referee were to call the game off an hour and a half before kick-off with the cameras already in place. It's hard enough refereeing in the Premiership without having to take decisions that affect so many people. Commercially speaking, calling off a live TV game at that late stage is a disaster. Not only are thousands of programmes and all the food ordered, but those involved in staging and tele-vising the game stand to lose a fortune. Add to that the time and effort that the police and health and safety organisations have put in. On this occasion there had been a security alert on the London underground causing chaos, though the fans, never wanting to miss a match, had overcome the transport problems and were on their way.

With a potentially dangerous pitch, it's not just the safety of the players that you have to consider. If the ball won't roll, then the game will be farcical. On this occasion, the main problem area was in front of the dugouts, where the pitch was seriously water-logged. I mulled it over, but knew that if I was going to call the game off the decision had to be made quickly. Nobody from Sky approached me. It was my call and I decided to play, mainly because the area that was worst affected was not a key part of the pitch. Spurs lost 1–0, and while it was not a great game, and the ball did not always roll as freely as the players would have liked, the decision to play had been the right one. I never did call off a Premiership game.

Towards the end of that season an outburst from Kevin Keegan set me thinking. The Newcastle manager launched into a televised tirade against Alex Ferguson, whose United side had whittled down Newcastle's massive lead and subsequently overtaken them to reach pole position. It was the infamous occasion where Keegan raged that he would "Love it" if his team beat Fergie's to the title. It made me realise that managers get more and more wound up as the season reaches its climax, but referees tend to go the other way, with early season nerves evaporating as the season progresses. That's how it had been with me, and while the big clubs battled it out for the honours I felt calm and in control.

7

THE SEARCH FOR CONSISTENCY

I was pleased with my first season in the Premiership. I felt part of the scene, but it was now up to me to keep my place, and I knew it could not be taken for granted. In some ways, I felt like a manager who has had a season to settle into his new club but then knows that he has to produce good results. If the team starts to falter, then the manager comes under pressure, worries about the sack, and lives on a knife-edge from week to week.

Consistency was the referees' watchword. The FA wanted us to stick rigidly to the rules and to show yellow and red cards accordingly.

You would have thought that every referee would be focused only on their on-field performance, but the growing profile of the Premiership was beginning to affect some referees in the same way it affected the top players – they were developing big egos and would walk all over their colleagues to be seen as top dog. That's natural enough in any organisation, but in refereeing age seemed to counter ability, some senior referees overlooking their own failings to pass judgement on others.

When I got on to the senior list it was David Elleray who appeared to assume the mantle of top dog. I was not alone in feeling, at our get-togethers, that he, rather than refereeing supremo Ken Ridden, was running the show. We would look at video incidents from games and David would offer strong views on the decisions other referees had made. And he would do it in a way that suggested he knew more than we did. Instead of asking why we had made a certain decision, he would say, "You shouldn't have done that." He was at the same level as the rest of us, but was telling us how to do the job.

Dermot Gallagher then emerged as a challenger to David's unofficial position, but that threat disappeared when he suffered an injury at Newcastle in Euro 96. Paul Durkin seemed to spot his opportunity but he reckoned without a major threat lurking in the wings – in the shape of Graham Poll. If I had doubts about Elleray's role, they were nothing compared to how Graham Poll felt about him. The two came from opposite sides of the tracks. David was the eloquent, non-drinking, well-spoken Harrow housemaster; Graham was one of the lads, rough and brash. He liked a laugh, and a beer. They were linked by ambition, but Graham felt his style angered David, and he was right. Graham is not unlike me, yet in fact I got on much better with David. David and I had early feelings of mistrust towards each other. Along with other young referees I had laughed at his school-masterly tone. He once said to me, as if I were one of his more senior pupils, "Do you know, Winter, you're the better for knowing." With time, though, our misgivings about each other evaporated as we got to know and respect each other. I've read David's book, *The Man in the Middle*, and while I disagree with his insistence that a Cup Final referee must be on the FIFA list, it's probably my only gripe. I know he is moving up the FA hierarchy these days but his book reminded me of his principles and attitude to refereeing, and if two people from such diverse backgrounds as David and I can agree on most things, then it shows that there is hope for the future management of the game.

Canny referees sought not only to please the top referee, but also the assessors and the match appointment secretary. Referees learnt very early in their careers that if they had the right assessor appointed to their game they could progress quickly. In other words, there was more to progressing than making the right decisions on the pitch. Call me naive, but I settled for trying to referee every game to the best of my ability. While the politics and machinations behind the scenes annoyed me, I tried not to let it affect me. Easier said than done, of course.

I had taken charge of a few derbies since arriving on the Premiership stage and didn't think that a game between Spurs and West Ham would be any different. While a derby between those two London clubs doesn't have quite the intensity as Spurs against Arsenal, they're still passionate and fiercely competitive affairs, and sometimes it's difficult to keep the game flowing when the tackles are flying thick and fast. That was the case in this game, with frequent interruptions when there was no alternative but to award a string of free-kicks and speak to players. There were no particular exchanges that I remember, because none of the players argued back at me, and the tackles were keen, but not malicious. The players simply wanted to get on with the game and win it, which Spurs did, 1–0. In the changing room I felt satisfied with my performance in which, despite the nature of the game, I'd shown only one yellow card. But the smile was wiped off my face when there was a knock on the dressing-room door, and in walked the match assessor Philip Don.

Philip had retired from refereeing a couple of years earlier, bowing out after he had taken part in the 1994 World Cup finals in the US. He'd been England's only representative, following in the footsteps of top officials of their day such as George Courtney and Pat Partridge. I had tremendous respect for Philip because he'd been at the top for years. He questioned two of my decisions, and stated that under the laws of the game, they should have both been yellow cards, so I had not taken the correct action. I put my case but Philip was adamant and said he was going to report my failure to show yellow in his report.

I felt he was too hard on me on that occasion. When I had left the field, there were no complaints from either manager or any of the players about my handling of the game. I felt that I had contributed to the flow by allowing play to continue wherever possible, and instead of raising the temperature of the game by showing cards, I had decided to settle for a quiet word with players. My decisions, I felt, were further justified by the fact that Spurs and West Ham weren't the dirtiest of sides, and there was respect between them. But Philip didn't take those factors into consideration. He wanted to look at my performance purely from a consistency point of view and he analysed the two tackles in depth.

He said that guidelines had been laid down and even though I was being consistent in my own way, other referees might have produced yellow cards. His point was that players might make the same illegal tackles in their next match and be booked, and then wonder why in my game I hadn't punished them. He felt that players needed to know exactly where they stood, and yellow cards should therefore be dished out whenever there was a bad tackle.

I suppose that he felt he needed to stamp his authority as an assessor, at a time when laying down strict and consistent rules was the FA's mantra. But his actions didn't do much for my morale, because I was still relatively new to the Premiership, and criticism stung me. I still felt that he should have handled my match analysis better. It was a relief that my next game was in the Cleveland League at Cargo Fleet. There were no red cards, no yellows – and no Philip Don.

Buoyed by a return to my roots, I was soon back on the big stage, taking charge of Manchester United, at Southampton. United's visits to the Dell were often full of incident – they lost 3–1 on their previous visit, the infamous occasion when the players changed from their grey strips at half-time because they claimed they had difficulty picking out their team-mates. They wore blue and white for my visit there, but it did them no good as they lost 6–3. They didn't help themselves by having Roy Keane sent off for two yellow cards for fouls in the first half, with Eric Cantona, Jordi Cruyff and Gary Neville following him into the book. Neville's protests were the strongest.

Keane cast a dismayed look in my direction but didn't argue, which was rare for him as he had a short fuse and always seemed ready to argue over the most trivial point. His dismissal didn't go down too well with his manager, however, who protested from the touchline. Later in his career, Keane, like me, seemed to mellow with experience and to be a touch more restrained when going for tackles, but I never had much of a conversation with him because, as Manchester United captain, he was totally focused. I think the most I got out of him was heads or tails.

Gary Neville and his brother Phil seemed to epitomise United's snarling and arrogant attitude in this era. They were always quickly in my face when things didn't go their way, but in the eyes of their manager didn't seem to do much wrong. I felt that my decisions showed the consistency that I was now focused on achieving in every game. In any case, United needn't have worried because they lost only three more league games that 1996–7 season, as they again beat Newcastle to the title, this time by a margin of seven points.

My performance at the Dell, however, had not gone down well with Alex Ferguson. I didn't referee another Manchester United game for over two years. I began to suspect that the opinions of the bigger clubs and the psychological pressure they apply could affect the appointment of referees. After a newspaper reporter did the stats, he told me that I had refereed around fifty Premiership matches during this sequence involving 100 teams. But not once did a match involve United.

While I was trying to establish myself in the Premiership, Boro were battling their way towards a first ever FA Cup final, and

David Elleray played a pivotal role. While referees try to make every decision in a totally impartial way, from a supporter's perspective there are only two types of refereeing decision – those that go in favour of their team, and those that are wrong. The FA Cup semi-final of 1997 was probably the best game I have ever seen. From the first whistle I gripped my seat high up in the largest stand at Old Trafford and watched the drama unfold. The game had everything, with teams that were two divisions apart, one with journeyman professionals, or youngsters like Kevin Davies, the Chesterfield striker who was just starting a career that was to lead to the top, the other packed with top international stars including Italian striker Fabrizio Ravanelli and Brazilian maestro Juninho.

Yet Chesterfield went 2–0 up, got pegged back to 2–2, went 3–2 behind, then equalised in the dying seconds of extra time. The game had two penalties, a red card for Boro's Vladimir Kinder and, of course, the moment of controversy when Chesterfield were denied what would surely have been a decisive goal that would have put them 3–1 ahead. David refereed the game well, defying the tension and adrenalin of the occasion. He had been faced with the sort of decision on which a referee's reputation can be broken. It was a career-defining moment when he ruled "no goal" after Jon Howard's shot appeared to cross the line. Television replays showed that the whole ball was over the line, but once a decision is made, it stays made. David is such a well-respected referee that his reputation remained intact. It was an honest decision – and that's what matters. He did everything an official can be expected to do to ensure he got it right.

His authority during the match was never in question, and that's not easy to achieve in such a tense atmosphere. To try to explain how charged semi-finals are, I'll tell you a tale from that day that demonstrates it perfectly.

The Chesterfield fans filled half the stadium, round to the press box. Right on the end of the press seats was a sportswriter, alongside the Chesterfield masses. He later told me what he saw. One of the fans, clothed from head to toe in blue and white, was particularly animated, his face contorted with the agony of seeing his side desperately trying to hang on after Boro had pulled it back to 2–1. He shouted, screamed, buried his head in his hands, threw his eyes to the heavens, burst into tears when Boro equalised, and generally went through the full gamut of emotions. At a break in play, thinking that the fan was so wound up he could suffer a heart attack, the sportswriter tried to calm him down by making a general comment. Pointing out a Chesterfield player, the journalist said, "He looks a hell of a prospect. How's he done this season?" The supporter replied, "Dunno, I'm really a Spurs fan. I live in Chesterfield, but this is the first time I have seen them play for twenty years." If a man with only vague affiliation to the team could feel like that, God knows what the diehard Spireites were going through!

Boro romped to a 3–0 win in the replay, and it was off to Wembley to face Chelsea. Much as refereeing had taken over a huge part of my life throughout that era, Boro's Cup Finals were proud and hugely important times for me. I was drawn into refereeing by my general love of football, but my roots remain the basis on which my life has been built, and success for Boro brings the sort of joy that few things can match.

That Cup Final was a strange affair, partly because I was to referee on the famous turf the very next day, in the FA Trophy final between Woking and Dagenham & Redbridge. So the Saturday was a sober day for me. I watched from the posh seats (though I paid for my tickets for both the final and semi-final). I was horrified when Boro were struck a mortal blow with the quickest ever Cup Final goal, Roberto Di Matteo's shot floating over keeper Ben Roberts in the first minute. We lost 2–0, and I couldn't even drown my sorrows because of my appointment the following day. So along with the other officials for the Trophy game, I went to a quiet restaurant. At least we thought it would be quiet.

Steve Lodge, who had refereed the final, was there with his linesmen. They were boisterous and elated after the day, and were winding down with the wine flowing. It was a strange scenario. People often view referees as robots, but Steve and I could not have been further apart in the emotional stakes that night.

I enjoyed the Trophy final. Woking beat Dagenham after I had sent off a Dagenham player for use of the elbow. I didn't spot the offence myself. The linesman did. Sky television commentator Martin Tyler was a happy man that night for he is a Woking fan. No doubt he raised a glass or two, and so did I. I could drown my sorrows at last. But I had got used to Wembley disappointment, for the FA Cup final defeat was Boro's second heartache of that memorable season. In April we had suffered against Leicester in the Coca-Cola (League) Cup final, Emile Heskey scoring a last-gasp equaliser for Leicester, who won the replay with a Steve Claridge goal.

At least there was one happy referee after the final, for colleague Peter Jones is a Leicester fan. We arranged to meet up before the Wembley game, and walked down Wembley way together, decked from head to toe in our team colours. A few fans recognised us, and smiled.

Peter had the fan's bragging rights for a while, but what bothered me more was whether I could maintain my refereeing standards. I started to have doubts about my ability in my third season, and wondered whether I would survive in the Premiership for I seemed to lurch from one crisis to another. I'm not all that superstitious but I should have known what was coming when I was invited to referee the first ever game at the Stadium of Light in Sunderland in July 1997.

There was a race against time to get the stadium ready for the friendly against Ajax, and even as the minutes ticked away there were workmen finishing off all over the place. I arrived four hours before kick-off, but had to keep out of the way, or I would have been handed a plug to wire, or a floorboard to nail down. After a rigorous inspection, the council awarded the safety certificate and gave the game the go-ahead, but it was a close call. Clearly, however, the council officials hadn't inspected the match officials' changing room because there was masking tape on the windows, and no door on the toilet! But that didn't bother me. I put it down to teething troubles, because I was eager to referee in a brand-new ground. After all, you have these sorts of problems when you move into a new home and you soon get over them.

After inspecting the lush green pitch of the 40,700 all-seater stadium, we decided to go for a cup of tea in the officials' refreshment area. To get there, we had to go up in a lift, but unfortunately when we reached the right floor, the door closed in front of me as I was about to step out of the lift behind the other match officials. Despite pressing all the buttons I was trapped inside. I'm not claustrophobic, so it was no problem, and I knew that I would soon be rescued. However, Tyne Tees Television, who was covering the build-up to the first match in the new stadium, heard that I was trapped and broadcast the news to an amused North East public.

I was freed twenty minutes later, to an embarrassing round of applause from the other match officials who had waited outside the lift to see my expression as I emerged. The game finished a goalless draw in front of a packed house and I disallowed a goal "scored" by Sunderland defender Kevin Ball, who was annoyed that he was denied the recognition of being the first player to score a goal in the new stadium. To this day he reminds me of it.

I don't know whether my spell in the lift was a bad omen, but my season seemed to go downhill from around October. The campaign had started without any problems. I refereed Liverpool at home to Leicester, and for the third successive match at Anfield with me in charge they lost. In my next game, I sent off Sheffield Wednesday's Benito Carbone as they lost 7–2 at Blackburn, although I thought it a little odd of the authorities to give Uriah Rennie the fourth official's role, considering that he lives just outside Sheffield. By that time the FA did not allow refs to take charge of games within their local area. What would the reaction have been if I'd had to pull out for any reason and Uriah was obliged to replace me? I think somebody must have forgotten where Uriah lived when they arranged the appointments. I can't recall a situation like it since.

After that game, things began to go wrong, starting with the Worthington Cup tie between Carlisle United and Tottenham at Brunton Park. For the one and only time in my career, I was struck by an object thrown from the crowd. Carlisle fans were furious that I hadn't awarded them a penalty in the first half, and as I was leaving the field at half-time, a youngster, just a few yards away behind the barrier, threw something that hit me just a fraction of an inch below my eye. It was painful and left a mark. The object was possibly a coin, and definitely not a Mars bar. I reported the incident to the police, and I believe that they arrested somebody, but it was a reminder to me how vulnerable match officials can be, and in stark contrast to my debut there in the Football League many years before.

If I was worthy of no more than a zero in that spectator's eyes, I was probably less than zero in the opinion of the *Sun* reporter at Newcastle versus Blackburn a few days later. I had never read much into match marks given by journalists until then. It's too easy for somebody watching to give a mark based on one incident in a game. There are so many things going on in a game that the ref has to keep an eye on. Spectators and reporters can't be aware of them all. If somebody feels that an incident hasn't been handled properly or, for example, a penalty or goal should have been given, then their judgement is impaired, especially if that person attends every game of a particular team. There is always going to be a feeling of bias and sympathy to the team in those circumstances. In the Sunday newspapers every week my mark was either six or seven, but in the *Sun* that Monday morning it was a big fat zero.

After the Newcastle game the reporter justified his mark by saying that both sets of supporters sang "You don't know what you're doing", as I booked eight players, two from Newcastle and six from Blackburn. I allowed the mark to affect me, even though I shouldn't have done, and began to question myself. Did I really not know what I was doing? Should I have booked those players? Should I have let the game flow more? Should I have joined in the singing? On reflection, if six was an average, then I put myself at either four or five. But I drew consolation from the fact that the assessors weren't all that critical. And it was they who were under the instruction of the FA, who wanted referees to consistently clamp down on foul play by flashing cards.

Nevertheless, the mark meant that I was under the spotlight. When somebody gives a zero mark, no matter whether you're a player or a referee, people wonder what's happened to cause it, even allowing for an element of bias. So I needed to restore my confidence immediately – which I was determined to do in my next game: Crystal Palace against Aston Villa. Things were fine until my assistant flagged for a free-kick against Villa, right in front of the Villa dugout. I held my whistle, waiting for a Palace advantage, but it didn't come because Villa committed another offence a few yards away. So I blew my whistle and awarded a free-kick to Palace, who took it quickly and scored an equaliser. I didn't think there was a problem until I looked over and saw the Villa boss John Gregory arguing with my assistant over where I'd allowed the free-kick to be taken from. He thought I should have given it from where the first offence occurred, whereas I'd allowed it to be taken from the place of the second foul. I raced back to my assistant and explained the decision, but while I tried to keep my cool, neither John nor his equally angry assistant Alan Evans accepted my explanation. At the disciplinary hearing, however, in a less fraught atmosphere, my version was accepted. The *Sun* gave me two out of ten for that match, so I was improving!

Sometimes my mark from the assessor was above average, on other occasions it was below. The FA wanted consistency above all else, but it seemed I wasn't providing it. If I couldn't find an acceptable level of consistency, would I be axed from the Premiership? On Boxing Day, I was given Sheffield Wednesday against Blackburn in the Premiership, and the same teams again a couple of weeks later in the FA Cup. The assessor on both occasions was Keith Hackett. Keith gave me an excellent mark in the first game but a poor one for the second, and I couldn't have agreed with him more. My performances were starkly contrasting. I felt in control of the first game, but not the second, when I was hesitant. My indecision filtered through to the players, which made it even harder for me. At least it proved that Keith gave honest assessments and was prepared to hand out both criticism and praise. My inconsistency was down to a lack of confidence, and I was feeling the pressure from above. I was handing out yellow cards in bundles of five, six, seven and even eight per game, brandishing them to try and assert my authority.

I even covered up an injury when I pulled a calf muscle in charge of Bolton against Leeds at the Reebok Stadium, because I thought that if I pulled out of a game, either before or during it,

It was some journey: As a schoolboy (*right*) in 1966 and (*below*) at the pinnacle of my career – as a referee in the best league in the world.

Below: Like most Premiership referees, I was often surrounded by stewards – and by controversy – as I left the pitch.

Above: Roy Keane sees red in 1996 against Southampton at the Dell, where I also booked another three Manchester United players – and for whatever reason didn't referee another game involving United for two years.

Above: Booking Duncan Ferguson in the cauldron of the Merseyside Derby at Goodison Park in 2001. I also had to arbitrate when Duncan himself came in for some pretty rough treatment at times.

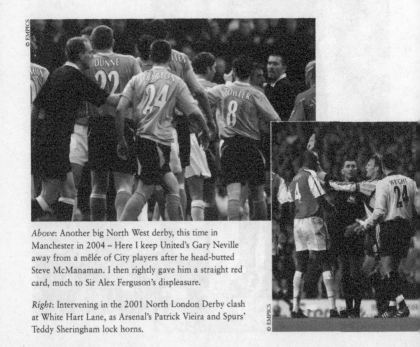

Above: Another big North West derby, this time in Manchester in 2004 – Here I keep United's Gary Neville away from a mêlée of City players after he head-butted Steve McManaman. I then rightly gave him a straight red card, much to Sir Alex Ferguson's displeasure.

Right: Intervening in the 2001 North London Derby clash at White Hart Lane, as Arsenal's Patrick Vieira and Spurs' Teddy Sheringham lock horns.

Left: Who, moi? I told Thierry Henry that Arsenal's dazzling skill was making me forget to referee the match, so he promptly committed a foul to check I was concentrating! The Gunners put five past Pompey in this thrilling FA Cup quarter-final in 2004, which made me want to continue refereeing for ever.

Right: Yellow-carding Roy Keane after an incident with Patrick Vieira in another fired-up clash between Manchester United and Arsenal – this time in the FA Cup in 2003. I wasn't the only official that had to contain the two captains' less-than-friendly relationship down the seasons.

Right: Lee Bowyer makes his feelings quite clear at my decision to send him off in the Arsenal–Leeds clash in 2001 for two bookable offences. Lee was on the wrong end of another decision the next season when I decided that David Beckham had elbowed him accidentally (*above*). TV replays had the benefit of hindsight – but in the heat of the moment, I felt I'd made the right decision.

I had many tangles with Sir Alex Ferguson: As fourth official in Manchester United's home clash with Arsenal in 2002 (*left*) and again in 2003 (*right*) against Newcastle at St James's Park, where ref Uriah Rennie sent him off for abusive language and making accusations that officials had "cheated" – which led to disciplinary action against Fergie by the FA.

Left: Another fiery character, Sam Allardyce – He and I had a good relationship in my refereeing days, but the Bolton manager fell out with me after I spoke about the El Hadji Diouf spitting incident in the media.

Above: I had a few run-ins with Gordon Strachan as a player and a manager. Here he brands my decision a "disgrace" in typically colourful language in the Chelsea–Coventry clash in 1999. Perhaps he'd have been a little kinder if he'd known I was missing my daughter's eighteenth birthday to ref the game.

Left: With a couple of young trainees during my trip to Canada, where I was invited to help educate Canadian officials in 2000 – a very pleasurable experience all round.

Below: Officials running a different kind of line for a change – with my fellow referees at a charity line-dancing event.

Below: Mark Halsey collides with me at the fitness programme at Staverton Park in 2004. The resulting injury to my leg was extremely painful and might have kept me out of the FA Cup Final had Mark not thrown me straight into a bath of freezing cold water!

© EMPICS

After the Celebrities versus Legends match, with two bona fide legends of the North East, Gazza (*left*) and Sir Bobby Robson (*below*), one of the managers for the day.

In La Manga for *Superstars* with (*left*) Steve Claridge and the broken nose from head tennis that Dennis Wise found so amusing, and (*below*) Olympic silver-medallist Amir Khan.

Left: Insert the obvious joke about referees... Saying hello to a guide dog after refereeing my final Nationwide League game between Nottingham Forest and Wigan in 2004.

Right: In disguise at the 1997 League Cup Final with sons Craig and Mark.

The FA Cup Final 2004 was a proud day that I was lucky enough to share with my family: with Lynette on the Millennium Stadium pitch before the game (*above*) and with son Mark, daughter Emma and son Craig (*right*).

Above: My last game in charge, the FA Cup Final 2004 between Manchester United and Millwall, with (*left–right*) fellow officials Roger East, Matt Messias and Tony Green.

Giving Dennis Wise the only yellow card of the Final after one too many of his old tricks (*left*) and him giving me a hug after the game (*right*). The Millwall player/manager graciously substituted himself late on to allow sixteen-year-old Curtis Weston to become the youngest ever FA Cup Finalist.

it would be considered a weakness. The game flowed from end to end, and was highly competitive. Maybe I should have come off, but I felt my fourth official wasn't experienced enough to take over, so I carried on and finished the ninety minutes, keeping up with play all the time. My assistants didn't notice and, more importantly, neither did the assessor, who gave me a good mark. That was my main aim now, to satisfy the assessor, even if some of my decisions angered players and managers. The assessor held the key to my future in the Premiership.

At Liverpool against West Ham late in the season my heart was in my mouth when I learnt that Philip Don, who had just been named as the new referee's supremo, and therefore in charge of which refs got which Premiership games, was going to be the match assessor. I was surprised to learn this; Philip lived near London, so what was the point of coming the best part of two hundred miles to see me at Liverpool when he could have seen me nearer his home on another occasion? Was he running the rule over me in order to make a final decision about my future? Was this going to be my final game in the Premiership? I was very apprehensive, especially considering our encounter at White Hart Lane the previous season.

All these thoughts were racing through my head as I drove through the Anfield gates. I loved refereeing there, because of its status, and wondered if this was going to be the venue where the final curtain came down on me. Certainly some of the fans mingling around the players' entrance were hoping so. "Fuck off, Winter, we never get anything when you're in charge!" they ranted. One thing about Scousers, they have a very good knowledge of all aspects of football. They knew I'd been to Anfield three times, and the opposing team had won on every occasion. I have always ignored comments from fans. There is no way you can start arguing with them. Stop to make your point and you will be surrounded in no time, so it's a case of walking briskly past them and into the sanctuary of the stadium.

But the Winter hoodoo was broken, as Liverpool won 5–0. I felt I'd had a good game and Philip, much to my relief, agreed. There was no criticism at all – and then he revealed that he'd been visiting relatives on Merseyside, which is why he'd arranged to come to the game. There'd been no hidden agenda, just my paranoia. A few weeks later, I received a letter saying that I was going to be retained in the Premiership. After the season I'd had, it was a huge weight lifted. If I'd been kicked out of the Premiership, it would have been a major anti-climax to drop back into the Football League. Nevertheless, I would have carried on refereeing. Despite the intensity I was loving it.

I was not alone in finding it tough. There had been a huge amount of pressure placed on every referee in the Premiership, because of the search for consistency. I wasn't the only one worried about job security. The "benefit of the doubt" approach on the field hardly existed, and out of self-preservation, referees followed the motto "When in doubt, get the card out", which sometimes didn't help the mood and spirit of the game.

Personally, I didn't think this approach was always the answer, because prudent man-management sometimes brought better results. What was wrong with a few quiet words to players when things looked like getting out of hand? I felt that they would respect me more for that than for being card-happy. Yet it was regarded as a sign of weakness by the powers-that-be if you weren't controlling games by dishing out red and yellow cards. They had made that perfectly clear in the pre-season get-together. Referees had to toe the party line, and unfortunately some very good refs who couldn't cope with the high expectations were removed from the list. Happily for me, I was still a part of the best league in the world – but I had to make sure I stayed in it.

While I was sometimes given flak by angry managers and players for my performance, fans would criticise me in games I wasn't even refereeing. Whenever I was free, naturally I would go and watch Boro. On one such occasion, we played Manchester City at the Riverside and had Steve Vickers sent off for violent conduct. There was no doubt about it, he'd used his elbow on an opponent. However, the Boro fans gave Vickers a standing ovation as he left the field, and that was a reaction that, to be honest, still baffles me today. If a player is guilty of violent conduct on an opponent and gives his side a disadvantage by being red-carded, why should he then be applauded for his indiscretions as he leaves the field, especially if his team goes on to lose or draw the game, and he ends up with a three-match suspension? Maybe it's a show of loyalty to the player by fans, but I think it's misguided.

After the match, several fans came up to me and complained bitterly about the dismissal, as if I could do something about it – like going to the referee's changing room and telling him how wrong he was. I gave them short shrift. The referee, Alan Wiley, had been quite correct. I felt that I was seeing things very clearly now. I must have been – I wasn't going to be swayed even by Boro fans. I was to need that unwavering eye in the seasons to come.

8

DEALING WITH THE STARS

A rather unlikely version of *Beauty and the Beast* in front of a partisan audience early in the 1998–9 season helped firmly establish me on the Premiership map. The venue for this production was neither Broadway nor the West End of London, but the gritty northern theatre of Elland Road. The cast was Leeds United and West Ham, and the starring role of the Beast was taken by renowned hard man Neil "Razor" Ruddock of West Ham, while Beauty was played by Leeds forward Harry Kewell.

Let me make it clear that by describing Kewell as "beauty" my sexual preferences are not being brought into question. He is beauty in this instance purely because of his footballing skills, which contrast sharply with those of Ruddock. Ruddock was nutmegged by Kewell, and every one in the ground, me included, collectively held their breath. I might as well have brandished the red card there and then and told Ruddock that I was sending him off for intent. Unfortunately, I couldn't do that and had to wait for an offence to be committed. It was not a long wait. Razor felt he had been humiliated by the jinking skills of Kewell and decided to take the law into his own hands.

If Kewell knew it was coming – and he ought to have done – then he either didn't or couldn't take evasive action. He was unceremoniously sent spinning into the air by a challenge I can describe only as horrendous. If Kewell defied gravity on the way up, he didn't on the way down, and the grace he had shown in beating his man a little earlier was nowhere to be seen. Ballet it was not. The card was out before Kewell had hit the ground, and as Ruddock's red mist evaporated he saw the red card. He didn't have any argument with me and I don't recall a word being exchanged between us. He knew, as I knew, that he had to go. On his way off the pitch he asked the fourth official, "Was it that bad?" The answer was straight. "Oh, yes." Without Ruddock to stop him Kewell inspired Leeds to a 4–0 win.

In the 36,000 crowd was my senior refereeing coach George Courtney, refereeing chief Philip Don, and match assessor Keith Hackett. The job of the coach was to motivate and encourage refs, and they could take issue with assessors on behalf of the refs. The trio are among the best referees this country has produced and I had relished the opportunity to show them that I was in charge. I had no choice but to show red, but if I could have avoided it I would have done. When Kewell knocked the ball through Ruddock's legs, I was praying for the ball to go out of play before retribution took place. Had it done so, I would have had a word with Razor to try to diffuse the situation. But before I had any opportunity to stop play, the act of revenge took place and the outcome was inevitable.

A year earlier I would have been intimidated by having three such senior figures there to judge me, but I was already growing comfortable in the spotlight and saw their presence as an opportunity. Though I do recall thinking to myself before the game, "This is shit or bust, Jeff! Your reputation will be enhanced or in tatters after this one game."

Ruddock is a brilliant character, the sort football needs. He is loved by the fans of his team, but hated by the opposition. He wears his heart on his sleeve just as I do, and always gave an edge and an atmosphere to a football match. If his name was on the team sheet, fireworks were likely. I don't think he was a nasty guy, but sometimes in the heat of battle, he couldn't contain himself. And he got his own back at a charity event. I was there at his invitation, and had to take my turn at karaoke. Razor is a much better singer than me – and it showed!

There were few trouble-free games in the Premiership. And when Gordon Strachan was involved, it seemed there were no trouble-free games. Being accused of incompetence is just one of the many insults that referees face. We're often told that while we know the rules, we don't understand the game, or the pressures of playing or management. We are also accused of acting like machines.

In January 1999 I was in London for a Chelsea versus Coventry game. I remember the occasion well, because it meant missing my daughter Emma's eighteenth birthday. There is no room for sentiment, and refereeing duties have to come first. Strachan disagreed with one of my decisions, jumping up and down, swearing, and gesticulating from the touchline. "That's fucking disgraceful!" was one of the phrases I heard. I asked him to calm down, but he persisted, so I sent him from the dugout, even needing the help of a police officer.

I couldn't see Emma the following day either, as I had to compile my report on Strachan, and attend a get-together of referees in the Midlands. But I hadn't forgotten. When a racehorse, called Bobby Grant, owned by a friend of mine, won at Haydock, I could afford a nice present for her out of my winnings. I occasionally have a flutter on the horses, but have always steered clear of betting on football matches. Emma certainly appreciated my efforts a lot more than Strachan did.

Less than two months after our altercation – and the subsequent disciplinary hearing – Strachan and I we were together again, for a relegation battle at Highfield Road, Charlton being the visitors. My relationship with him worsened when I had to dismiss Coventry striker John Aloisi for violent conduct, for the use of an elbow on Charlton full back Danny Mills. Post-match we were treated to Strachan at his eloquent, entertaining best, declaring to the *Match of the Day* viewers that, surprise, surprise, refs know the laws but don't understand the game. He added that it is impossible to jump for the ball without using your arms to propel yourself. I knew I had been right, so was relaxed while watching the highlights that evening. I was pleased when Alan Hansen said that he agreed with my decision, and stated that Strachan would be embarrassed by his comments because he couldn't fail to see the recklessness with which the elbow was thrown. I don't get carried away by the opinion of pundits. If you take them too seriously you will be affected every time they criticise you, and you can't afford to be that sensitive. You analyse decisions, but mustn't be haunted by your mistakes. Still, endorsement is always welcome.

Nor can you be haunted by individuals. I crossed swords with Sir Alex Ferguson again on my next visit to Old Trafford, for an FA Cup fifth-round tie in February 1999 when Fulham, then managed by Kevin Keegan, were visiting. After twice narrowly losing out to United in the title race, Keegan had quit Newcastle who had subsequently slipped, and splashed the cash at Mohammad Al Fayed's Fulham. United were lucky to win a caution-free game 1–0, but while Keegan took it on the chin this time, and shook my hand, Fergie was unhappy – I could tell by the glare in his eyes. He was about do a television interview in the tunnel, and just as I was walking past him, he shouted, "Back to your usual self, Jeff, fucking useless."

I hadn't a clue what he was talking about, and allowed the comment to go over my head. I could have reported it, but thought better to put it down to the heat of the moment. If every such incident were reported there would be a steady stream of managers and players going to FA disciplinary hearings every week, and we wouldn't have time for anything else. However, Fergie wasn't completely wrong that I was "fucking useless" because when I arrived at my hotel the night before, I realised that I hadn't packed any shoes. It would have done me no good at all turning up at the plush Old Trafford reception wearing a pair of trainers with my match-day suit, so I phoned one of my assistants, Ian Blanchard from Hull, who hadn't left for the game, and he lent me a pair of his size nines. They were a bit tight, but I got away with it.

Around that time Fergie was far from my only critic. Criticism is part and parcel of the game but there are boundaries that I don't feel should be crossed. I felt that Alan Oliver, who covers Newcastle United for the city's *Evening Chronicle*, overstepped the mark after I had refereed Newcastle at Nottingham Forest. Forest were having a torrid time and were to finish bottom that season. And this game was certainly one of their bad ones. I issued a red card to Forest's Matthieu Louis-Jean, cautioned another four of their players, and awarded a penalty for a foul on Tyneside hero Alan Shearer. You would have thought that the Geordie media would have been happy, especially as Newcastle won 2–1, but in his post-match article Oliver included my car registration number – which is personalised – and implied that I was a poser. I felt that my car registration had no relevance whatsoever to how I had handled the game, and have often seen number plates blanked out in newspaper and television pictures to protect the owners. I took the matter to the Press Complaints Commission. They decided my privacy had not been invaded. My view now is the same as it was when I received the letter. "Bollocks." But I had to accept their decision.

A referee's privacy should be protected as much as possible, but sometimes it's difficult. Nowadays only the county, rather than the home town, of a referee is printed in match programmes – this is to prevent them being tracked down in the telephone directory and receiving abusive calls. Some referees have panic alarms linked to their local police station, and I recall that Alan Wilkie had to move out of his house because of death threats following one controversial Manchester derby. Luckily it has never happened to me.

Sometimes, though rarely, there is almost complete harmony in a stadium, and I had the privilege of refereeing at Anfield on one such occasion, the nearest Saturday to the tenth anniversary of the Hillsborough disaster. There was scarcely a dry eye in the house, and I felt the occasion keenly. I was feeling fragile as we emerged from the tunnel, and it didn't help emotionally that goalkeeper Mark Bosnich, who led out the Aston Villa team, placed a bouquet of flowers behind the goal at the Kop end. We held a minute's silence, impeccably observed. It seemed a long minute. I could hardly wait to blow the whistle and get on with the game. The build-up had affected me outside as well as inside the ground, as, on arriving at the stadium, I had visited the shrine to those who had died. I stood alongside fans in the street outside the Anfield Road end of the ground to look in silence at the tribute. Villa won that day.

My season ended in pain, as I struggled through a Newcastle versus Blackburn fixture with my recurrent calf injury, and I doubted whether I would be able to complete my season by taking charge of the FA Premier League Academy under-19 final at West Ham. Fortunately, I knew a chap who could help. I travelled by train from the North East to London and on the way dropped in on physiotherapist Paul Cross. Not many football people will have heard of Paul, who was one of those players who never hit the heights, but who was a model professional, and is a super person. He played for Barnsley, Hartlepool and Darlington, where a knee injury brought his career to a premature end. In fact, it was Paul who inadvertently gave me my break as an after-dinner speaker, which I was later to make a career out of. I was at his benefit dinner after he had hung up his boots and the speaker didn't turn up, so Paul pulled me aside and asked me to step in. I didn't want to let him down, so I quickly scribbled some notes and grabbed the microphone. I had nothing to lose, because if I had flopped, people would still have appreciated me for giving it a go. In the event it went well. My first story was well received and my confidence grew. Paul even offered a fee, which I turned down. I didn't feel he owed me a thing, and if he did, he has paid me back since by helping keep me on the pitch. For my part I was honoured to referee his testimonial.

When his days on the pitch were over, Paul settled in Darlington and took up physiotherapy. He treated my calf injury so well that I got through the ninety minutes at Newcastle comfortably – and the extra thirty, for, as luck would have it, the game went to extra time. Calf problems were to trouble me throughout my career, though on this occasion I had a full summer to rest and recuperate. And while I didn't need to be physically sharp for my next appointment, it was above all a day for mental toughness, for I was back at St James's Park on the opening day of the 1999–2000 season, as fourth official for Uriah Rennie.

It was to prove a controversial start to the campaign. With each season new directives came from the FA, and we had been ordered to clamp down on all misdemeanours by club officials in the technical area outside the dugouts. Before each season referees gathered to be told of any new laws and how we ought to apply them. We were also given advice on how to interpret existing laws if there had been any inconsistencies with them the previous season. It was mainly a case of listening and taking directives on board, though we often asked questions to clarify points, so that all of us were on the same wavelength. There were never any major arguments at these meetings.

Villa were Newcastle's opponents that day, so the volatile John Gregory was under my watchful eye. The home fans were delighted when I made my mark by calling over Uriah to send the Villa manager to the stands for his aggressive behaviour. But the Toon Army had soon forgotten all about that, for Uriah made a very brave decision. He sent off their hero, Alan Shearer, early in the second half. There was absolute uproar, especially as it seemed an innocuous offence. Yet he had already been booked and been guilty of a series of other fouls. One more foul was deemed by Uriah to be sufficient for a second yellow – it was the cumulative effect on this occasion. The foul was minor in isolation, for all Shearer did was lean a little heavily with his arm on an opponent when going for the ball. No doubt that's why 52,000 fans reacted as they did.

The lid came off and the feeling of hatred towards Uriah increased as the game went on. I agreed with Uriah. The decision was brave, but correct, and was in keeping with what we had been ordered to do to clamp down on persistent misconduct. Newcastle fans have a collective blind spot towards Shearer. For ability and a winning mentality there have been few equals in the game. His goal-scoring record and his qualities of leadership have spoken for themselves down the years. But he was not an easy player to referee, because he was an aggressive challenger, and had learnt all the tricks of the trade. Add to that his god-like status in the eyes of the fans, and the task of the official was made even harder.

All good referees will give what they see. But such was the profile of Shearer that if you booked him, disallowed one of his goals or even blew up for a foul by him, you were automatically vilified by the fans. To send him off was a crime, nothing less. What made it even worse was that it was the first red card of Shearer's career, and came in his one-hundredth game for the club. It was the start of a bad month for him, as before the end of August he was subject to an even more controversial decision. He was dropped by manager Ruud Gullit for the derby game against Sunderland.

As Shearer left the field shaking his head, he glanced up at me as if to plead for my support, even though he knew it was too late. I didn't react, though I was about the only person in the ground who didn't. I knew as I stood on the touchline, being yelled at by fuming fans, that our problems would not be over after we left the pitch and right on cue the chief steward came into our dressing room and said, "Gentlemen, there is quite a crowd outside, and in the interests of your safety it is best not to go out the front door. We will go out another way."

He contacted our chauffeur, told him when and where to park, and the steward escorted us under the stands, through a side entrance, round the back of the club shop, and to our waiting people-carrier. We didn't have the opportunity for a drink or a chat with the players. It was as if we were escaping from a prisoner-of-war camp, looking over our shoulders for the guards. Fortunately, around that time the FA had decided to provide transport for the officials to ensure their safety. Philip Don had introduced the scheme because of an incident when West Ham fans in a pub had spotted the referee at a set of traffic lights and piled out on to the streets to confront him. Who knows what would have happened after the Newcastle game if we had all been left to make our way to our own cars. It was bad enough as it was. As we left the ground, with hundreds of fans still milling around, we immediately hit red traffic lights. Uriah is instantly recognisable, and I lost my cool. I politely told the driver to "Hit the fucking floor with that pedal, and sod the lights." Some of the Newcastle fans, had they latched on to us, would certainly have gone into thug mode. For me it was like being a young Boro fan all over again. We had marched into enemy territory, done our job, and were now legging it.

For every down, however, comes an up. In Uriah's next match he walked out of the tunnel to a standing ovation from another full house. He was the most popular man in Sunderland's Stadium of Light, for just a few miles away from Newcastle, the decision to send Shearer off had gone down a storm. Someone, somewhere, has a wicked sense of humour, for the next time Uriah was at St James's, I was again his fourth official. I can't remember whether we told the driver to keep the engine revving and pull right up to the stadium exit but what I do remember is that Uriah decided not to take to the field to warm up, because he didn't want to inflame the fans. I did, however, and it one of my warmest ever welcomes at Newcastle. I was asked countless times as I warmed up, "Why can't you be the ref today, Jeff, instead of that XXXX." It was great to be popular on Tyneside at last, but this was at rather too high a price. Generally speaking, when I refereed at Sunderland or Newcastle I couldn't win.

I was soon back at the Stadium of Light to take the middle for a game against Watford, another team that had been promoted to the Premiership that season. After the game I was strongly criticised by Watford manager Graham Taylor – who was on the losing side that day. He claimed that I was too familiar with the Sunderland players as I lived so close by. Using this argument no London referee could ever referee a team in the capital. The following day I was approached by complete strangers in the streets of Middlesbrough ready to have a go at me because they felt I should have made sure that Sunderland didn't win. The locals were speaking tongue-in-cheek but I think Graham Taylor really meant what he said. I had generally got on well with him, and respected his views. But he had spent too long in the south and needed a geography lesson, as many people south of Watford do. They tend to brand all northerners as if they come from the same village.

I wonder what Taylor would have made of it when I crossed swords with Peter Reid twice in quick succession. His Sunderland team had raced into a 2–0 lead against Manchester United, before United rallied, pulling a goal back. I then awarded United a free-kick near the touchline and in front of the dugouts, a decision given in agreement with assistant ref Jim Devine – also a Teessider. Sunderland failed to clear, and United equalised. Naturally Reid felt it wasn't a free-kick – especially after United scored. But he could hardly blame me for his side's defensive frailties. I thought, here we go, I'm going to be accused of wanting Sunderland to lose because I'm from Middlesbrough again. I was wrong. He saved that one up for a short while later, after I had refereed an FA Youth Cup tie at Newcastle which Sunderland lost 2–1.

I can say with hand on heart that I have always given every decision as I have seen it. The locality of the teams, my familiarity with the players, and whether I like or dislike certain players or managers is all an irrelevance when it comes to controlling games. For a start, refereeing requires such high concentration and quick decision-making that there is quite simply no time to think about anything other than the tackle that has just happened. Of course I often mulled over my style of refereeing and whether I was going about things the right way, but that was always done off the pitch, perhaps when driving, or relaxing at home.

Every season has its watersheds, and this was no exception. England striker Emile Heskey, who was by now with Liverpool, had built a reputation in some quarters for the ease with which he went to ground. In a game against Aston Villa, Heskey twice went down and both times the defender was shown a yellow card. As the offender was Gareth Southgate in each instance, his second yellow was followed by a red. Southgate is very polite but he lost his cool when I showed him the red card. He forcefully questioned both cards and for the one and only time with him I had to take a stern approach, insist that the decisions stood, and warn him that he would make it worse for himself if he persisted.

I felt that each offence was a foul, and worthy of a booking, but was Heskey guilty of exaggeration? I decided he wasn't, so Southgate was handed a red card, and his out-of-character protests to me later earned him a fine from the FA. However, with hindsight I feel I may have been wrong to send him off. Even though he felt aggrieved, he should have known there was no point in arguing. In fairness to him, the next time I saw him, he apologised for his outburst.

After that game I made a big effort to assess whether fouls were bad enough to warrant the reaction they received from the victim. It's a pity referees are faced with such decisions, but such is the nature of modern-day football. Of course the introduction of so many foreign players has made the job of the officials harder still, because different standards are applied in different countries, even though we are all supposed to referee to the same rules. The players of some nations find the feigning of injury, diving, and exaggerated reactions more acceptable than those in other countries. The influx of overseas players has certainly made the game more interesting, and added talking points.

It was a foreign import who was at the centre of events when I was involved in more controversy at Old Trafford, but this time I had one of Fergie's entourage to thank for saving me. I showed the red card to Newcastle's Nikos Dabizas for foul and abusive language. The Greek was furious but instead of walking off the pitch towards the changing rooms he strode menacingly towards me, swearing at me even more. It was the first time in my career that I had felt seriously threatened by a player as he continued to make a beeline for me, despite my gestures towards the changing room.

Just as I was starting to think how I would defend myself, Fergie's bodyguard, Ned Kelly, raced on to the field, grabbed Dabizas, and wrestled him off the field. Ex-SAS man Ned was used to looking after people who upset others. You can't please all the people all the time, however, and as Man United won 5–1, a Newcastle fanzine, in listing ten things to hate about that day's game, put me at number one, describing me as "Stockton Lardarse and Magpie-hater Jeff Winter".

Manchester United were absolutely flying at this time. They had won the treble a few months earlier, and went on to retain the title, winning it by eighteen points from Arsenal, despite seventeen goals for star French striker Thierry Henry in his first season at Arsenal. United went through the season unbeaten at home, and won eleven straight games at the end of the campaign, scoring thirty-seven goals in the process. You can't keep a good man down, though – despite his early-season problems Alan Shearer scored twenty-three Premiership goals to enhance his already legendary status. Newcastle, however, could not regain the momentum of the Keegan era, and finished eleventh.

Dabizas was one of relatively few Premiership stars to be sent off for foul language, which is not as prevalent in the professional game as it is lower down the ladder. Those who do swear, Ian Wright and Wayne Rooney being examples, tend to do it instinctively. By contrast, in park football such language is rife. At grass-roots level players tend to be worse than managers, but in the Premiership it's the reverse and it's the managers who are more likely to lose their cool and hurl obscenities from the dugout. Look at the number of times a camera picks up a desperate manager, yelling at his players or the referee. It's not difficult to decipher some of the words they are using. Occasionally the cameras pick up on a player issuing a brief expletive, but the managers' rants are longer and more colourful. For me, that's worse than if a player does it; managers spend more time within earshot of impressionable young fans and are supposed to be setting an example to players and fans alike. During that season I sent off managers Mel Machin and Gary Brazil for abusive language in a game between Bournemouth and Notts County, yet there were virtually no problems with their players.

Shortly after that game, Tranmere manager John Aldridge berated me as we took the walk to the dressing room at half-time in a match at Birmingham. His team were 3–0 down, partly because of a first-minute penalty and the dismissal of Tranmere's Clint Hill for violent conduct. I was hardly surprised that he was upset, but I was stunned when he said that I had revealed before the match that his team would get nothing. I was so bemused I couldn't think how to reply to him, so I didn't. Then, as I sat in the dressing room, it dawned on me why he had come out with such an outrageous accusation.

Just before the game started Tranmere's Andy Parkinson had asked me whose kick-off it was. He had missed the result of the toss of the coin. I smiled and said, "Theirs. The home team gets all the decisions." It was a jocular, throwaway remark, and I didn't think for a moment that he'd taken it seriously. But when the game swung Birmingham's way, I realised he had obviously passed on my comment to his manager, probably grossly embellishing it. I blamed myself. It was another lesson learnt. Don't give anyone the chance to doubt your impartiality – even if you are joking. I then explained what had happened to Aldridge. This time he didn't reply, but neither did he look entirely convinced.

There was no respite, and before long I was on the receiving end of another ear-bashing, this time from Huddersfield manager Steve Bruce who, along with 13,000 fans, felt I had denied Huddersfield a last-minute penalty in a Worthington Cup fourth-round defeat against Wimbledon, the Londoners going on to win in extra time. Fair play to Bruce. What he came out with was no more than the usual tirade. "Everybody in the ground could see that it was a penalty, except the referee," he said. He was over-shadowed by his club chairman, however, who threatened to sue me for loss of revenue! I know it was said in the heat of the moment, but people in authority should know better. It was another example of giving what I saw – or in this case not giving what I didn't see. It would have been far easier to give the home side a penalty, please the vast majority of the crowd, and get myself off home rather than play extra time.

Rarely do managers admit they have got it wrong, though there are exceptions, Harry Redknapp being one. I've always liked him – a Londoner who doesn't need to study geography. I was handed a West Ham versus Aston Villa game in unusual circumstances that season, a replay having been ordered after the Hammers had fielded an ineligible player – Manny Omoyinmi – without realis-ing he had already played in the competition for Scunthorpe. Harry was red-faced when he handed me the team sheet for the rearranged game and I said to him, tongue-in-cheek, "I hope all these players are eligible," to which he replied, "All right, I fucked up. In fact it was such a bad mistake it was even worse than the ones you normally make." He is a gentleman, fair-minded, and always honest even though he takes the game seriously and is as animated as the next man. I was impressed by his prompt action in the 2004–5 season, after he had switched to Southampton. He dragged one of his players, David Prutton, away from trouble after the player had been red-carded and was heading for the assistant referee in a threatening way. Harry reacted in a flash to diffuse the situation, then in his television interview refused to defend the player, saying that he would be disciplined. Football needs more managers in that mould.

More often than not managers will stand up for their players, almost no matter what they have done. And if they don't feel they can defend them, they often use the get-out clause of temporary blindness, claiming that they didn't see the incident. It amuses me how the top managers and coaches can dissect a match in precise detail when it comes to seeking ways to improve their team – yet somehow miss a punch-up.

Leicester City boss Martin O'Neill was very upset after a Leicester versus Everton game. He'd already leapt from his bench to dispute some of my decisions, and was on the field protesting when I awarded Everton a goal which arose from a quickly taken free-kick when the Leicester keeper picked up a back pass inside his area. Everton took the free-kick from outside the penalty area and scored. Leicester were furious, saying that I shouldn't have allowed the free-kick to be taken from there.

Ironically, it was in another Everton against Leicester game, this time in January 2000, that I got on the wrong side of O'Neill again. One of my assistants had to be stretchered off after he was upended by a tackle from an Everton player as he went for the ball, in the same way that I had been cleaned out at Newcastle years before. I awarded Everton a second-half penalty, which they converted to make it 2–2, and this remained the score at full time.

On the final whistle, O'Neill shrugged off a steward as I approached the tunnel, and looked as if he was going to throw a plastic bottle at me. He maybe didn't realise he had the bottle in his hand, because everybody tends to have a drink at the end of the game, and fortunately he was held back by another steward. In his post-match press conference he said, "I wish the referee had been stretchered off instead." His comment surprised me, as there had been nothing controversial during the game.

Sometimes you can smell trouble coming. It's important to go into games mindful of where problems might lie, by being aware of players' reputations, though without pre-judging them – and that's a delicate balance. In an important derby game between Manchester City and Stockport County, when City were chasing promotion back to the Premiership, Jamie Pollock and Tony Dinning set their stall out early in the game and it was clear to me that they were both working their ticket by having sly digs at each other. Pollock would say to Dinning, "That pass was crap," or some other insult, and trouble was clearly brewing. So I called them over and showed each the yellow card. In unison they pleaded, "What was that for?" I replied, "Nothing, but it's the only way to ensure that you two behave yourselves." It worked. There was not a hint of further trouble.

I felt able to use my discretion to bring a calming influence to games. When there are equal aggressors, it is easier to handle, because you can mete out equal punishment. However, there are occasions when one player is determined to rile another, but the feeling is not mutual. I sent off Frank LeBoeuf of Chelsea in a game against Leeds, then found I was also in charge of the reverse fixture. This time LeBoeuf was as good as gold, but Leeds striker Alan Smith was not. It was obvious that Smith was out to intimidate the Chelsea man, and fuelled by the crowd's venom – there has been animosity between Leeds and Chelsea ever since the 1970 FA Cup final, which Chelsea won – he ensured that I was faced with an ugly situation. LeBoeuf showed the sort of discipline that had been missing at Stamford Bridge, where I had sent him off for two bookable fouls. I kept a close eye on each potential flashpoint between the pair and, in doing so, learnt that the more a player focuses on the ball and the pattern of the game, and the less he is worried about making his mark in an aggressive way, the better he plays. LeBoeuf was outstanding, Chelsea won and Smith was eventually booked. I'd done my job, LeBoeuf had done his, but Smith had failed to do his properly. He was young, hot-headed and paid the penalty. I realise he is a player who performs on adrenalin and passion, but the more it is controlled the better he is likely to play.

On another occasion Smith came to the touchline for treatment to a minor injury, but he remained standing on the pitch. As I was fourth official I politely walked over and asked him if he was staying on the field or coming off, to which I got a four-letter tirade. Brian Kidd, the Leeds assistant manager at the time, turned round to me and said, "I know you used to be a hard man, Jeff, but don't talk to him like that." I was flabbergasted. Why was I being cast as the villain? Leeds boss Terry Venables just shrugged his shoulders at me and said, "You know what he's like."

Dealing with a volatile young player like Smith, however, was chickenfeed compared to coping with the atmosphere generated at one particular Burnley versus Millwall game that season. Millwall fans were intent on causing pre-arranged trouble and the police were prepared. The build-up to the game was of military proportions, the visiting hordes of fans being well marshalled. A police helicopter circled the ground, the rise and fall of the noise from the blades adding background tension to the scene.

I had been called to a meeting by the police to forewarn me of the potential for trouble. Match officials and the police work independently, but courtesy and mutual respect demands that we keep each other in the picture. I smiled as I entered the meeting, for it reminded me how I had changed over the years. Football intelligence had been a new concept when I first took an interest in the game – and I knew it was unruly youngsters like me who made it necessary. Yet here I was co-operating with senior officers, who seemed to respect me as much as I did them. They told me how many visiting fans they expected and where the trouble was likely to occur away from the ground. They reassured me that they would contain any problems inside the stadium. In turn I told them that I would endeavour to calmly control things on the pitch, which might help minimise the risk of the crowd getting overheated.

I didn't have a word with the players beforehand, as I would never try to influence them in terms of the way they played. If I had done I would have strongly advised Burnley not to race into a 4–0 lead. To the Millwall fans, squeezed in their thousands behind the goal, the scoreline was like a red rag to a bull. A large number of them decided to try and join us on the pitch but the police and stewards were brilliant and prevented an invasion.

The Millwall players helped to soothe the situation by hitting back and scoring three goals. The crowd was now fully focused on the action, and I began to feel that we would get through the game trouble-free. Then two players – one from each side – squared up to each other right in front of the Millwall supporters. A cordon of police was all that separated us from the snarling mob. I quickly stepped between the two players, calmly asked them to glance over their shoulders at the crowd, then asked them to face me.

Raising my voice so that the duo could hear me above the baying crowd, I uttered what any rational person would have said in the circumstances, "Are you two trying to get us fucking killed?" It is a pleasure to see two faces reveal that they have suddenly joined your wavelength. The red mist cleared, calm descended, and the pair shook hands. The game finished without further incident but, as I sat in the dressing room, I could hear sirens outside the ground. I felt satisfied that I had done my bit. Now it was up to my new mates – the boys in blue.

I could have done with a quiet game to follow that one, but my luck was out – I was handed a relegation battle between more Londoners and northerners in the shape of Wimbledon's trip to Bradford. The fans were all right this time; it was back to the regular job of dealing with the players. And the atmosphere among the players before the game was as bad as I've ever known it – for two reasons.

First, the tunnel area at Valley Parade is very narrow. Despite the ground being redeveloped following the dreadful fire of 1985, the dressing rooms are crammed into the corner between the main stand and the visitors' end. There is barely room for the two sides to line up and, to make it worse, on this occasion the two teams were hurling insults at each other from the word go. It started with an accusation that Wimbledon striker John Hartson had given Bradford skipper Stuart McCall the sort of tackle that Vinnie Jones once famously made on Paul Gascoigne. For those who don't recall the famous photograph, let me put it this way: Hartson allegedly made McCall's eyes water with a strategically placed grip.

It was a relief to get out on to the pitch but, as is often the case, the mood had been set and so it continued. I had to send Hartson off in the second half for aiming foul and abusive language at assistant referee Alan Sheffield. Alan has had worse. He was the linesman at the centre of the controversial disallowed goal in Boro's FA Cup semi-final involving Chesterfield. The difference that day was that it was in my power to red-card Hartson, whereas David Elleray could hardly have banished the thousands of Chesterfield fans who took a dim view of Alan's decision. At least with Hartson leaving the scene early I didn't have to worry about him in the tunnel afterwards.

Later in the game the Wimbledon keeper Neil Sullivan raced out of his penalty area to confront me about a decision. That sort of behaviour was something I always clamped down on, and I made it clear that he would be in big trouble if he didn't retreat immediately. That did the trick, and back he went. By the way, the other reason why there had been such a bad atmosphere in the narrow tunnel was that match officials and players all had to share the same toilet.

I had more trouble with Bradford that season, though in a more light-hearted setting. Sometimes the referee is on the receiving end and I was given a bit of stick when I made a sudden appearance in the "What Happened Next?" section of the BBC's *A Question of Sport*. The game was between Liverpool and Bradford. I had awarded Liverpool a penalty and a Bradford player lashed out at the ball in frustration. That was where the film was frozen. What did happen next was that the ball hit me on the back of the head. I turned round to see that Dean Windass was the guilty man. At first I thought it might be retribution, not only for the penalty award, but for his red card at Hull some years earlier. But I decided that it couldn't have been a deliberate act – because the ball had hit me, and if he intended it, he would have missed. I didn't book him.

After a season of trouble from players and fans alike, I bowed out for the summer on a much better note, as fourth official at Wembley for England's final friendly before jetting off for Euro 2000. England beat the Ukraine but the significant moment for me was when I held up the board to declare a substitution and so signal the arrival on the international scene of Steven Gerrard.

By chance I had been the referee when he made his Liverpool debut as well. As he stepped off the bench for England, the Three Lions on his chest, I whispered to him, "You deserve this. Best of luck." I thought no more of it, but he obviously did, and some years later he brought a lump to my throat with a marvellous gesture. When I came off the pitch having refereed my last ever game at Anfield, there was a knock on the dressing-room door with a special delivery for me. It was Gerrard's autographed shirt.

9

IN THE FIRING LINE

The silence was deafening, for nobody could quite believe what they had seen. Then, after a few seconds, an audible gasp broke collectively from the crowd of several hundred. The goalkeeper, head bowed, trudged off to the dressing room for the early bath. There was not a hint of dissent, partly because that is not the way of things on the other side of the Atlantic, and partly because the keeper was too shocked to speak. Like the Canadian Mountie, the referee always gets his man.

The game was between two Calgary sides, the Dinosaurs and the Villains. Even after a tough Premiership season there was no time to relax, for I accepted an invitation to fly across the Atlantic to spend three weeks delivering lectures to Canadian officials and to referee a few games. The pressure was on me in this derby match. Not so much because it was a derby, for it was nothing compared to Villa against Birmingham or Man City against United, but because I was a top English referee under the spotlight, my every move being studied by a host of Canadian referees.

I suppose I needn't have worried, because they were there to learn from me. In that sense, as long as I could persuade them that I was demonstrating how it was done in England, whatever decision I made was right. The keeper's sin was committed after just five minutes. He had rushed to the edge of the penalty area to collect a through ball, misjudged it and handled outside his area as a striker closed in. It was a straightforward case of denying a goal-scoring opportunity so I had no choice but send the keeper off, but clearly in Canada he would normally have been given a second chance. My explanation was accepted nevertheless, and the Dinosaurs were brought into the modern age.

I made wonderful friends in Canada in that summer of 2000. Their hospitality was marvellous and their enthusiasm for the game considerable. If I was jaded after a long hard English winter, they refreshed me and put the spring back in my step. Fortunately, later on I was given a chance to repay their kindness with a gesture that stunned and delighted them, in the very last game of my career.

They say football is a universal language and for referees that's certainly true. Wherever you are in the world, the rules have to be applied. After the Canadian trip, I swapped the piercing, clear blue mountain air for the taste of sulphur from the chimneys of Middlesbrough. OK, it's not quite that bad, but the area around Boro's Riverside Stadium has always been grim. The Boro ground-staff make up for it though, and when I stepped out to referee Robbie Mustoe's testimonial against Borussia Dortmund, a game that doubled up as a pre-season match in the build-up to the 2000–1 campaign, the green sward was testimony to their skills.

Robbie was one of a breed of players that rarely exist now, yet it's only a couple of seasons ago that he retired. He was not only extremely loyal to his club, he was also a gentleman. Brought up in the rather genteel Oxfordshire town of Witney, he played for Oxford United before being snapped up by then Boro manager Lennie Lawrence. Robbie adapted to Teesside like a duck to water, and was a model professional. Nothing was too much trouble for him. He did all the things that so many footballers have done without an ounce of recognition from the national media. Hospital visits, school events, fund-raising for charity and other worthwhile causes were carried out with a smile.

On the pitch he was a tenacious, hard-working midfielder, a box-to-box player who snapped into tackles and refused to let the opposition settle. Yet he was never a problem to referees. He was living, playing proof that you don't have to be nasty to be effective in a team's engine room. It was an honour to be invited to play my part in testimonial matches for the likes of Robbie, Curtis Fleming and Clayton Blackmore. All three spent a considerable time at one club, and were prepared to work their socks off to back up the big-name stars, without ever gaining the same recognition as some of their team-mates.

The same could be said of Dickie Ord at Sunderland and John McDermott of Grimsby who also asked me to referee their testimonial games. But none would compare to the testimonials I took charge of for players at non-league level, such as Paul Pitman's game at Whitby Town, Ged Hartley's at South Bank and Andy Harbron's at Billingham Synthonia. I still have a strong affinity with the non-league clubs from where my career progressed, and it was always an honour to be invited back to do their pre-season games. For these players it's not about money, or glory. It's about being a dedicated man who will not let his team down. When I'm asked to help players like them, I never hesitate.

Mind you, there's a job to be done too, and in Robbie's testimonial I booked five players in the opening twenty-five minutes. Boro duo Hamilton Ricard and Jason Gavin went into the book, as did three Borussia lads. Some of the players were taking liberties because it was a pre-season match, but I was determined to referee the game the way I would have done had it been a competitive fixture. The Boro players felt that I went out of my way to give them nothing. I told them that I refereed without fear or favour. When they asked why I booked so many of them in testimonials and friendlies, I replied, "Because I know what you buggers are like." With hindsight, maybe my knowledge of them did work against them at times. These games were warm-ups for the long season ahead not only for the players, but for me too. Perhaps I wanted to get the bookings in for that reason.

Before long I was back in competitive action, handing out cards when necessary, but settling for a quiet word where possible. The 2000–1 season was my sixth season in the Premiership and my early self-doubts about whether I would be able to cope with the demands of the world's greatest league had evaporated. I felt that I was an integral part of it all. I had the experience and the ability to deal with all situations in a highly tense atmosphere. Huge amounts of money were at stake, and there was pressure on every club. Those at the top knew that to win the Premiership guaranteed them a place in the Champions League, and a chance to equal Manchester United's achievement of winning that competition. Those at the bottom knew that they had to stay in the Premiership, otherwise face huge financial problems. The television money for the Premiership clubs is far greater than for those in the Football League.

The large amounts of money at stake made it even more crucial for the referee to be the voice of authority when tempers and emotions ran high on the field, and to possess a sense of understanding and sympathy. Never more so than in my first game of the season when Ipswich staged their home fixture with Manchester United. The newcomers played so well on their return to the Premiership that United had to hang on grimly for a 1–1 draw. United were under the cosh as the crowd got behind Ipswich, and they didn't like it one bit. I booked Jaap Stam for a foul, as well as David Beckham, Dwight Yorke and Gary Neville – all for dissent.

Cautioning Beckham almost got me into trouble. It was the first season of the new rule of advancing the ball ten yards if a player showed dissent when a free-kick was awarded. In the heat of the moment, with all the arguments going on, I forgot about the new law, even though we had spoken about it several times in our pre-season preparations. I was just about to allow Ipswich to take the free-kick, when I heard the buzz from my assistant's electronic flag in my earpiece. I quickly realised why, so I grabbed the ball and walked forward ten yards before placing it down again. United players moved menacingly towards me to protest, but I was ready for them, and flashed the yellow cards, which did the trick. The players retreated and got on with the game.

The following day, the feedback from the United camp was that their players thought I was arrogant. But I think the reverse is true and it is United who believe that they are above the law and have the right to bully refs. Sir Alex Ferguson glared at me as I walked off the field at the end of the game, but didn't speak.

United were up against it as they sought to yet again retain their title. An away draw may seem a decent result but it was rare for them to drop points, especially against a newly promoted team. And with Thierry Henry now firmly established as an Arsenal goal machine, United knew they would be pushed all the way. If the pressure was already showing on the manager, it didn't on David Beckham. He provided the equaliser that day at Ipswich, and even on what was an off day for the team, it was great for me to be out there on the pitch with him.

Beckham looks every bit the superstar at close quarters and to be alongside him seeing his silky movement and precision passing is awesome. At ground level, his skills are even more evident than they look from elevated camera angles; the ref can see the game unfold as he does. The way he swings crosses in is incredible to see. While referees are charged with controlling games, we still see the big names as stars, even though they chat to us and we are virtually in touching distance as they unleash their skills. To the fans they may be even bigger stars than they are to us, but don't believe any referee who claims he is not delighted to be on the turf alongside the giants of the game. We can't be star-struck of course, because there's a job to be done.

One of my earliest red cards that season was for Coventry's Paul Williams in a Carling Cup tie. He had already been booked when he chased a Preston player who was running towards the goal line. The Deepdale pitch was wet, and although the ball stayed in play, both players slid out over the line. The Preston lad was on his feet first in the scramble to get the ball, and Williams pulled him back. Even though both players were off the pitch, it was a bookable offence, so I produced a second yellow followed by red. In such situations the game should restart with a drop-ball but it was easier all round to award Preston a free-kick, so I did. I was still reflecting on the decision when I heard an almighty clatter. Williams, in heading up the tunnel, had kicked out in anger at the fourth official's electronic board. The kick was so violent that it smashed the board, and I included the incident in my report to the FA. To add to his red card, therefore, he was handed a £4,000 repair bill. Not surprisingly, I earned one of Coventry manager Gordon Strachan's glazed stares, and compounded his anger by booking Craig Bellamy for dissent. It was not the last time that Bellamy would in trouble in a stormy career. I later got to know him off the field, and he's nowhere near as fiery away from the pitch.

My approach to games had been changing gradually over the last few seasons. I had always disliked sending players off, as it tended to spoil games. At times, however, their behaviour meant that I had little choice. The next pair to go were Chelsea's Graeme Le Saux, and Sunderland's Kevin Kilbane, for violent conduct. Le Saux was one of those players whose personality changed as soon as he stepped on to the field. He was a pleasant, articulate man and a pleasure to be with off the field but a complete contrast and difficult to handle when he was playing. What made the incident unusual was that it happened right in front of the assistant referee, Martin Atkinson, in his first Premiership game. Martin didn't get a clear view of it, but I did. I was at least fifteen yards away, but sometimes peripheral vision enables you to see more clearly than when something occurs right under your nose.

Martin didn't react, but I swiftly took control to give Le Saux and Kilbane no time to start trading punches. The result was that Martin got terrible stick from the crowd for failing to see something that happened so close to him. The problem with running the line is that you get abuse from the fans behind you for what you give and what you don't. But you can only react to what you see clearly. Martin is now on the Premiership list of referees and deserves to go a long way in the game.

Before long, I was back at Old Trafford to referee what is always a tough and highly charged fixture, United versus Leeds United. There is a history of bad-tempered games between the two clubs but I managed to avoid any sort of repetition and only had to show the yellow card to Alan Smith and Lee Bowyer of Leeds. However, I realised that my booking of Smith was harsh when I watched the television replays later. I duly informed the FA, who withdrew the caution. Sometimes clubs asked me to review dismissals and bookings, through the FA, but a ref can decide to review his decision himself, and I did so on this occasion. I had reached a stage in my career where I felt confident enough to admit my mistakes, and no longer feared being dropped from the Premiership, even if those mistakes could alter the destiny of the title. This game took place in October and Manchester United were top of the table, but they'd already had a reminder that Arsenal were on their trail, for the Gunners had inflicted a first defeat of the season on United two games earlier.

The Premiership games came thick and fast, but I was occasionally asked to take charge of lower-league matches. Premiership refs did not work exclusively in the Premiership, but also refereed key Football League, play-off or Cup tie games. Lower-league clubs often viewed top referees with suspicion, feeling that either we hand out far more cards because we care less for the reputation of lower-league players, or that we are arrogant, know it all, and that returning to their level is beneath us. I know that some fans, players and officials of Football League clubs are angered when a referee is dropped from the Premiership list but is allowed to take charge of league games. They claim that if he is not good enough for the top level, he is not good enough for them, for the same rules apply at all levels of the game. I disagree. Not because the same rules should not be applied – they should – but because in some cases referees have found the Premiership too hard to handle. They are good referees, but the pressure from the cameras, the media scrutiny, and dealing with top-name players and managers is too much for them. Take away the intense glare of the spotlight, and they are excellent officials, who are objective and of a very high standard. Equally, I suppose, some Premiership refs may be off their game when they are handed a lower-league match.

So to Wrexham versus Cambridge in Division Two in front of 1,500 hardy souls on a night of lashing rain. It was my first visit to the Racecourse Ground since 1974, when Wrexham knocked Charlton's Champions out of the FA Cup. I arrived early, and wondered if I had got the right night, as the ground was in darkness only three hours before kick-off. But a dim light and the sight of a shadowy figure moving past a window pane revealed that there was indeed to be a match on. The rain was so heavy that a pitch inspection was needed, though the surface was in surprisingly good condition, considering that it was surrounded by a moat that should have been a cinder track. I had to paddle through it to reach the pitch.

For the first time in a long while I struggled to motivate myself, a fact that the assessor picked up on and mentioned in his report. However, I must have been awake for part of the game as I cautioned Darren Ferguson, son of Sir Alex, for dissent.

The next time I was handed lower-league duty, there was nothing low-key about the game. Carlisle was where I had made my Football League refereeing debut, so I was glad of the opportunity to make a nostalgic return. Lincoln City, known for their direct football and robust style, were the visitors, and the 1–1 draw was played at a hectic pace, with five cautions and a few flashpoints. I felt I handled it well, being on the ball from start to finish. Assessor Terry Heilbron thought otherwise and his assessment slated me, but Philip Don supported me. One of the major problems facing young referees coming through the ranks is when someone who was known in his own refereeing career for his leniency on the pitch suddenly becomes a hatchet man as an assessor. It is confusing and unsettling for young referees and an example of poacher becoming gamekeeper.

It's a good job the FA don't take too much notice of whingeing managers, or I would have been taken off an FA Cup tie between Everton and Tranmere. John Aldridge, the Tranmere manager with whom I'd previously had trouble, had complained when I was given the fixture. The FA didn't tell me, but I heard about it on the grapevine. In the event Tranmere hit their Cup form, and turned over their glamorous rivals 3–0 in front of a full house at Goodison Park. Aldridge was all smiles, and as an ex-Liverpool player was probably thinking that there were now only two teams on Merseyside.

Much as I like Scousers, they can be a raucous lot. The police had been busy before and during the game, and the officer in charge had a furrowed brow when I spoke to him afterwards. "Your work's done," he said. "You can escape home for a quiet evening. We can't. I've got a feeling we haven't seen the last of the trouble." I smiled and said, "There's no quiet evening for me. I'm stopping over in the city to have a night out."

He looked alarmed. "You're not serious are you?" he replied, his jaw dropping. "I've got enough on my plate without the ref wandering around the streets antagonising the fans." It had been many years since a police officer had advised me to get off home before there was further trouble. I hadn't taken any notice of such advice in my youth and I was not about to start now. After all, one of the joys of being a Premiership referee is that you get the chance to sample the atmosphere of big cities, not just during the game, but afterwards. That evening Lynette and I enjoyed a meal out with friends in a bustling Albert Dock. I didn't antagonise anybody, but I did enjoy the banter of the locals. Liverpool is a great city, the people's humour is widely recognised, and I always feel relaxed there – even when the crowd are baying for my blood. I'm not surprised that footballers love a good Saturday night out. The adrenalin is still flowing after games and it's great to hit the town. In that respect some referees are no different from players.

And it's the big games that provide the adrenalin, as a Worthington Cup semi-final second-leg game at Birmingham City proved. Previous experience had taught me that St Andrew's is a tough ground on which to referee. When people talk of the great soccer cities, Birmingham is not often on the list. Liverpool, Manchester, Newcastle and Leeds would all spring to mind before the country's second city. Yet Birmingham can be an intense and hostile place during a match and this semi-final was one of the most frightening of the lot, even if the problems were caused by enthusiasm rather than aggression.

I'd been offered this game against Ipswich as a replacement for Graham Barber, who was double-booked and had opted to do a Premiership game. Such a situation would not normally arise, but the Cup game had been rearranged at short notice. I jumped at it, as it was a chance to referee a major semi-final for the first time.

Birmingham were a goal down from the first leg, and the atmosphere was highly charged and a test of my authority as they set about levelling the tie. Each time Birmingham scored on their way to a 4–1 win, the fans invaded the pitch from all four corners. It was good-natured, but it was clear that the police and stewards couldn't cope. The game went to extra time and I knew that the drama would only heighten. I said to Ipswich coach Tony Mowbray, one of my heroes, that whatever happened he should get his players off the pitch as quickly as possible at the end of the game.

The St Andrew's dressing rooms are in a corner of the ground and some of the most animated fans were in that corner. Fortunately, the old tunnel that led to the dressing rooms when they were under the main stand was still there, so I arranged with my colleagues and the Ipswich team that we should use the old exit as the escape route from the pitch. Birmingham scored in each half of extra time to book their place at the Millennium Stadium. Despite the dangerous atmosphere, Andy Johnson, the scorer of the fourth goal, raced to the fans to celebrate. Players do not realise the reaction that their actions can provoke. When he emerged from the throng, I booked him for an over-zealous celebration. I may have been worried, but not too worried to do my job.

On the final whistle I broke into a sprint, the shrill sound still cutting through the air as I did my Linford Christie impersonation. As I reached safety I looked behind me, and could hardly see a blade of grass. The entire pitch had become a mass of celebrating Brummies. The tannoy requests for the fans to stay in their seats had gone unheeded, and the stewards were engulfed. King Canute would have had a better chance than they did of turning a blue tide. I shudder to think what would have happened if Birmingham had lost, or if I'd had to give a highly controversial decision against them.

I was mightily relieved to reach the security of the stand. A referee does have some responsibility to ensure the safety of the players and his fellow officials, but on this occasion I had genuine concerns for my own safety. Besides I had already warned the players to get off as quickly as possible. It was clearly a case of every man for himself. I had a brief word with Tony Mowbray after the game. His team had lost, but as always he conducted himself impeccably. He overcame personal tragedy, losing his wife to cancer, with great honour. He is a super guy and a very good player and manager. Bruce Rioch summed up how valued Mowbray is as a companion when he said that if he had to fly to the moon, Tony is the man he would chose to accompany him.

I have always been able to stick up for myself, and have not automatically gone running to the authorities to report people who have had a go at me. It's not my way to grass, and even though I have felt compelled to at times, there are many others when I have chosen to turn the other cheek. One such incident arose after I had refereed Derby County, fighting for their lives at the wrong end of the Premiership, twice in quick succession. There was not a cross word spoken in the first game between County and fellow strugglers Manchester City at Pride Park.

Derby were in sixteenth place in the twenty-team Premiership of 2000–1, and had won only five games with the season well over halfway through. Not surprisingly, they were desperate for points. I took charge of their game at Leeds and have never seen such a negative display as the one Derby put in. From the kick-off they were hell-bent on earning a 0–0 draw. Time-wasting was top of the tactical plan. I booked two players for that, and another three for dissent, but they didn't waver from their plan, and fair means and foul were used in a desperate backs-to-the-wall performance, which I couldn't help but admire. There were several minutes of added-on time, as you would expect. Derby held on, took their goalless draw, and set off home down the M1.

I thought no more of it, and was totally relaxed when I answered the phone the following day. It was Colin Todd, the Derby manager. It was unusual, but not unheard of, for a manager to phone on a Sunday – club secretaries have contact numbers of all referees, in case of emergency, or to arrange pitch inspections. And when the phone did ring, it was not always to criticise. Sometimes managers simply wanted a point clarified, and on one never-to-be-forgotten occasion, at the height of my disputes with Peter Reid, the man himself phoned to compliment me on my handling of an Arsenal versus Spurs game.

Toddy, meanwhile, started off pleasantly enough, before suddenly embarking on a tirade of foul-mouthed abuse. "Why did you book five of my players yesterday?" he snarled. I tried to reason with him, but he would have none of it. I tried to tell him that his game-plan had worked, and so had mine. He had come for a point, and I had come to apply the laws of the game. When I managed to squeeze a word in edgeways it was obvious that I was wasting my time, so I suggested that we call a halt to the conversation, if you could call it a conversation.

I don't recall ever having a cross word with him before that Leeds game. Similarly, I have seen Toddy many times since, and he has never referred to the call. I knew Colin well. Before he took charge at Derby he was assistant manager to Bruce Rioch, who often invited the referee into his manager's office before games for a cup of tea. It was a strange thing to do, but Rioch was a gentleman from the old school. (The FA doesn't allow it these days, because they feel such interaction means the referee might be putting himself in a compromising position. I wonder what current Chelsea manager Jose Mourinho would have made of the opposition manager inviting the ref for a pre-match cuppa?) In other words, I had met Toddy in all manner of circumstances without a hint of trouble. Had I reported him for his phone call he could have faced a serious FA charge, so I took a view and simply put it down to the intense pressure all managers feel. There is nothing in football as stressful as being a manager embroiled in a relegation battle, especially if he's just had a look at the league table. I wasn't angered by the call; surprised maybe. Overall, I think the incident did me a favour, because it furthered my understanding of the pressures the game can bring. I don't think you can be a top referee if you fail to recognise that, and little reminders do you no harm. I often used to call my friends to have a reassuring chat after I'd been involved in controversial games. This was no different really.

Sometimes I do feel that managers needlessly put themselves under pressure by fielding weak teams in FA Cup ties. Blackburn and Arsenal left out some of their top names for a quarter-final tie. Blackburn were in Division One, so you would have thought that a game with Arsenal would have been huge. But promotion was their priority, and it showed as soon as I looked at the team sheet. Arsenal treated it with equal contempt, but still won 3–0.

They may have changed their approach for that game, but the pressures on me were the same. I still had to apply the laws in front of a big crowd, and the players who were on the field were taking the game seriously enough as they were only two games away from the final. I turned down a penalty appeal for each side within the space of twenty seconds. Blackburn appealed loudly for one, and I waved play on. Arsenal counter-attacked in typical rapier-like style – even without their star men – and had their own shout rejected. Yes, I had kept up with play! The video technology that so many people call for would have been useless in circumstances like this, and I am convinced it should never be considered. If we had stopped the game and decided I was correct to turn down Blackburn's claim, then Arsenal would not have had the chance to counter-attack. Alternatively, if I had given an Arsenal penalty, and the "video ref" had decided that Blackburn should have had one, all hell would have broken loose. Rather than helping the referee, the technology would have been a huge burden and made the job nigh on impossible. Television pundits often can't make their mind up about incidents they have watched several times over. To me it's just another illustration of why the referee's instantaneous decision should be final.

Rarely have I taken such stick as when on FA Cup semi-final duty and that season I was fourth official for Wycombe Wanderers' big day, the Villa Park clash with Liverpool.

The game ought to have been another magical FA Cup occasion, with the minnow taking on the big fish. Wycombe were so short of strikers they had even advertised for one. Even though I was fourth official rather than in the middle, I was greatly looking forward to the game. But Wycombe manager Lawrie Sanchez put me through hell; the worst forty-five minutes I have ever had the misfortune to experience.

I was aware of his reputation as a hard man, though I'd had no previous experience of him as our paths had not crossed. Let's just say we made up for lost time.

It's a good job the Liverpool bench was well behaved or I would have had to call for reinforcements. Sanchez stepped out of his technical area early in the game, and I politely asked him to go back, only to be met with a tirade of foul-mouthed abuse. I tried a more abrupt tone. No effect. Then I tried telling him rather than asking him. No joy. In fact I made it worse. Eventually he turned to me and yelled, "Will you fuck off. This is our big day. It has nothing to do with you." What baffled me was that his behaviour was so out of keeping with what was happening on the pitch, for his lowly side were holding their own in a drab game. At least I think it was drab. I had no chance to see more than the occasional kick as I had my hands full with Sanchez.

One course of action open to me was to signal to the referee, Paul Durkin, and have him send Sanchez to the stand. But I didn't want to go down that route. First, I wanted to fight my own battle, and second, it would have looked ridiculous, because in terms of the game there was nothing for the manager to get worked up about. The crowd – apart from those behind the dugouts – and the millions watching on live television, would have wondered what all the fuss was about. So I bottled it, and just put up with the irate manager. In other words, I gave in to the pressure.

However, at half-time I had a word with Paul. He thought I was winding him up. A referee is normally aware of problems on the sideline but there was no reason, in this instance, that he should have been. Fortunately, the FA referees' secretary Joe Guest had watched the first half from the main stand and told Paul that the problem was obvious from up there. Paul had a quiet word with Sanchez, telling him that I had reported him, and told him to calm down for the second half.

I winced at the prospect of facing Sanchez after half-time but I needn't have worried – he calmed down and spent most of the half discussing tactics with his side-kick Terry Gibson. To be honest, he would have been better off shouting at me, as Liverpool won 2–0. I saw Sanchez a year or two ago, and he breezed up to me with a broad smile. "Hello, Jeff," he said. "Good to see you again." The semi-final was never mentioned. I reckon it was the "Colin Todd syndrome" all over again. Sanchez was probably worried that his under-strength team would get battered by Liverpool, and the last thing he needed was me acting like a jobsworth.

Not all managers are trouble, as I was reminded two games later when I took charge of my one and only Liverpool versus Everton derby, another intense occasion with both clubs experiencing highs and lows. This was an occasion when it really was impossible to keep the card count down and the match saw my highest ever Premiership booking count. Everton were winning 6–5 in the yellow card stakes, when Liverpool's Igor Biscan "equalised" with his second yellow, and was sent off. I awarded a penalty to each side, before Liverpool finally won 3–2 with a late goal from Gary McAllister, who scored from a quickly taken free-kick. I allowed the goal to stand despite huge Everton protests. They surrounded me, claiming that I shouldn't have allowed the free-kick to be taken. After the match Gerard Houllier knocked on the dressing-room door, popped his head round and thanked us. "That was not an easy game, but well done," he said. I believe he would have said the same had Everton won.

By now United had romped to yet another title triumph. They refused to let up, however, as they sought to win it by the biggest margin they could. As it turned out, they came unstuck at bogey ground the Dell when they lost 2–1 to Southampton. I booked Ronnie Johnsen for delaying the restart after Southampton equalised. Fergie was unhappy that I had allowed the winner, though I couldn't see the slightest problem with it.

Meanwhile, Derby had escaped relegation by eight points, so Colin Todd's plan had worked. He was no doubt much happier now, and relishing the following season in the Premiership. And so was I, for rumours were rife that Philip Don was seeking a select group of referees to turn professional.

10

PROFESSIONALISM –
THE BIG SACRIFICE

The big orange sun sank slowly below the horizon until the last shimmering segment slipped away. It had crossed the divide that separated day from night – and I didn't need the assistance of a linesman to tell me that it was completely over the line. Even David Elleray could not have got that one wrong.

The Masai Mara settled sedately down for the night. In this wilderness I ought to have been reflecting more on the wonders of nature and less on the Premiership, but I was unable to get the idea of being a professional referee out of my head. My fortnight's break in Africa had taken me well away from phone calls, the media and all the hype that surrounds football, yet I couldn't help wondering what was happening back home.

Being self-employed, I was perfectly placed to become a professional referee. When we were all amateurs, we would have to beg, borrow or steal time away from our day jobs. The idea was that as professionals, we would form a dedicated, salaried group that would meet fortnightly for three days to train together. Our fitness would improve, as would our focus, and there would be more time to liaise with others, so in theory the standards, and therefore the game of football, would improve.

As I sat in Africa reflecting on this, there was only one problem – I didn't know whether I would be on the list. If not I would be facing a return to the Football League, and would be heartbroken.

When I got home from my travels there were two weeks' worth of *Evening Gazette*s waiting on the doormat. I started flicking through the sports pages looking for news of Boro signings. To my surprise, on the back page of one edition there was a picture of me, and a story which I could hardly take in quickly enough, suggesting that I would be on the elite list and be offered a professional contract for the forthcoming season. Just as my eyes were quickly skimming over the final few words, the phone rang. It was referee and close friend David Pugh. I could just about decipher from his excitable babble that he had made the list, even though he had yet to referee in the Premiership. Eventually I managed to tell him that I had heard nothing, and would ring him back as soon as I had spoken to Philip Don. I rang Philip immediately and he asked in a cheery tone whether I had had a good holiday. I said "yes" but had no intention of telling him about it at that point. I wanted to know if I was on the list.

He continued, "There is to be a select group. I have tracked people down all over the world, and think I have now been in touch with everybody." But he hadn't contacted me in Kenya. He then went into chapter and verse about how the system would operate, and said that all those selected would attend a meeting in

London to finalise all the details. My heart dropped. I thought I had been overlooked. Then he said, "You'll get a letter giving you the details." I was still not sure whether this meant I was included, or whether the letter was to be circulated to all referees out of courtesy, to let them know officially what was happening.

"Am I on?" I blurted out. "Of course you are," he answered with a hint of surprise, to which I replied, "But you said you had contacted everybody." He explained, "I didn't need to worry about you. I knew you would be up for it because your work would make it easy to join up." It was nice to be so highly thought of. And he was right. For me it was no decision. But for some of my mates it was not so straightforward.

Eddie Wolstenholme, for example, was on a secondment in China at the time. He had been tracked down by Philip and given twenty-four hours to make up his mind. It was a tough call for Eddie, because his wife and family were with him in the Far East and he was earning more than he would as a professional referee. Also, he was forty-six, and had just two years left as a referee. No one could have blamed him for declining the offer. But, as with most things, when you are made an offer that appeals, you take the plunge and do it, worrying later about the consequences.

It was still possible to do some work outside refereeing, and those able to take reduced hours found adapting to the new professional set-up no problem. Others had to try to hold on to jobs by persuading their employers to allow them to work for perhaps twenty-four hours a week. And that's what Eddie did. The commitment to turn professional was massive, and risky, because there was only a one-year contract, with no pension, and no company car. Yet for most, common sense, not to mention the family, came in firmly in second place. The potential salary was bandied about in several newspapers, and ranged from £50,000 a year to £70,000. In reality it was £35,000, plus match fees. Before professional refs, the match fee was £1200 but that dropped to around £700 per game when professionalism came in.

There was no room for negotiation. It was take it or leave it. We all took it – bar one – and in doing so showed our commitment to football, because a lot of referees had accepted pay cuts in order to take the plunge. The exception was David Elleray, who was in his final year. As I understand it, Philip did not want him on board unless he turned professional, but was forced to make an exception, and allowed David to continue for his final season on a match-fee only basis. Philip never hid his dislike of that decision, but it was taken by those above, who felt that David was the number one referee, even though he put his teaching career before football. I had no problem with that. He was an excellent referee, perfectly capable of officiating to the highest standard while concentrating on his career at Harrow. He willingly became the outsider in the select group of twenty-three.

The FA accommodated David, but other referees were treated in an unacceptable way. One aspiring young ref, Andy Hall, who had created a good impression in the Football League, received a call from Philip Don asking him to join the list. Andy quickly consulted his family, weighed up the implications for his career outside the game, and decided that he would like to take on the challenge. So imagine how he felt twenty-four hours later when he was told that the numbers had been rechecked, and there was no longer a place for him. How an error like that can be made is beyond me. To his credit, he knuckled down, and a year later was again offered a place. As he was in his early thirties, Andy had many years ahead of him as a referee. He understood that going professional could open all sorts of doors for him, leading to top domestic and international games, so he put the previous year's snub to one side, and accepted.

Philip had suggested that financially referees did not need to have any job outside the game, especially as it was necessary to be totally dedicated to football. Andy duly wound up a thriving business. He knew that in his first season he would not be asked to referee many Premiership games, but in the event he was not handed a single one, despite exemplary behaviour. He gave everything in terms of attending the training camps and get-togethers, and his enthusiasm shone through, but the nearest he got to the Premiership middle was fourth official, and the rest of the time he remained on Football League duty.

Frustrating through it was, he was prepared to bide his time. However, at the end of his first season in the professional ranks, without any warning, he was dropped from the list. He took legal advice but decided not to press for damages. Instead, he made the decision to continue his refereeing career in the Football League. I admired him incredibly for doing so. Many a man in his position would have given the FA a bloody nose in court. It showed that he is a gentleman who deserved to be treated as one.

I too had taken the plunge and was fortunate to fare better than Andy, whose demise upset me, and reminded me that I was in a perilous profession. Now that I had become a professional referee, I was expected to forsake some of my home comforts to concentrate on my full-time career. More days away from home at a training camp, more training – and a sex ban before matches! So my appointment meant a big change in my lifestyle and my approach to refereeing, not least because we were expected to attend a three-day training camp once a fortnight at a country retreat in Northamptonshire. The village of Staverton is in the perfect location, hidden away, yet close to the M1, and therefore easy to reach for referees from all parts of the country.

No arrangements like this had ever been made in our amateur days. Previously we would have the occasional meeting to discuss latest developments and issues but never anything on the scale that Philip was proposing. He had worked long and hard, against much opposition, to set up the select group of referees, determined that the best refs in the country would be able to devote most of their time to serving football, instead of getting accused of being amateurs in a professional game. We had long argued that our dedication to training and our high standard of officiating had proved that we were professional enough, as we juggled our football, domestic and full-time working lives. Looking back, though, we could never really have hoped to be as effective, given the circumstances.

Philip's vision had created an environment in which we could devote our time solely to preparing for top-level matches. We would be able to train professionally, instead of having to cram training runs into the lunch hour or after the kids had gone to bed, and we would be able to prepare for duty with nothing else on our minds. To me, the sacrifices were worth it.

Philip had laid the foundations for building a generation of fitter, more educated and more professional referees. However, his ideas didn't meet with universal approval. He was accused of creating an elitist group, which didn't go down well with Football League officials, and he also had had the problem of integrating a squad of officials who previously had only seen each other at brief weekend get-togethers into a proper and united team.

The format was that we would meet fortnightly on a Wednesday at Staverton, train on the Thursday and Friday, and the rest of the time have video reviews and discuss the latest innovations. We would then leave after lunch on Friday before our weekend match. This meant that if we had a midweek game or a trip abroad, we could be away from home for five or six days at a time – tough on the domestic life but, then again, this was now our job. I will always remember the huge feeling of anticipation of a new way of life and a new adventure on the eve of the 2001–2 season, the first of professionalism. Millions dream of being a professional footballer, and now we were being given the opportunity to enjoy the same lifestyle, albeit without the huge financial rewards.

The problem facing Philip, as in any dressing room, was getting twenty-three people from different backgrounds to gel together. It was clear from the very early days that there were friendships and differences within the group, and in that ours was no different from any workplace. Within the twenty-three there was a small group of refs brought together by standing friendships and FIFA involvement, and this group comprised Graham Poll and Graham Barber – nicknamed the Tring Triads (even though there were only two of them) – Paul Durkin, Steve Dunn and Rob Styles. Then there was a handful of others, like Andy D'Urso and Mike Dean, who flirted with this group, believing that their careers would benefit; Uriah Rennie and Dermot Gallagher kept themselves to themselves; Alan Wiley was in the middle; and then there was the rest of us, or, as we called ourselves, the good guys. All we wanted to do was enjoy our privileged positions and, assuming we got a fair crack of the whip, develop our careers. There were two occasions when everybody pulled together – training sessions, which were always great fun, and where we all encouraged each other to build up our fitness levels, and social occasions.

As a group, we were strongest on the social side. Our social secretary in the first year, Peter Jones, organised a multitude of events that were a laugh a minute, although I appreciate that a game of Connect Four might not sound like the most side-splitting thing on earth. We also got involved in fund-raising events for local charities and sports clubs, and you have to admire Paul Durkin for dressing up in green tights to be a pixie, and Mark Halsey for donning his Santa Claus outfit.

Despite all the good times, however, it was difficult to readjust. It always amuses me when people express surprise that footballers are free in the afternoon – what do they expect them to do, train physically for eight hours a day? It is impossible, and the train, rest and recover theory is sensible. After juggling our working lives and football, it took some time to realise that following a tough training session it wasn't wrong to have a lie down for a couple of hours. Yet it was during those hours of relaxation that the little gripes started to come out. The major issue was that some people in the group seemed to enjoy an element of favouritism with regards to the major appointments, and our mood wasn't helped by some of the media interest in us. One photograph, in particular, of us all in a sauna really annoyed us, as it wrongly suggested a holiday-camp atmosphere at Staverton. We enjoyed a sauna, but only after a hard day's training. Within the game, the initial disquiet was increasing. People like Jim Ashworth at the Football League did not see why so much had been spent on the select group when money in the game, especially at the lower end of the Football League, was tight. I always referred to Jim as "Rules is Rules" because of his desire to stick rigidly to the regulations.

I'm not saying categorically that the best officials in the country were in the select group, but many things would determine a place and those selected had to satisfy all criteria. They included constant availability, and the desire to be part of the group, as well as pure ability and experience. As the year progressed, there was the need to learn from our early experiences and follow up ideas. On the training front, we tried a variety of initiatives to improve our fitness, including activities such as aerobics, yoga and Pilates. I couldn't get my head around yoga though, as there's something strange to me about looking through your own legs.

Pilates is a discipline that strengthens core muscles, especially around the stomach and pelvic area, to improve balance and poise. There were times in my early sessions when I questioned my sanity as I lay on an exercise mat at Bannatyne's gym in a room full of women, stretching muscles I didn't know I had, and initially doing it badly. But I warmed to Pilates, and under the patient, expert guidance of Angie, the instructor, my frame became much more flexible. I have a lot to thank her for, because when I started I was about as supple as a plank of wood.

To help me build my overall fitness and sharpness for the coming season, I visited Keele University to help in a young referees' course and officiate in the pre-season tournament. They were happy to listen to older referees, like me, David Elleray and Martin Bodenham. Young women, as well as men, are now showing potential and one in particular, Amy Rayner, is following in the footsteps of the first ever female official at league level, Wendy Toms, and has made the national list.

We all had to pay careful attention to diet as well. While a footballer's life can last until his mid- to late thirties, if a referee wants to last until the retirement age of forty-eight, looking after himself is obviously very important. Dieticians recommended that we had our own menus, but chicken and pasta without any sauce pissed us all off. Alcohol is the one thing that doesn't go with longevity, as anybody will tell you, and I felt it started to become a problem with some in the group. I freely admit there was one night when the good guys enjoyed more than their fair share of red wine, but with good cause.

The two cliques in the group had begun to move further apart. Graham Poll was the unofficial leader of the smaller group, who tended to get more of the big matches, and I was the spokesman for the rest, who were less high profile. Graham had proved himself to be an excellent referee, but he was not the most popular among us. The desire to be top dog was becoming increasingly evident, and would intensify as the big international tournaments loomed. Everyone wanted to represent England.

Closer to home there were some new rules, which were ridiculous, and an example of the professional set-up getting too serious. We were warned to be careful who we socialised with, and who we spoke to about football. I was even advised to be careful what I said to Lynette when I was on the phone to her work – in case it was overheard. I wasn't allowed to discuss incidents in matches I'd refereed in case somebody mistakenly thought I'd been deliberately biased against a player or team. It was football's version of the Official Secrets Act.

Fully prepared, I felt relaxed as I breezed into my first game of the 2001–2 season as a professional. It was at Liverpool and the home fans were clearly thinking, "He's here again" when I awarded West Ham a penalty in front of the Kop. Liverpool came back to win 2–1.

Two days later, I was in charge of Arsenal against Leeds at Highbury, and my performance was put under the media microscope when I red-carded two Leeds players, Lee Bowyer and Danny Mills. I sent Bowyer off for two bookable offences, and there was a photograph in one of the national papers the following day of his foul-mouthed attack on me as I showed him the card. He just completely lost control and had to be escorted off the field. The card I held aloft did my talking. A few minutes later, Mills also came out with expletives when I gave him the red card for deliberately and venomously kicking the ball at Arsenal's Robert Pires after I'd awarded a free-kick to the home team. I was delighted when Mills signed for Boro, because it meant that I wouldn't have to referee him any more. I had no doubt that both red cards were exactly what the FA was looking for.

Leeds still won 2–1, and one of their goals was unusual. Full back Ian Harte scored direct from a free-kick outside the box after he'd asked me if he could take it quickly. As a delay would have been an advantage to the team that had offended, I agreed, and he scored while Arsenal were still sorting out their defensive wall. Keeper David Seaman didn't move and Arsenal claimed that the free-kick should be retaken because I hadn't blown my whistle. But I allowed the goal to stand. The Leeds manager at the time, David O'Leary, agreed with my interpretation – although he didn't agree with the red cards. Arsenal midfielder Patrick Vieira wasn't too happy with the goal and protested strongly. Vieira was a player who snarled and sneered at every decision that went against him, and that led to him being red-carded by other referees. In response, he said that he was being victimised either because he was French or because he was black. It was never the case.

Two seasons later, O'Leary wasn't quite so agreeable when Thierry Henry scored from a quick free-kick against Aston Villa. The manager criticised referee Mark Halsey for allowing the game to continue. It seems that it's fine when the referee allows a quick free-kick in your favour, but against the rules when the same decision is applied to your opponents.

Meanwhile I was appointed David Pugh's mentor during his first season at the new level, and I was his fourth official for his

Premiership debut at Newcastle against Leicester. We introduced a mentoring system in the select group as a means of support and advice for the newcomers, and it all added to the team spirit and group morale, which was still quite strong despite the cracks that were beginning to appear. The idea worked both ways, because the newcomers also encouraged and supported the older referees. David refereed the game well in front of a 50,000 crowd, and was a happy man as we travelled to Staverton the following day. When we watched the match video afterwards, however, his elation changed to dejection when Philip Don pointed out that his early non-award of a penalty was the wrong decision.

A heated debate followed between those who agreed with Philip and those who agreed with David. He's a strong character, and put it behind him. I could understand the situation from Philip's point of view. He wanted to achieve consistency, and "Trial by TV" (as we nicknamed the sessions) was his means of demonstrating to every select group ref exactly what was required. The increased focus on mistakes wasn't meant to be personal, and refs had to be thick-skinned when it came to frame-by-frame analysis. Though perfection would never be achieved, Philip was trying to get as close as possible to it. So while the group didn't always reach agreement, at least it showed how dedicated we were.

The mentoring system also worked for Mike Dean from Merseyside. I was fourth official to Mike for Bolton against Nottingham Forest in a Worthington Cup tie at the Reebok Stadium. Even though he had a good game, I thought he lacked experience in certain situations. But with the support and encouragement of all the other referees, and by listening to their experiences, by the next time I was fourth official to him at a Newcastle game six months later he was much more confident and accomplished.

In September 2001 I was in charge of one of the best games of my career in terms of the exciting football it produced. Manchester United were visitors to Spurs. I booked Nicky Butt, Denis Irwin and David Beckham in the first half as Spurs scored three times without reply. Their fans in the 36,049 crowd were ecstatic with the half-time lead, following goals from Dean Richards, Les Ferdinand, and Christian Ziege, but they struck with their only chances of the half, while United's flowing play suggested they could save the game if only they could convert their chances.

I told my assistants and fourth official at half-time that the next goal would decide the match, and sure enough within seconds of the restart United pulled one back to ignite the game and further electrify the White Hart Lane atmosphere. I was caught up in the atmosphere. This was the sort of game that made the Premiership so special – a packed house enthralled by the contest. I could feel the unease of the Spurs fans and the renewed hope of the United contingent, and I knew that the game was building to a crescendo.

As we returned to the centre circle for the restart, I looked across to my assistant on the far side and gave him a clenched fist sign, the usual signal between officials to increase their concentration because it was definitely game on. The signal was spotted by Spurs' former United striker Teddy Sheringham, who immediately misinterpreted it. "What the fuck are you doing? Celebrating their goal?" he snarled, waving his arms about. "No, Teddy, it's a signal to my assistant." "Looked to me as if you were celebrating," he retorted. If a clenched fist was supposed to be a celebration, I would have been doing somersaults at the end of the game, because United scored five times in the second half, to complete a remarkable fight-back.

In that dazzling forty-five minutes, Ruud van Nistelrooy scored one of his twenty-three goals that season, and Andy Cole, Laurent Blanc, Juan Sebastian Veron and David Beckham were also on target as Spurs wilted. But United's joy was not to last that season, for Arsenal finally snatched the title, Thierry Henry leading the way with twenty-four goals.

I found Darren Anderton of Spurs difficult to referee in that game, as I usually did. Anderton was a right moaner and I couldn't get any sort of understanding going with him. He always appeared to have a surly look. On one occasion, when he approached me to have yet another whinge about something minor, I said to him, "Go on, smile, you can do it even if it's only wind." All was to no effect, however. Other referees, like David Elleray, had the same problem with him, though I don't suppose David would have tried my approach.

I was soon given another high-profile and potentially fiery game, West Brom against Wolves in a Black Country derby. As I was enjoying a beer after the game, which ended 1–1, one of the fans pointed out something that hadn't clicked with me. West Brom's Neil Clement equalised direct from a free-kick that Wolves claimed I'd signalled as indirect. After reviewing the video, I saw that the fan was right – I did raise my arm, and should therefore have disallowed the goal. I crossed my fingers, hoping that it wouldn't be picked up by a television camera because I knew that

I would be criticised for my lapse at the next training camp. Fortunately, Philip Don didn't spot it either – which was rare for him – so on this occasion it didn't turn up on the video nasties. Needless to say, there were one or two remarks from my fellow referees when Philip wasn't around!

Another derby match followed a few days later, this time between Spurs and Arsenal. There was even more tension than usual in this fixture because this was central defender Sol Campbell's return to his former club Spurs in the colours of Arsenal. No Spurs fan wanted to see Campbell leave the club, so you can imagine their anger and frustration when he not only left but moved a few miles across North London to their despised rivals.

I knew it was going to be a match with a difference when we arrived at the ground two hours before the kick-off in our chauffeured people-carrier. There were more fans than usual in the streets, all determined to make their feelings known to Campbell as he arrived at the ground. It's a good job players don't walk to matches like they did fifty years ago. There was a sense of real venom in the air, and some dreadful abuse hurled at Campbell from the fans that used to idolise him. For his own safety he had to be escorted off the Arsenal coach. The abuse continued as he walked on to the pitch, and I must admit it was hateful, among the worst I'd ever heard. Usually when a player is given stick by the crowd I have a quiet word with him on the field, just to make sure he keeps his cool and doesn't allow the provocation to get under his skin. I needn't have worried about Campbell. He is nicknamed the Iceman, and I could understand why. The Spurs fans booed him every time he touched the ball or went near the touchline, but he never flinched. One player who did find his way into my book for a foul that day was Arsenal's Martin Keown. He was probably one of the most intimidating players in the Premiership, not just because of his strength and anticipation in Arsenal's defence, but also because of his eyes. He always seemed to glare with hatred at me, but I suppose it was the same with every opposing player.

By now I thought I'd seen it all. In my next FA Cup tie in January, Macclesfield against West Ham, however, something happened to me for the first time. West Ham midfielder John Moncur was a feisty player and always seemed to catch the referee's attention. Near the end of the game, he clattered into a Macclesfield opponent from behind, leaving the player flat out on the ground. I put my hand into my top pocket to reach for the yellow card and while I was doing so, he bent over the player, grabbed hold of him, and tried to drag him to his feet, shouting, "Stand up, I hardly fucking touched you."

Then came my two-card trick. I showed him a yellow for his challenge, raised the card a second time for his unsporting behaviour, and then brandished a red because of his two yellows. Everybody was confused by my card-shuffling skills, as they were unaware of the second offence. The *Match of the Day* pundits agreed with me in their post-match analysis after the benefit of replays. I also showed a yellow to West Ham defender Tomas Repka for a foul. He was one player who didn't need the English language to make his feelings known. I never sent him off, but there were times I wish I had. Whenever I tried to talk to him or even caution him, he just sneered and looked at me with total contempt. It was as much as I could do not to follow a yellow card with a red purely for his arrogance and disdain.

A few days later, in a midweek match at Cambridge, who were entertaining Wycombe Wanderers, I dismissed another player, but that wasn't the cause of the delayed finish to the game. I showed a red card to home keeper Lionel Perez, for a professional foul. In the second half, two players collided, leaving one unconscious. I didn't wait for the ball to go out of play. I frantically waved for the physio to come on, who was quickly followed by other medical people. Fortunately, the player came round after a worryingly long time and then there was a further lengthy delay while we waited for an ambulance. When the moment came to tell the fourth official how long was left, he nearly didn't have enough fingers to acknowledge my signal – nine minutes. To cap it all, there was then another lengthy injury stoppage, because another player suffered a head injury. All in all, an accident-prone match. What fans, players and managers sometimes don't realise about extra time is that the amount of time added on at the end of each half is the minimum, not the maximum. That's in case of further stoppages, and in this game I added on fifteen minutes. I think quite a few fans left early to catch the last bus, and we struggled to catch last orders, because we didn't finish until just before ten o'clock.

As well as refereeing, I continued to do my share of fourth official work, and it was while on that duty in a Blackburn versus Arsenal game that I made a sudden switch to running the line again. At half-time, when we got back to the dressing room, one of the assistants, Andy Butler, said that he had a calf problem and was struggling. "You've got to be joking," I said. I just thought it was a mickey-take. I'd done it loads of times to other people when I'd been a linesman. But then realisation dawned. He wasn't joking. I suggested that we went outside for a fitness test, but a short sprint suggested that more running would simply do further damage.

So I was forced to make a comeback as an assistant, nearly ten years after I'd last run the line in a competitive game. It was a reminder of how difficult running the line can be. You need to stay with play, keep an eye on the last defender for offsides, and at the same time watch when and where the ball is kicked. The concentration needs to be intense because of the speed of the game (and the speed had increased since I'd last been a linesman). I must have done well, because volatile Blackburn manager Graeme Souness didn't complain once to me. Naturally, for weeks afterwards all my assistants had to take it on the chin when I ribbed them that they weren't as good as me.

By now professional football had ceased to become only a Saturday game. In an attempt to be different, the Football League signed a deal with ITV Digital to screen games on Sunday nights. There were already games on Sunday afternoons and on every other night of the week. Televised football had reached saturation point. We had to be flexible; there was no other option. It was novel at first for many clubs and fans, and I thought I'd refereed every conceivable day and time until Burnley played West Brom at Turf Moor on a Sunday evening at 6.15.

The West Brom fans joined in the spirit of the day and sang one of their anthems to the tune of "The Lord is my Shepherd". Despite the unusual kick-off time, 15,800 people crammed into Turf Moor. The noisy travelling support added to the atmosphere and the Baggies were rewarded with a 2–0 win. Yet the Sunday night game ruined the weekend not just for me, but for my wife and family too. At least when I refereed a Sunday afternoon game there was still some time for relaxation, but with this new schedule I felt as if I hadn't had time to myself at all that weekend, especially as it was back to training on the Monday morning.

Night matches have a great atmosphere because of the floodlights – when they work. At Anfield, where Liverpool took on Newcastle, they sadly failed. It was a big fixture and the tension I was feeling increased the longer the delay went on. Eventually the power was restored and I was as relieved as the players to get the game under way. Liverpool won 2–0. The following Saturday, when I was fourth official at St James's Park for Newcastle against Arsenal, Newcastle manager Sir Bobby Robson congratulated me on my Anfield performance. I was chuffed to bits. It goes to show that not all managers are driven solely by results. I only wish more were the same as Sir Bobby.

After that game, I felt totally drained, because eight months of training and matches had taken their toll, physically and mentally. Everybody else's stamina and adrenalin seemed to have dried up as well and we were all in danger of burn out. Philip Don and trainer Matt Weston realised this and our high-intensity sessions the day before a game were cut out. While the training had been excellent at times, we were working just a little too hard. Just like players, referees can run and run some days, but on others that extra little bounce is missing. How many times, for example, have you thought that a player is all over the park and the next week he isn't as prominent?

There was, happily, a lighter side to refereeing and our professionalism still allowed for a laugh. Wendy Toms was my assistant for a game at the Dell between Southampton and Fulham. After giving a decision against Fulham, she started getting some stick from the visiting fans.

Football fans have always been, and always will be, quite inventive with their humour, and they quickly burst into song, suggesting that Wendy should be "doing the washing-up at home". I couldn't help laughing and I glanced over towards Wendy, who was clearly suppressing a giggle. After the game, we left the officials' changing room, and the gentlemen let Wendy lead the way. As we followed her we repeated the song. Wendy burst into laughter. She knew that playing jokes on each other was part and parcel of refereeing, and kept us sane.

Towards the end of the campaign Graham Poll was appointed for the World Cup finals in Japan, an honour he deserved for his refereeing skills. No one had yet been appointed for the Carling Cup final between Blackburn and Spurs, though there was a rumour than I was to be handed the game. After training one day I was in the sauna with Graham and the subject cropped up. "Yeah, I reckon you're odds on for it," he said. In the event, he was given the game.

The season ended with a huge game, the title decider between Manchester United and Arsenal on 8 May 2002. I was fourth official to Paul Durkin, and watching Paul in action from the touchline was a valuable experience. There was plenty of friction between the sides, partly because of what was at stake and partly because of their history of squabbles.

I was pictured in the papers in a touchline confrontation with Fergie, as he raced from his technical area to berate the officials over a decision he disagreed with. At least it gave my boot sponsors A-Line some free publicity! It was difficult to understand exactly what Fergie was saying, what with his broad Glaswegian accent, his anger, some expletives and the crowd noise. I persuaded him to return to his technical area, although he went very reluctantly. If I had been able to make out anything coherent I would have buzzed Paul Durkin and brought it to his attention.

Arsenal won 1–0, a result that obviously didn't go down too well with the home fans, especially when the Arsenal fans sang "We won the league in Manchester", as they celebrated after the final whistle. Fergie said no more to me on that occasion, but I understand he had a few negative words about Paul Durkin, despite his outstanding performance. In fact, it was performances of this quality that left people in no doubt that professional refereeing was here to stay. Just as well after what we had been through that season in adapting to all the changes.

11
REPRIEVED

My career seemed to be rushing by at breakneck speed, one season merging with another. But in the summer of 2002 I realised how lucky I was that my birthday falls on 18 April, because it unexpectedly earned me an extra year doing the job I love. At the end of the 2001–2 season I thought that I had only one campaign left because of the age limit. I would be forty-eight after 1 August 2002 and, at that age, referees had to retire, no matter how fit or alert they felt.

However, the FA made one of their best decisions ever, in my eyes, when they changed the qualification year, so instead of the "referee's year" being from 1 August to 31 July , it became 1 March to 28 February. So I was given an extra year. What a bonus. Though it didn't go unnoticed with the rest of the referees, and some joker handed me a walking stick at our next get-together.

I was fit thanks to full-time training, so the dreaded pre-season fitness tests shouldn't have been much of a worry. However, I couldn't help having nagging doubts. I was more nervous on test day than when refereeing at Old Trafford, because a sudden injury could ruin everything. In the event I breezed through, without having to resort to the walking stick.

I was now more relaxed than when I started refereeing in the Premiership, and I felt that man-management on the field would be much more beneficial than brandishing yellow and red cards. Despite directives from above on how games should be refereed, I felt confident enough to make decisions using my own initiative, and I never received criticism from above for doing so. But there were still situations in which I had no alternative other than to book and dismiss players.

My first game that 2002–3 season was Wolves against Burnley in the Football League, and it was a memorable occasion in more ways than one for former Wolves player Paul Cook, who was Burnley skipper. His children were mascots, but unfortunately he had more quality time with them that day then he bargained for, because I showed him the red card after only six minutes. It was one of the easiest decisions I'd ever made because Cook was guilty of a bad foul on Alex Rae. Burnley lost 3–0, and their colourful manager Stan Ternent looked daggers at me as I left the field.

So you can imagine my surprise when Philip Don told me that Stan had given top marks for my performance in his club's report. Perhaps it was sarcastic Stan's attempt to make sure I stayed in the Premiership, out of Burnley's way! Philip, not realising what had happened at Molineux, was delighted with my mark, but Stan and I knew better.

One of my best friends, fellow Boro referee Graham Frankland, saw the other side of the marking system and started to have mixed feeling about the game. He had become established in the Football League but decided he wanted to pack in refereeing in the summer of 2002 because he was no longer enjoying it. I spent a long time trying to persuade him to change his mind, pointing out that one game can rekindle enthusiasm and get adrenalin flowing again. I implored him not to be hasty, because he still had a good few years left in the game, and to give the new season a chance. Refereeing to me was the be-all and end-all, but to Graham it wasn't. He had family and sporting interests that he wanted to devote more time to, one of them being to return to football as a fan. I couldn't believe that he wanted to pack it in. I wished that I was forty again, with eight years left of my career, but I suppose everyone is different, and it wasn't my job to judge.

Still, Graham took in what I said and decided to give it a while longer, but by the middle of September still wasn't enjoying it. We had shared many a post-match conversation on the mobile phone from different ends of the country, talking about our respective match-day experiences as we made our way home. After a game as fourth official for Manchester United versus Bolton at Old Trafford, I phoned Graham on my way to Staverton for our next training camp. He had been refereeing a Carling Cup tie at Macclesfield that had gone into extra time. He had been more than happy with his performance and in his opinion had controlled the game well, without any complaints from players or managers. His match assessor, however, had commented on what he thought was Graham's lack of fitness. That was a bit rich coming from the assessor, who had hardly been the most mobile of officials during his refereeing days.

It proved the last straw, and Graham told me right at the start of our conversation that he was retiring. Try as I might, I couldn't persuade him to change his mind again, even though we spoke for over two hours until I reached Staverton. I admired him even more for his honesty to pack in the game there and then, instead of going through the motions and not enjoying himself. Refereeing in that sense is just like any other work – if you're not enjoying it, you'll never get job satisfaction.

Luckily, I was still enjoying refereeing immensely, and there was no way I was going to quit before I had to, even though the controversy continued. At Leeds that season I decided that an elbow by David Beckham on Lee Bowyer was accidental. So, too, you won't be surprised to hear, did Sir Alex Ferguson. Television pundits suggested later, with the help of slow motion, that the act was deliberate, and should therefore have resulted in a red card. But I was happy with the decision I made at the time. That's all you can do.

My next game at Villa Park was my introduction to a new precocious teenage sensation who had just hit the Premiership – and it was Villa defender Steve Staunton's first meeting with him too. After just thirty seconds of Villa's home game with Everton, Staunton was clattered by the young Everton striker – the calling card of Wayne Rooney.

I gave Rooney the benefit of the doubt because it was so early in the game, and settled for handing him a warning, in keeping with my new more lenient approach. He looked at me when I first spoke, then stared down at the ground as I continued talking. But even from that first glance into my eyes, he belied his age. There was a determination and strength there that you don't expect to see in one so young. There was not a hint of dissent from him, but he had a presence that I could see from close quarters more clearly than the fans could. Even among the great talent in the Premiership, you can tell when you are out on the pitch in the thick of it that some players have that bit extra. It was clear in this game that Rooney was one such player. His speed, vision, crunching tackling, and sheer strength immediately told me that he was something special.

My lecture didn't seem to do much good, however, because by the end of the first forty-five minutes, he was the only player on the field to be shown a yellow card. He didn't swear during the game but it was evident that he had an edge to him that I thought might make or break him.

As for Staunton, in the same game he raced half the length of the field to remonstrate with me, even though I'd given a free-kick Villa's way. I had to defuse the situation by quipping, "Where I come from, you get a smack in the mouth for talking to people like that." He just looked coldly at me. At the end of the game there was a knock on the dressing-room door, and one of the home club's officials told me that Staunton was the club's PFA union representative, and was intending to take action against me because I was alleged to have said, "I'm going to smack you in the mouth." I sought Villa boss Brian Little and explained the context in which I'd made the statement, adding that in future any Villa player who ran towards me and spoke to me in the same way that Staunton had would receive a yellow card. I learnt a valuable lesson that day, in that a few words and actions can be misconstrued and leave you with egg on your face.

In my next game, Fulham versus Arsenal at Loftus Road, Fulham striker Luis Boa Morte swore at me, and he had some justification, as I realised afterwards when I became the subject of the dreaded "Trial by TV". Boa Morte ran into the Arsenal box, where he went down under a challenge from Arsenal defender Sol Campbell. The Fulham fans and players bayed for a penalty but in my eyes they were wrong. Arsenal went on to win 1–0, and I was given non-stop abuse by the Fulham fans for the rest of the game. As it turned out, they were right. It should have been a penalty.

At the time I wasn't sufficiently convinced, however, because Boa Morte was a player with a reputation of going to ground at the slightest touch in the penalty area, so maybe he was a victim of that perception. All referees had noticed it. It's always a tricky one. You try not to let your view be clouded by a player's reputation while at the same time you can't ignore the fact they have that reputation for a reason. In fact, it could have been worse for him, for he could have been sent off for using foul language, but I decided not to reach for the red card.

The Fulham fans didn't forget the incident, because in their next game, when they entertained Bury in the Carling Cup, and my mate David Pugh failed to give them a penalty, they chorused "Are you Winter in disguise?" I didn't get any mercy from my refereeing colleagues either. Philip froze the action frame by frame to analyse the incident, and there was no hiding place. Sometimes the group could be split 50-50. This time, even my close friends couldn't defend me, and several people said, "How couldn't you give that?" My sheepish grin said it all – it was clear I had dropped a clanger. I didn't dwell on it, though, because you can't afford to let self-doubt creep in. It's a game of instant decision-making and you have to accept mistakes and get on with it.

I've seen many young referees progress through the Football League to the Premiership and one I became particularly good friends with was Rotherham's Howard Webb, who gained the dubious privilege of becoming my room-mate in the select group after the retirement of Eddie Wolstenholme. Howard has the potential to become one of the top English referees, and also be at the forefront of European and World football.

Howard was my fourth official for another fiery game between Leeds and Sheffield United in the Worthington Cup, a meeting that proved that neither players nor referees should stop concentrating until the final whistle. Leeds led 1–0 going into stoppage time, but Sheffield United scored twice within a minute and won 2–1. Emotions ran high among the fans after the game – it's not very often your team loses a game in those circumstances – and Howard, a police sergeant, was fortunate not to be called upon for post-match duty, as the fans rioted and spoilt a great night of football.

The following Saturday, I had another local derby, on a smaller scale but which turned even more dramatic. Notts County versus Mansfield sounds innocuous enough, but there is animosity between the two sets of fans that has its roots in the miners' strike from two decades earlier, when miners from Nottingham and Mansfield had contrasting opinions on whether or not to strike.

In this game, I experienced, for the first and only time, a black player claiming that he was racially abused by a white opponent. I didn't hear anything because I was following play, but that isn't to state that nothing happened. Something may have been said with me out of earshot, or the noise of the crowd had drowned it out, but the black player lost his self-control for a few minutes. Something had upset him but I couldn't act because I needed evidence. If I'd managed to hear anything abusive and establish who had said it, then I would have red-carded the culprit. Racial abuse has no part to play at all in our game. I'm pleased that progress has been made to stamp it out.

The game ended in more controversy when Mansfield scored a late equaliser that appeared to be offside. In the absence of my assistant's raised flag, however, I let the goal stand, as he was in a better position than me. As I returned to the centre circle, my attention was drawn to somebody shouting "you fucking bastard" and I turned round to see a large, animated Notts County fan marching towards me. He had already walked twenty yards on to the pitch, and was well within earshot. I looked over his shoulder towards the stewards for assistance, but none of them was taking any notice.

I started to approach the fan, and he must have realised that I was bigger close up than I looked from his seat in the stand. He thought twice about coming any closer, turned round and was eventually taken away by the stewards. God knows what would have happened – he could easily have been armed with a knife – but I would have had no hesitation in taking him on if he'd kept walking towards me, and protecting myself, just as I'd done in my boot-boy days. I would have made sure I got my retaliation in first. It was lucky I heard him swear, otherwise I wouldn't have known that he was there, and might have been assaulted from behind.

After the final whistle I told the club stewards and officials exactly what I thought of their lack of prompt action and used some choice words in doing so. One of the club officials got quickly to his feet and accused me of saying that Notts County was a "Mickey Mouse club", when what I actually said that the stewarding was "Mickey Mouse".

I reported the incident to Jim Ashworth, the referees' secretary of the Football League. When there had been trouble between Leeds and Sheffield United in my previous game, Jim had been very forceful in his advice to me that the incidents involving the Premiership club's supporters – Leeds were still in the Premiership then – should be reported in full. Jim always gave me the impression that he was anti-Premiership and very protective of the Football League clubs, therefore it doesn't surprise me that I didn't receive any feedback regarding the Notts County matter.

I did get feedback, however, after I issued what turned out to be my last red card in the Premiership two days before Christmas 2002, even though I was eighteen months away from retirement. And it was probably one of the easiest and daftest I'd had to show in the whole of my career. I dismissed Spurs player Christian Ziege, who had left Boro for Liverpool under a cloud of controversy a couple of summers previously. There had been a bitter legal battle between the two clubs over the legality of the move and eventually it had ended up in the High Court, with Boro winning their case. Ironically, Ziege didn't stay long at Liverpool, and soon moved to White Hart Lane.

Ziege was a good player, but moody with a streak of typical German arrogance. Spurs had taken the lead at Manchester City and Ziege kicked the ball away to prevent City from taking a quick free-kick as they tried to get back into the game. He ran away from the incident, and wouldn't come back to me so that I could show the yellow card. People think that referees are being awkward in those circumstances, but it is a chance to warn the player not to get himself sent off. I tried to meet him halfway but he still wouldn't walk towards me, despite the fact that I was pointing at him. His arrogance annoyed me and so I waved the yellow card in his direction, even though he was about twenty yards away.

A few minutes later, he conceded a throw-in and knocked the ball away again, forcing another delay. I ran past and had quiet words with him but he didn't make eye contact or acknowledge me. A minute later, he did the same again, toe-poking the ball away from the City man just as he was trying to pick the ball up. It was too stupid for words. I showed him his second yellow – and there weren't any arguments from Spurs. I was frustrated that I'd had to send him off, but I had no choice. When I went shopping the next day, though, I realised that the incident made my popularity soar on Teesside, because several Boro fans commented. "Good old Jeff, you got one back for us there," one said. I hadn't had any ulterior motive but that red card saved me a fortune in lieu of Christmas cards for the people of Teesside.

That season match officials were discouraged by the authorities from giving post-match interviews. Previously the media had rarely been interested in getting the ref's point of view, but now they were clamouring for every angle. I would have appreciated an opportunity to give my version of events after I'd given Arsenal a penalty at home to Liverpool. It was a game of two penalties. I awarded Liverpool one that they converted, and it looked as if they would hold on for three points to keep them in the title race. Late in the game, however, Arsenal substitute Francis Jeffers turned in the box and Liverpool's John Arne Riise pulled his shirt. Even though Jeffers made the most exaggerated dive, I awarded a penalty, which Thierry Henry put away. Liverpool protested furiously. They felt that I'd been taken in by ex-Evertonian Jeffers's dive.

I usually got on very well with former Liverpool manager Gerard Houllier, but most uncharacteristically, I got the dog's abuse from him this time. Houllier had by now recovered from his heart surgery of 2001, but was clearly under pressure. I saw a different side to his nature. He ridiculed me for being apparently conned, and for a long time afterwards made reference to the incident. When you come face to face with a manager you respect as much as I respected him, it is a little harder to take when they have a go at you than when it's from someone who is constantly having a dig. But I felt it reflected on Houllier, rather than me. No one else asked for my opinion, and if they had, they would have been surprised by it. I agree that Jeffers had dived in an exaggerated manner, but it wouldn't have made any difference had he had done a somersault, for Riise had committed a foul in the penalty area.

Before long I was back in the thick of it in an explosive Old Trafford FA Cup tie between Manchester United and Arsenal. The first ten minutes of this game were possibly the most difficult I'd ever officiated. It was clear from the off that the players were prepared to rile each other with niggling fouls and face-to-face insults. I don't think there was a player on the field who wasn't more wound up than usual. So much so that I can't recall who were the main aggressors. I felt I needed eyes in the back of my head to spot everything.

It's easy to sit in an armchair at home watching on television and criticise a referee's performance after slow-motion replays, but high-profile games such as these between United and Arsenal are a million miles away from run-of-the-mill matches. There are so many different things to watch out for, so many players eager to be stronger and better than their opposite number, and so many highly strung personalities ready to snap at the slightest hint of trouble.

The game won't be remembered for Arsenal's 2–0 win, or for the bookings of Patrick Vieira, Paul Scholes, Roy Keane and Ruud van Nistelrooy, but for what happened after the match in the United dressing room – the infamous boot-flying saga, whereby a furious Fergie allegedly threw a boot at David Beckham, an incident which was to be the beginning of the end for the England skipper at Old Trafford. I wasn't aware of what had happened until I read about it in the media, and saw the pictures of Beckham's cut face.

My performance was given plenty of praise, but not from Fergie, who accused me of letting myself be bullied by the Arsenal players, and thereby give decisions against his team. But he must have known from the list of yellow cards his players had collected from me in previous seasons that I wasn't easily swayed.

Arsenal went on to win the FA Cup, but with just over one season to go it looked as if my chances of refereeing a major final were disappearing, because I was handed the second-leg of the Worthington Cup semi-final between Blackburn and Manchester United. If I was in charge of the semi-final, there was no way I would be given the final as well. I would only have three more chances of refereeing a major final before my retirement.

I was soon in charge of a Chelsea versus Leeds game again, this time at Stamford Bridge. Chelsea full back Graeme Le Saux had a habit of indulging in my pet hate – dashing across the pitch to mouth off at a decision from an assistant. In those situations, an assistant has nowhere to hide. He can't run away, all he can do is stand still, trying not to listen to the abuse coming his way. In the Leeds game, Le Saux did exactly that, turning on assistant referee Russell Booth. I ran over to stop the incident getting out of hand, showed Le Saux a yellow card, and warned him that if he continued I would show him another. He put his hands on his hips, and said, "Well, go on then, send me off." I was sorely tempted, but I wasn't going to give him the satisfaction. It's not very often you come across players asking you to send them off!

It was a week of crazy cautions. In my next game, Premiership-bound Wolves were comfortably beating Sheffield Wednesday 4–0 at Hillsborough in a game that had been virtually trouble-free when Wolves decided to make a substitution, although why manager Dave Jones decided to do that, I don't know. There was no need to run down the clock, given the scoreline, and we were already into time added on. A tired Paul Ince headed mistakenly towards the changing room, but stopped in his tracks when he realised that he wasn't actually the player who was to be taken off. He muttered something under his breath. Within ten seconds of the game restarting, Incey wiped out an opponent with a wild tackle, earning himself a yellow card. I asked him what that was all about, and he replied, "I'm upset at not being subbed. I'm knackered."

I could always have a laugh with Incey, and my lasting image is of him haranguing me or one of my officials. I always found a quick "Fuck off, Incey" did the trick and calmed him down. Players are not allowed to swear, but I did if I felt it would calm a situation, which usually meant saying it in a light-hearted way. In turn, if a player swore in a jocular way, or in a one-off outburst, I took no action.

With just over a season to go, the pressure was off, and for the first time in my career I was starting to enjoy the sort of freedom that referees only gain once they've put the years in. You have experience and confidence, as well as the long-awaited respect of most players and managers. I could now deal with most situations in a relaxed way. At an FA Cup replay between Blackburn and Sunderland, Blackburn manager Graeme Souness had one of his touchline rants at goodness knows what. Instead of steaming towards him and displaying my authority, I crept up behind him and whispered in his ear, "Graeme, why are you such an obnoxious get?" Smiling, he turned round and said, "Jeff, I just want to be out there." When you consider that Souness has played at the highest level and got the medals to prove it, it's not difficult to understand how frustrating it must be for him to see players who don't have the ability he had. It's not only tension and pressure that make managers rant and rave from the touchline.

My Dubai suntan – I'd just taken a short break with Lynette to celebrate her fortieth birthday – came back to haunt me in January of that season. Everton lost 2–1 at Charlton and their manager David Moyes wasn't happy. His post-match comments turned a little too personal when he said, "The referee should have stayed on his sun bed," although how a suntan can affect a performance, I don't know. Nevertheless, the remark stuck for a few weeks, especially when some of the referees at the next training camp wore sunglasses for my benefit. The media latched on to it as well, and they nicknamed me "the perma-tanned referee", which I suppose was one of the better comments about me – and at least I didn't get a zero mark.

When it comes to major games, a referee sometimes needs luck on his side. I was fourth official to Sheffield United versus Leeds in the FA Cup quarter-final that season, my second game involving these two clubs following the Worthington Cup thriller in August. Steve Bennett, widely tipped to be the referee for the final, was in charge. He's one of the nicest guys in football and an excellent official. Unfortunately, his Cup Final hopes disappeared that Sunday lunchtime and Danny Mills, the Leeds full back, unwittingly played a major part. Teddy Lucic, the Leeds centre half, had already been cautioned for a foul. In the second half Steve showed a yellow card to Danny Mills for a foul, and then to the player's astonishment showed him red. Amid strong protests from Leeds, Mills started to leave the field. Steve had mistaken Mills for Lucic. I quickly conferred with the assistant referee and frantically buzzed Steve. By now, with the Leeds protests, the assistant's flag and my buzzer, Steve realised what he had done, and called Mills back.

It was an understandable mistake to make, because the two players are fairly similar in appearance. Steve was distraught in the dressing room, for in those split seconds after a baffled and protesting Mills was about to go down the tunnel, Steve realised that his Cup Final chances had gone. It had happened in the heat of the moment. I felt so sorry for him. The referees' changing room at Bramall Lane is divided in two, and so I gestured to the two assistants to go into the other room as I tried to console Steve. Then there was the inevitable and dreaded knock on the door. The assessor came in. Steve, with tears in his eyes, knew what he was going to say. I was very sad for Steve, and still would have been, even though it had opened the door to the final for me.

A fortnight or so later, Philip Don approached me and asked if I would like to be a referee in *Superstars*, the TV sports competition which was being revived by the BBC. Apparently, the BBC had specifically asked for me – was it the athletic body, the good looks, or the luck of the draw? I wondered – and they gave me some dates in between the play-off semi-finals and the play-off final. In other words, Cup Final weekend. It was clear, then, that I wasn't going to referee the final. Nevertheless, I put *Superstars* on hold as I believed I had a good chance of getting the play-off final.

As for my refereeing tactics that final season, I continued to believe that players respected me more by defusing problems with a quiet word than by brandishing cards, and I didn't get any suggestions from the authorities that I should be less lenient. The next test of my man-management theory was with my mate Paul Ince again, at Molineux, where promotion-chasing Wolves were playing Midland rivals Stoke, who were battling against relegation. It was a tight game and in the closing stages tempers started to boil over, with Incey and the Stoke centre half exchanging verbal unpleasantries at close range.

I tried to break into the exchange, shouting, "If you two are going to have a fight, then I'll take you both on after the final whistle!" The Stoke player started to laugh, while Incey continued to shout. But when he realised that we were both laughing at him his red face of anger turned to one of embarrassment. I didn't need to show a card, and they restarted the game with the matter resolved. Plus there were no frustrated tackles from Incey when he got tired later in the game.

In my next game, Huddersfield versus Chesterfield, the visitors' Glyn Hurst showed his frustration by shouting, "Fuck off!" rather loudly in my general direction after Huddersfield had taken the lead from an early penalty. While the swearing wasn't necessarily directed at me, I felt that action was necessary. As I beckoned him towards me, he must have feared at least a yellow card. He stopped, head down, six yards from me. I beckoned him even closer, looked him in the eye, and said, "Now you fuck off." There wasn't another cross word exchanged. My colourful language had the desired effect – sometimes it's necessary – and Hurst knew that if he swore as loudly again in future games he could well be sent off. I hope he learnt from it.

I appreciate that it's not the greatest example to set young referees, and I hope none copy it. Swearing on the pitch is frowned upon by the authorities and rightly too. I wouldn't have been so easy-going when I was starting out, but by now I was feeling carefree and, what's more, it seemed to have a positive effect on the players, who realised referees were human. Maybe my action worked because of the element of surprise it generated in the heat of battle.

When FIFA referee Graham Barber was handed the FA Cup final between Arsenal and Southampton at the Millennium Stadium I made a quick call to the BBC, agreed to be their *Superstars* referee, and at the same time hoped that I might still get the First Division play-off final, if it could be squeezed in between *Superstars* commitments. Before the end of season play-offs, however, I had to fit in my final Manchester United game of that campaign. It ended in joy for them, for they clinched the Premiership title against Spurs at White Hart Lane.

In contrast to the eight-goal thriller we were treated to on the previous meeting between the two sides, this time the teams played out a tame goalless draw. A point was all United needed, so they were happy. I could have sent off David Beckham to join Real Madrid slightly earlier than expected. Beckham, who was to depart that summer, got involved with Spurs' full back Mauricio Taricco, who was trying to wind Beckham up throughout the game, and with some success, as he was beginning to bite. Becks swore at him, and I ran past him and said, "You would send your sons to bed early if they spoke to you like that," to which he replied, "I know, Jeff, but he's a fucking Argie!"

My final game of the Premiership season was a great honour – fourth official in David Elleray's last game, Newcastle United versus Birmingham City at St James's Park.

David had been a great referee, but wasn't one of Philip Don's favourites because of his refusal to go full-time. As a result, David wasn't given many high-profile games. In my opinion, he was still the country's number one. Despite his reluctance to join the select group on a full-time basis, David had refereed for well over thirty years, which in anybody's book is quite an achievement. He was probably the most professional referee I'd met, in terms of his preparation, attitude and control of games. And he'd never missed any of the pre-season courses at Keele University. To his credit, he didn't appear to allow the poor relationship between him and Philip get him down.

For the final game of his career, he asked for three particular officials to accompany him, and I was joined by Dave Babski and Phil Sharp. I'm sure David would have liked to have ended his career without taking his cards out of his pocket, but that wasn't to be. Birmingham centre half Matthew Upson committed a professional foul which was met by David's last ever red card. He did his duty to the end – I bet he would have sent off that Chesterfield player for swearing!

Before the play-offs began, I headed to Guernsey to referee the Muratti Vase final, which has traditionally been controlled by a Premiership referee. Although the game between Guernsey and Jersey wasn't high profile, and didn't attract the saturation television coverage of the Premiership, it was one of the most enjoyable games of my season. There were 4,500 people inside a recently completed stadium, creating a tremendously good-humoured atmosphere. We even had a streaker! An exciting game earned great credit for both sides and it ended all square after extra time. Mark Le Tissier, the refereeing brother of the famous Matt, asked me if I could take the replay but sadly I was unable to because of *Superstars*. That was a pity, because the social side afterwards was great.

There were two Premiership referees in the play-offs, myself and Steve Bennett. Philip Don confided in me that one of us would get the First Division final at the Millennium Stadium. I refereed the first leg of the Third Division semi-final between Bury and Bournemouth at Gigg Lane, and then the second leg of Bristol City and Cardiff in the Second Division play-off. I then flew off to La Manga for *Superstars*. I was hoping Philip would get in touch to say whether I was doing the final, but the call didn't come. I rang Steve, who told me that he had been given the game. I was therefore disappointed on two counts – I'd been overlooked for both the Cup Final and the play-off final. Maybe Philip felt that he'd done me a favour by opening the door to *Superstars* – which, make no mistake, I'm grateful for – and that Steve should have the consolation prize of the play-off final after missing out on the Cup Final.

So there were only two more chances of refereeing in a major cup final. But Boro were improving all the time as a Premiership force, and there was every possibility that they might reach two cup finals in one season, as they had done in 1997. Was my home town's success going to mean that I would be passed over for the big occasion again, and leave the Premiership stage with barely a whimper?

La Manga provided an opportunity to referee on a different stage, under different circumstances, and I was determined to enjoy it, even though part of my mind was on matters back home. After idolising footballers for years it was great to meet other sportsmen and women who earn a fraction of the amount, yet are exactly how the programme describes them – superstars. In terms of the effort they put into their sports, and the professionalism they show, they are almost superhuman. The boxer Steve Collins was one of the first I met on arriving at the airport. Steve was a larger-than-life character who both I and Lynette – for wives were allowed to travel – got to know very well over the following ten days. Sporting stars of all disciplines were involved, and football had its share of representatives.

The teams quickly integrated, and the camaraderie was excellent. There was one character I'd already seen quite enough of in his chosen sport – Steve Claridge. He'd scored a Carling Cup final winner against Boro. But what a great guy. Steve's a tremendous competitor but also humble. His dance routines with "partner" Steve Collins in the Hyatt Hotel after a few drinks did leave a question mark over his sanity, however. I later admired Steve Claridge as a media man, summarising at matches, and bringing the dullest of games to life with his humour and astute observations.

Stuart Pearce was there as well, another man who always played with an intense passion, but who is a quiet family man away from the game. Now Manchester City manager, he brings a refreshing honesty to post-match interviews; I have never heard him criticising other managers or referees. Dave Beasant was our regular keeper in matches at *Superstars*, but none of them could top little Dennis Wise. He almost suffered a career-threatening injury while at La Manga – nearly splitting his sides with laughter at me. We had retreated to a showpiece tennis ground for an impromptu game of football/tennis – a kind of volleyball without hands. Such was the team spirit of the gang that the others even let the old ref join in to display his footballing skills. I rose majestically to plant a match-winning header over the net, only to feel a sickening blow to my face as I collided with another player – and came off much the worse. Blood spurted from my broken nose, I couldn't open my eyes, and it took me a while to pick myself off the ground. The first person I saw was Ricky Hatton, the boxer. The pain suddenly eased as I realised that my "street cred" would go up no end when I told my mates that Ricky had broken my nose and blackened my eye.

Then I saw who had really inflicted the damage. It was a chap of around 4ft 11in, a mate of athlete Derek Redmond, and even smaller than Dennis Wise. My assailant had out-jumped me, and come off relatively unscathed. As the game was suspended to wash blood from the pristine court, Dennis couldn't help laughing. You can't put one over on some people, no matter how hard you try. Dennis was on the trip with his wife Clare and young son Henry, who had been carried up in his father's arms to the Royal Box at Wembley to collect the FA Cup in 1997 – after Chelsea had beaten Boro.

Sprinter John Regis got as surly as any footballer I have handled when I ruled out some of his dips in the gym competitions. But away from the competition he was brilliant, as were the likes of Jamie Baulch, Darren Campbell and Ewan Thomas. In our midst was the legendary Brian Hooper, a double *Superstars* winner, who was in La Manga to celebrate his 50th birthday, and the great Brian Jacks, who assisted me in refereeing the final – maybe because of my alleged dodgy adjudication in the gym tests. But my favourite guy of all out there was cricketer Jimmy Adams. He was the definitive West Indian, in that he was so incredibly laid back. Nothing flustered him.

When I returned home my refereeing friends gave me a ribbing. With their eagle eyes they had picked up on something on the TV coverage of *Superstars* that I hadn't been conscious of. When judging the squat thrusts, I had stood alongside the male competitors, but when it was the women's turn, I had taken up a position behind them – with a good rear view. As the competitors included Annabel Croft, Catherine Merry and top swimmer Zoe Baker, it was an easy mistake to make.

12

INTO MY FINAL SEASON

Lynette was dreading the final whistle. She had no idea how to live with me when football was over. Nor did I know what I was going to do, but whatever it was to be, it would be a major change for her too. No wonder she was worried. At least I would have a helping hand in adjusting. A sports psychologist had been appointed to help us adapt to the world of professional refereeing, so I asked him for advice on how to move into life after refereeing too.

His name was Craig Mahoney and he was a good man. As an Australian, Craig naturally had to cope with a bit of stick from us at first, particularly with reference to sheep. The more we got to know and like him, though, the easier we went on him, and actually started listening to his advice. And good advice it was too. He stressed the importance of looking forward, not back, and having no regrets. That applied to turning professional, but it was equally relevant in terms of retiring from refereeing and moving on to new ventures. Eventually I ended up enjoying every minute of the sessions with him. The need to have a positive mental attitude was as important as physical fitness. I proved that I was strong of mind and body for a gruelling season ahead, by taking on board what Craig said, while also passing the fitness test at my final boot camp before the start of the 2003–4 season.

Just before the season got under way there was time for a holiday, back in Canada, with Lynette and my younger son Mark. We had made friends with a lot of people there on my previous visit, so I was delighted to be invited back to lecture to referees in Edmonton and Calgary, as well as refereeing three games. I refereed the Villains again, and this time the keeper stayed in his penalty area, and on the pitch. We were all learning. The warm-weather training there and the time spent with my Canadian colleagues made for the perfect start to the new season. I returned home to a pre-season friendly at St James's Park, which turned out to be my last visit there to referee a Newcastle United game.

Over 32,000 turned out for the game with Bayern Munich – an astonishing crowd, but then, the Geordies are completely football-mad. After that match I took charge at Middlesbrough's Riverside for their warm-up game with Chievo Verona. I was aware that I would be visiting grounds as a referee for the last time, and managed to keep my emotions in check – for the time being. I also wanted to visit some for the first time, so handed Philip Don a list of non-Premiership grounds at which I had yet to officiate. He looked at it and said with a sarcastic smile, "If you want I'll give you nothing but Football League games," to which I retorted, "Well, that's what happened to David Elleray and Peter Jones, wasn't it?" Some of my fellow referees who were present cringed.

But I had always spoken my mind and wasn't going to change now. However, I can't have annoyed him too much, for I did get to some of the venues I'd requested, including Stoke's Britannia Stadium early in the season.

I took a deep breath before the first competitive game of my final season. It was an emotional moment; even though the season had not yet kicked off, I was already desperate for it not to end. I realised as I blew the whistle to start the game that the sands of time were already running down. In that 5–1 thrashing for Wolves at Blackburn there was just one caution, for Nathan Blake of Wolves, who made a typical forward's challenge in the last minute. It looked a lot worse than it was but nonetheless I felt it was worth just a yellow. The assessor disagreed and told me so. Even at this late stage of my career, I was still not immune from the guardian of standards. When I watched the tackle on television, I have to confess that the assessor was right. It was a red-card challenge. Yet on the pitch, from my angle, and that of the players, a yellow was sufficient punishment.

While accepting you're wrong is part and parcel of the game, so is standing up for yourself when you know you are right. And that's what I had to do after a feisty game between Newcastle and Manchester United that August. It was clear that I was not Sir Alex Ferguson's favourite referee, assuming that he ever had one. Nevertheless, I was determined to enjoy every game in my final season, and Newcastle at home to United was a plum appointment even as fourth official. Uriah Rennie was referee.

Something always seemed to happen when Uriah and I worked together, especially at St James's Park. Remember, he'd sent off

Alan Shearer for two bookable offences a couple of years previously when I was fourth official.

The Man United game started quietly and there had been little to concern me involving the two benches until midway through the first half – and then all hell broke loose in an incident which would grab the headlines for weeks. Manchester United forward Ryan Giggs was running in full flight towards the Newcastle penalty area and was challenged by Andy O'Brien. The defender slid into Giggs, who then fell to the ground under the challenge, with the United fans, players and coaching team screaming for a free-kick and a sending off for O'Brien, who was the last Newcastle defender, and therefore denying Giggs a goal-scoring opportunity – but only if the challenge was deemed to be a foul. It wasn't. Assistant referee Russell Booth kept his flag down, and Uriah waved play on. Fergie was incensed. The face turned its familiar shade of red as he leapt from his seat, ran outside his technical area, and screamed, "You fucking cheating bastard!" at Russell, who was level with play and perfectly placed to judge the tackle.

Fergie returned to his technical area but by chance the ball ran out of play into the dugout. Fergie furiously kicked the ball back on to the field, and again shouted, "You fucking cheat!" at Russell. I buzzed Uriah to come over to the touchline – although I think he had a fair idea of what had been going on – and I told him what Fergie had said. Without further fuss, Uriah dismissed the United manager from the dugout. As Fergie walked up the tunnel, he turned round to me and shouted, not once but twice, "You're a fucking joke." This time I had no problem deciphering exactly what Fergie said. There wasn't much crowd noise because the majority of the fans in the ground naturally weren't screaming for a free-kick and red card for O'Brien. I quickly scribbled notes of Fergie's outburst verbatim and later used them in my report. Despite the fact that these reports are meant to be private and confidential after they're sent to the FA and the club, within a few days details of my report were in the tabloids for everybody to see. How they got there, I wouldn't like to say, but it could only have been from somebody at the FA or at Manchester United.

By then, anybody who can lip-read had worked out what Fergie had said anyway, courtesy of the Sky television camera aimed at the dugout from the opposite side of the ground. The camera captured the whole incident from the moment of the challenge until he was banished from the dugout. Certainly most of the newspapers had worked out what he'd said from the pictures, and with the use of asterisks, headlined the words the following morning: "You f***ing cheat" – exactly the words I'd written down.

There is no way Uriah or his assistant would ever cheat, nor would they want to, and to have implied that they were by using the word "cheat" is out of order. It is an abusive personal remark that a referee or an assistant referee will not tolerate. Swearing is one thing, and can be overlooked at times, but accusing officials of cheating is a massive slur – probably the worst accusation you can make. Not only that, but Fergie swore pretty loudly several times in front of the main stand. Not exactly the example for a knight of the realm to set.

A few days later, the FA charged him on two counts. One was for alleged improper conduct, and the other for directing foul and abusive language towards match officials. He was instructed to appear in front of the FA at a disciplinary hearing. Then it all started to get rather naughty and, to my eyes, it appeared there was a campaign, orchestrated by United, to discredit me and thus get Fergie off the hook.

Now let me take you a step sideways. Prior to the start of the season and following my trip to La Manga to appear in *Superstars*, I had been approached by a production company with a view to a TV documentary being made of my final season. The idea was for it to be one of those fly-on-the-wall accounts of what was involved in training, preparing and officiating in the Premiership. I passed the request on to my boss, Philip Don, and then on to the Premier League offices. Discussions hadn't been concluded when the season started, but everybody was in agreement, subject to final editing rights. Nobody knew about this, apart from certain people at the Premier League, the television production company, and a couple of television companies who had shown interest in buying the documentary. Not even my fellow refs.

The arrangement was for a camera crew to film me preparing for a game later in the season, travel with me to a match, and then for me to do an interview. They would also use footage, supplied by Sky, of me in action. Pretty much run-of-the-mill stuff really but nevertheless a different angle on what it's like behind the scenes in the professional game.

Unbelievably, the Sunday following the Fergie incident, I received a phone call from my boss Philip Don, one of the few people who knew of the project.

"How does Fergie know about your documentary?" he asked.

"I don't know," I said. "What do you mean?"

"Have you read the papers?" Philip asked.

One of the Sunday papers carried a short story saying that "A Winter's Tale", the agreed title of a documentary, was being filmed and that the Fergie incident was going to be one of the featured items. From where did the newspaper get its information? Philip clearly thought that Fergie, or his connections, could be behind it. I didn't give permission for the news to be released, and neither did the small number of people who were involved in the original talks – unless one of them lied to me when I asked them later. It would appear that Fergie was already privy to the information. Had he released it to the press? I was speechless, because only a small number of people were supposed to know and they didn't include Manchester United representatives.

The disciplinary hearing that was originally scheduled for the FA's headquarters in Soho Square on the 9 October was cancelled, and then rearranged for the 20 October at the Crowne Plaza Hotel in Manchester. Quite often, disciplinary hearings are rearranged for the convenience of clubs, and referees and FA members have to travel all over the country to fit in with the clubs' requirements. It seemed a case of the tail wagging the dog.

Then, events took another sinister twist. Prior to the hearing, I was asked by the Compliance Department of the FA to make a witness statement, because there had been an inference from United that I had stage-managed the incident involving Fergie to help my proposed documentary. What a load of bollocks. As I said in my statement, Fergie's actions left me no alternative other than to alert the match referee. United were clutching at straws. That seemed to be the FA's opinion as well. The compliance officer told me that he had recommended to Fergie that he should accept the charge, and bearing in mind his previous good disciplinary record (obviously other referees had decided to ignore barbed post-match comments as I had done after the United versus Fulham game in 1999), he would probably only be reprimanded. But Fergie had his teeth into the defence of his case, refused the advice, and wanted his day in court. He appeared to have only two aims, to discredit me and to have the charges dropped.

I tried to forget about the growing furore, and went on refereeing games to the best of my ability. I must have done well for I avoided further controversy as the day of the hearing loomed. I booked into the hotel the day beforehand, which was fortunate because the following morning the national media had camped en masse, ready to pounce, in the hotel foyer. They snapped everybody who was taking part in the hearing – apart from me, because I was already inside.

The next few hours were the most traumatic of my career. The setting was like a courtroom, in that the prosecution and defence were on opposite sides of the room and the judges in the middle. The judges in this case were the panel of three set up by the FA to make the decision, all in their dark suits, sitting apart from everyone else, as if to protect their neutrality.

There was Fergie, looking stern and sober-faced, with the occasional icy glare in my direction. With him was Manchester United's barrister Maurice Watkins and two legal staff, all of them on the left-hand side of the room. They had a file of papers on the table in front of them. The FA had sent their own in-house prosecutor who, along with one of the disciplinary staff, would present their case. They were sitting on the opposite side of the room, and like their adversaries, had a briefcase and a wad of papers.

I was in the middle, taking it all in, thinking that this disciplinary hearing was certainly going to be different from all those hearings at North Riding FA for Sunday League offenders I'd been involved in during a long career. It was very formal, just like any court case. The spotlight was on me to withstand the intense pressure of the situation and hold my nerve under a bombardment of questions from United's QC. It was me versus Fergie, probably one of the biggest matches of my career. Fergie had brought Maurice Watkins with him for good reason. It was clear from the opening exchanges that they were putting me on trial, and not the other way round.

United brought in several witnesses and read out a number of statements, all saying that Fergie had not used the words I had reported. He did, however, admit to swearing, but felt that swearing at someone is not abusive language, but more everyday language. His arrogance shone through and he clearly thought he was above the law. He thought calling one of the officials a "cheat" was harmless and he couldn't see that he'd done anything wrong.

My testimony was dissected, line by line. My version of events was queried; my interpretation of what Fergie had shouted was held up for scrutiny. Witnesses were called, all stating that Fergie hadn't done anything wrong and suggesting that my attitude had been provocative towards him. Fergie's legal team even produced a letter from Newcastle United supporting him. But I wasn't too concerned. While I repeatedly fended off the accusations that I had ulterior motives, I just waited for the screening of the video that would show Fergie clearly using foul and abusive language.

However, I was in for another surprise. I expected the video to show the incident in its entirety, from O'Brien's tackle on Giggs to Fergie storming up the tunnel. But it didn't – the incriminating parts were missing. I was astounded. Why didn't the tape show Fergie swearing, when everybody watching on television previously had seen exactly what had happened? Had somebody edited it? Did this explain why I had come under such intense scrutiny from the United legal team, because there was going to be no other evidence? It was like a murder trial without the forensic evidence.

After the three-hour hearing, we all left the room to enable the FA people came to a decision. I decided to spend a penny, and who happened to be in the gents at the same time? Fergie, of course. He totally blanked me.

Before leaving the hotel – there was no need for me to hang around for the decision – I was thanked by the FA's prosecutor for my evidence.

"What the hell happened to the video?" I asked him, knowing that it would have been the most damning and conclusive part of the evidence.

"We couldn't get an unedited copy," he replied.

I suggested, "If it hadn't been a club with the power and clout of Manchester United, there would have been a proper tape."

He smiled and said, "Tell them about it in your book."

When you consider that the incident had been widely shown on television, and the FA couldn't lay their hands on an unedited version, his reply was unbelievable. Somebody must have taped the match. So who provided the edited version of the tape?

It had been a torrid experience for me because my integrity and honesty had been questioned so closely and so minutely. I suppose I shouldn't have been totally surprised by the day's events. I knew that I was going to come under intense pressure from the United legal team, but never to the extent that they would try to discredit me.

Fortunately, the FA disciplinary board believed my version – maybe they had seen the incident on television the same day like the rest of the country. Fergie was banned from the touchline for two matches and fined, but it was me who felt like the guilty man that day. The hearing provided more questions than answers as far as I was concerned. That meeting in the gents wasn't the last time I crossed paths with Fergie that season either. I mulled it all over for several days, and was pleased to get back into match action.

Wolves had won promotion the previous season, but struggled badly, and by the time I next took charge of them, on 4 November 2004, they had yet to win a game. I proved something of a lucky charm for them, however, and they broke their duck by beating Manchester City. In a frantic final five minutes I issued four yellow cards, including the obligatory ones to Paul Ince and Alex Rae, and thought that at least by exerting my authority I would have pleased Philip Don who was watching from the stands. Consistently applying the letter of the law was a stance he never wavered from. I later learnt that he had left with five minutes remaining, as he wanted to beat the traffic!

My following game was a Division Three derby between Scunthorpe and Lincoln City. The sides had met in the play-off semi-final the season before, and there was no love lost between fans or players. Lincoln took an early lead, scorer Ben Futcher being booked for excessive celebration in front of the Scunthorpe fans. That booking set the tone, and there were a further seven yellows and a straight red for Mark Bailey for a deliberate kick at former Boro man Peter Beagrie (whose sister lives across the road from me – though that didn't affect my decision). "Job well done," I thought, having managed to keep the lid on a rough game. But again the assessor disagreed; he thought there should have been a second sending off.

I was soon back on fourth official duty for a Sunday lunchtime clash between Birmingham and Aston Villa. It was a potentially explosive game, as the previous season in the meeting of the sides Dion Dublin had become a cult hero with fans around the country for putting the nut on Robbie Savage. Fortunately, the game was beautifully controlled by Mike Riley, who was having an excellent season, confirming me in my belief that he was one of the very best in the business. While it's a pleasure to be close to the star players, I also found it highly satisfying to work with the star referees. Sometimes I marvelled at their skills as well. Even Steve Bruce didn't give me any hassle this time. All I had to do was carry out my duty with the electronic board – though I was ready, willing and able if any trouble had brewed.

While there wasn't any during that particular match, trouble in general was never far away, and it duly arrived in the Leeds versus Liverpool game that came my way shortly afterwards. Leeds were fighting relegation, and lost 3–1. To be fair to Leeds manager Peter Reid, he never hid his feelings. He is like me in that respect. He had praised me earlier in the season for the way in which I'd handled his side's game at Leicester, even though Leeds were thrashed 4–0.

I had deliberately applied a softly softly approach to that game, which found favour with Reid. I felt that it was time referees put in some low-key performances, letting certain things go rather than reaching for the book at every opportunity. Sometimes you must look at the bigger picture. Around this time referees were getting a rough ride from the media – and fans – for dishing out cards left, right and centre. Matters had come to a head when Rob Styles had handed out cards galore in a match between Newcastle and Everton.

My more subdued approach had gone down well on the previous occasion but by the time I took charge of Leeds again, I found out that sometimes you can't win, whatever stance you take. Reid exploded with me because I let a Liverpool goal stand when my assistant had flagged for offside, and he told the media, "The sooner Winter packs in permanently and retires to *Superstars* the better for me." The thing about Reid was that he could switch from blind rage to calm reason within a second. This time he stuck to that view, but whenever he criticised me I was half expecting him to withdraw it immediately. He once had to be dragged away from me by stewards, but then shook them off, bounded up and put his arm round me.

However, he'd had his say to the media, and I decided to have mine. I felt that it was time the voice of refereeing was heard. Perhaps I was subconsciously getting some practice in for the media career that was awaiting me. I felt that fans needed to know why certain decisions were made. I also felt that by appearing on camera, or being quoted in the press, referees could show their human side, and perhaps hold their hands up to mistakes they had made. Not that I was wrong to allow the controversial Liverpool goal, but by speaking to the media it gave me the chance to explain the interpretation of the law.

Ray Gould, my assistant, had rightly flagged a Liverpool player offside. From his angle the player appeared to be interfering with play. But from where I was I could see that goalkeeper Paul Robinson's vision was not impaired, even though he fumbled the ball into the net. I was convinced that the position of the attacking players had not influenced him, and therefore the goal was good. If I had been anywhere else on the pitch when the Liverpool scorer cut in from the left and shot, I would have accepted the flag. But by now my experience had taught me the most advantageous positions to take up. Robinson thought he had got out of jail when he saw the flag. But he hadn't. I ran over to Ray to explain my point of view. Consultation with the linesman comes first, then the players, then the media. I wondered whether the decision to disallow the goal, or my decision to speak to the media, would be brought up at the next meeting at Staverton, but it wasn't.

I was loving every game now, and particularly enjoying the freedom to apply my own interpretation. I was going easy with players in the hope that they would go easy with me, and that the fans would see a better game. In my next match, for example, I let Everton's Tobias Linderoth off with a quiet word after a bookable offence against Chelsea. When I didn't produce a card, Chelsea's England midfielder Frank Lampard came over to me and said, "Surely that's a yellow!"

I told him I was giving everyone a chance, and added, "Let's see if we can get through the game without a card." We did, which is credit to the players, because they responded to my challenge and played fairly without letting it affect their determination to win. My reputation was now that of a referee who would let the game flow. Therefore, when I did produce a card, the players knew it was because I had no choice. I had learnt that you are more likely to lose control when you issue cards galore than when you don't produce a single one.

I guess it's like much like a schoolmaster's job. If he sends one child to the headmaster, the head invariably ends up with a queue outside his door. I felt at ease with myself though I'm led to believe that some others, players, managers and fellow referees included, felt I was de-mob happy, and should have refereed as strictly as I did at the start of my career. But I wanted to finish my career leaving behind the perception that not only had I been a very good official, but that I'd understood the game and those involved in it too. I believe I became a better referee in that final season. Sir Alex Ferguson, Steve Bruce and others may not agree. I no longer felt in the hands of other people. Now I could be me. And that meant that when I wanted to have a laugh, I could do so. I took the job seriously, but could be more relaxed about match days.

Within a month I was back at Everton for a boring 0–0 draw with Manchester City, an afternoon livened up by one memorable incident off the pitch. The local police chief had instructed his motorcycle division to pick up the Manchester City team coach belonging to the Finlandia company, and provide an escort to Goodison Park. They duly rode to the M62, and the story goes that the outriders saw the coach coming, flashed the driver and indicated that he should follow them. The coach driver followed the orders, and made his way through the Liverpool streets to the players' entrance at the ground. Imagine the surprise of the police when a mass of grey-haired folk climbed carefully down on to the tarmac. The police had picked up a group of pensioners, using the same bus company, on a day trip to Albert Dock. I guess the driver had no reason to suppose it was mistaken identity. He obviously felt that the Merseyside constabulary were being particularly helpful. The City team managed to make their own way there, but the way they performed they would have been better off fielding the pensioners.

All sorts of strange things were happening as my career neared an end. I even had a civilised conversation with Gordon Strachan, when I was fourth official as his Southampton team suffered an extra time Carling Cup defeat at Bolton. Gordon resigned shortly afterwards so maybe he was feeling de-mob happy as well. The relaxed, humorous manner that he went on to display as a television pundit was completely at odds to the persona of Strachan the manager. Maybe it was the pressures of the job. He is not only relaxed and funny on television but displays an acute knowledge of the game. His assessments come under the category of compulsive viewing. Mind you, to a neutral, his tirades at me were probably much more entertaining.

Not quite so entertaining were the shenanigans at Staverton, where matters were coming to a head. Since the start of my final season, referees in the select group had become employees of the PGMOL (Professional Game Match Officials Ltd). This came about because there had been a long-running dispute with the Inland Revenue as to whether professional match officials could continue to be classed as self-employed. It was decided that as we were getting all our income from one organisation, we should not be. There were benefits to being employed. It meant that all tax was deducted at source, rather than us getting hefty bills at the end of the tax year. However, the downside was that many of our allowances were reduced in line with employment law.

We did have greater rights as employees though. If, at the end of the season, a referee was no longer wanted on the list, proper disciplinary procedures were applied. That meant performances on the pitch had to be fully assessed and written warnings issued. There was a desire among the FA bosses to show that the system of professional referees was open to scrutiny and was being properly applied. For example, it was necessary to remove, or relegate some referees, otherwise it would have been seen as a closed shop where a referee's job was safe no matter how badly he performed. This is all well and good in theory. Yet, in contrast to a football team, for a dismissed ref there is no way back. Having an axe hanging over us was not conducive to giving good performances – in what was already a high-pressure job.

By my final season the pressure on some people had increased to the point where it was almost impossible to do the job. On the face of it, things were fine. Philip Don held regular one-to-one meetings with each of us and was forthright and honest. If you were performing well you got the big games, if you weren't you didn't. I had no complaints with the matches I was handed, but some of the other referees felt aggrieved.

The problem was that a revised assessment system had been introduced, with new interpretations of how a referee should view his responsibilities. Both referees and assessors were uncomfortable with it. Basically, a referee could now lose marks for anything and everything that occurred in a game. It soon became clear that some assessors would delight in docking marks for what appeared to be trivial matters. For example, it was stressed to us that at kick-off every player had to be in his own half. That's a long-standing rule that had never been strictly applied. If a player was a foot over the halfway line at kick-off we'd never paid too much attention to it. But now, suddenly, we had a situation where a referee could be controlling a high-profile game superbly – making a correct penalty call, sending a player off, getting all the major decisions right – but if he transgressed on minor points he would get a lower mark than a referee who had got crucial decisions wrong but had been a stickler in making sure that nobody had a toe over the line when kicking off after a goal had been scored.

It was petty in the extreme, but even such a hard line might have been acceptable if all assessors were robots. They're not. Some are strict, others easy-going. Both approaches can work. And some assessors are overawed by having to mark referees who are at a far higher level than they ever reached. In short it was flawed, though I admire the way Philip Don tried to apply it. He wanted a system of 100 per cent uniformity, one that everyone had cried out for, so that players, manager and fans knew where they stood and had no cause for tirades against referees.

As I see it, the problem is that the more you seek consistency, the less scope there is for referees to apply common sense. I wanted to draw on my wealth of experience and apply it to help keep games flowing and entertaining. In general, referees were starting to show annoyance at the new procedures, and the pressures behind the scenes were increasing. It didn't help that Philip Don appeared to me to have his favourites, though no doubt he would counter with his usual mantra that it was the best referees who got the biggest games. Still, there were anomalies.

By now the system was in place whereby we knew only a few days in advance which game we had been allocated for the coming weekend. Yet Graham Poll, now widely regarded as number one, seemed to know before the official announcement which games he had got. There were rumblings of unrest and bad feeling towards Graham, but he brushed them off. In fact he was quite happy to let it be known that he had advance information. It showed to the rest of us that he was "top dog". This inevitably led to divisiveness among us, when what we needed was unity.

If the pressure was building on Philip from within, it was also increasing from the outside. With players, managers and supporters growing more uncomfortable with the way red and yellow cards were being handed out like confetti, the Professional Footballers' Association, and League Managers' Association were beginning to kick up at Philip's hard-line approach. The result was that there was less consistency than ever in refereeing. Some were applying the letter of the law and brandishing cards galore while giving free-kicks for the most trivial things. Others, myself included, were trying to apply common sense, and control games without using the five-card trick. With two different groups at the refereeing get-togethers, the friction was growing.

Rob Styles had the ability to alienate nearly everybody. I have never come across a referee so roundly criticised by players, managers and supporters. And among referees he found few friends. He had a ruthless streak that surpassed anything I, and many others, had seen. Plus he seemed to be joined at the hip to Philip Don. I wasn't the only one to notice, for Rob earned the nickname of "Thrush". No explanations needed, I hope. The anti-Don feeling had become intense, but it still came as a huge shock when we reported for our fortnightly get-together at Staverton to find that he had been axed. We were told that Philip had arrived but then gone straight home. Rumours that he had left the job were rife. It was Richard Scudamore, the Chief Executive of the Premier League, who delivered the truth.

Scudamore arrived on the Friday morning, thirty-six hours after the rest of us had gathered, to tell us that Philip Don was no more. He said that while he had always supported Philip, he had become aware that Philip had "lost the referees". It was a straight-forward talk but the rumour mill then went into overdrive. Who had spilled the beans? The fingers of suspicion pointed at certain referees, especially those perceived to be keen to take over from Philip. There was little time to discuss it with the others though, as we all had to set off for our games. I headed to Lancashire to ponder the dramatic events, though I spent most of the journey on the phone. Not to colleagues, family or friends, but to Philip.

Just like any employee I hadn't always seen eye to eye with the boss. However, I have always been a people person, and don't like to see fellow humans being badly treated.

I know how much refereeing meant to him, and since his dramatic departure I have always kept in touch with him. His only crime was trying to rid the game of cheats and bring in a consistent level of refereeing performance. He had failed on both counts, because it was those he had tried to help who had ultimately been instrumental in his downfall. He summed it up to me in one succinct sentence, saying, "I trusted the wrong people." I felt dreadfully sorry for him, but life went on, and I had to concentrate on completing my final season as smoothly and efficiently as possible.

That was never easy with Fergie around. Midway through the season I had my first encounter with him since we had met at the court hearing. I refereed United's Carling Cup tie at West Brom. After I'd finished warming down on the field after United's 2–0 defeat, I came across Fergie in the narrow corridor. I was ready to exchange pleasantries, but he bowed his head, didn't acknowledge me, and just walked past.

He was back to his usual self after another Cup tie, United versus Manchester City in the fifth round of the FA Cup. United won 4–2 at Old Trafford but finished the game with ten men because I sent off Gary Neville. I showed him a yellow for diving in the City penalty area and, in the arguments that followed, a straight red for a head butt on City's Steve McManaman. Fergie didn't say anything in the tunnel after the game but in his press interviews he said Neville's red card was all my fault, though I can't recall head-butting anybody in the game. It seemed he could talk about me, but not to me. "The referee, as usual, was on his next after-dinner speaking date," said Fergie.

I have tremendous respect for Fergie's achievements as a successful manager and he richly deserved his knighthood for transforming United into one of the major forces in the football world. If and when he retires, his successor will have a hard act to follow. However, my personal experiences of Sir Alex don't make me one of his fans. His mind-games, while at times amusing, don't enhance the image of the game, and his arrogance has led to him being an unpopular figure.

13

BORO'S CUP AT LAST

On New Year's Day 2004 for the first time in years there was no football, so I grabbed the chance of four days of relaxation in the warmth of the Mediterranean in Majorca before returning to the banks of the River Medway to take charge of a Gillingham home game. You might think that North-Easterners don't bat an eyelid when cold winds cut through them. Wrong. The icy blasts that hit Kent come from the same North Sea that brings grey, bitter days to Teesside.

I was bloody freezing. I cannot ever recall being so cold, and even a rip-roaring FA Cup tie, with Gillingham knocking out high-flying Premiership boys Charlton, brought no comfort to my rattling bones or chattering teeth. It was a far cry from the sunny May days of FA Cup finals, but part of the magic of the Cup is that games are fought, won and lost in the mud, slush and cold of winter on the journey to a glorious, balmy final.

For some clubs, however, survival is the top priority, as it was for my neighbours Darlington. They had suffered horrendously under the ownership of maverick chairman George Reynolds, one of the most extraordinary characters ever to find his way into football. The former safe-cracker had built the club a magnificent new stadium, the 25,000 capacity being far too large for a club of Darlington's stature. Reynolds was very much his own man, had refused to listen to advice, and had alienated the locals. The inevitable outcome was administration for the club, which all but went under because of massive debts.

However, team manager David Hodgson, a man of strong character and a talent for lost causes, set about rejuvenating the community and saving the club. Part of his master-plan was a big fund-raising game involving all the stars he could muster from his contacts. He had played for Liverpool and been an agent, so had a bulging address book. I was invited to referee the game, which involved Paul Gascoigne, Kenny Dalglish and Bryan Robson. Darlington is just fifteen miles down the road from Middlesbrough and I dearly wanted to help, partly because of my memories of when Boro nearly folded in 1986. However, I was forced to decline, because I had been handed the role of fourth official at an FA Cup tie between Manchester City and Spurs on the same day. I could have asked to be let off that duty, but professional commitments always took precedence. Had I asked for the switch – and as it was my final season there might have been nothing to lose – it could have proved a huge mistake, because in fact the FA Cup was to play a massive role in the short remainder of my career.

The City versus Spurs game ended in a 1–1 draw, and led to the incredible replay in which City trailed 3–0, only to triumph 4–3. An amazing turnaround maybe, but not as amazing as the one

David Hodgson engineered at Darlington. A crowd of over 14,000 flocked to their stadium for the fund-raiser, the money generated going a long way towards saving the club.

In a season of incredible twists, turns and incidents, I was soon back at Leicester City, where the locals were pleased to see me as I had taken charge of their 4–0 win over Leeds earlier in the campaign. This time Leicester lost 5–0 to Aston Villa, though the attack on Leicester City keeper Ian Walker, rather than the score-line, was the real story. The incident occurred in the second half, and highlighted the slowness of stewards in dealing with potential trouble. Instead of nipping it in the bud, they allowed it to become actual trouble.

Walker was guilty of a howler that led to a Villa goal. Along with the players, I took up my position for the restart, before noticing that one of the teams wanted to make a substitution. As I dealt with that, I heard a roar from the crowd behind the goal, and turned to see a supporter on the pitch. He was making his way towards Walker. At first I assumed it was a celebrating Villa fan, as they were behind that goal. I waited for the stewards to lead the fan away, as I assumed they would, and was stunned when this didn't happen.

The intruder was in fact a Leicester supporter angry at Walker. In the confrontation that followed, Walker started to push his adversary. As the stewards still refused to react, I hurried over to intervene. I may not have been the quickest of sprinters, but my feet and my brain reacted quicker than anyone else managed on that occasion. As I got nearer I could see that Walker was becoming increasingly agitated. I grabbed hold of the angry keeper and wrestled him from the fan, before stewards finally reacted and led the intruder away.

The reason I went for Walker rather than the fan was because my job was to be in charge of the players, and also because I sympathised with him, which showed how I had changed over the years. In my youth I saw things from a fan's perspective and would have been angry myself if my team was getting hammered and the keeper was at least partially to blame. But now I remembered how I felt when a fan had confronted me at Notts County. I had been sorely tempted to thump him, and could see that Walker felt the same on this occasion. Had he done so, I would have had to send him off for violent conduct, whether I sympathised with him or not. With such an outcome, God knows how the stewards would have coped if crowd trouble had followed.

Remember when former Manchester United star Eric Cantona assaulted the Crystal Palace fan with that amazing "kung fu" kick? On that occasion, the player was already off the pitch, but Walker was still on it. If he had assaulted the fan, the Football Association would have thrown the book at him. By reacting as I did, I potentially saved Walker, who is an honest professional, from serious trouble.

At the end of the game, the scoreline was the least of Leicester's worries, as it appeared that there had been a dispute between police and stewards as to who was responsible for what. It's a grey area that should have been ironed out long ago. When I was first on the terraces, the police did a good job, but the lines later became blurred when police costs meant that there were fewer officers and more stewards were on duty. The police are more of a deterrent to trouble-makers than stewards are. Besides, stewards are part-time, not as well trained, and less likely to want to put themselves on the line when major trouble breaks out. In these days of litigation, incidents of this nature should be stamped out at all costs. The fan could have sued Walker for pushing him, because technically it was assault. The knuckles on my right hand were bruised, and I realised I must have made considerable contact with Walker when grabbing him to restrain him. So I suppose I could have sued him too. Then again, he could have argued that I'd assaulted him and therefore sued me. That we should even think of such things shows that the football world has gone mad.

In the end I was relieved to get out of it relatively unscathed, but I couldn't help thinking about how I would have reacted had it been my first season as a referee. The incident had the right ending. The fan was banned for life, while Walker signed his shirt and presented it to me for saving him from big trouble. I'm pleased I didn't pull his shirt hard enough to rip it!

Ironically, before long I was a fan again – at the Riverside where I was in the crowd to see Boro reach the Carling Cup final by beating Arsenal. Jim Ashworth had implied that had Boro failed to reach the final I would have been selected to referee the game. But if it came down to a choice between me refereeing a major final or Boro winning their first major trophy, there was no contest. I was 100 per cent behind Boro that night, and joined in the celebrations.

"Never mind," said Jim, as if I needed consoling. "There's always the Division One play-off final." "What if Sunderland get there?" I asked. He turned rather red and admitted that such a scenario might create a problem. For some reason, he always insisted that I should not take charge of Sunderland or Newcastle, even though I had done so in the Premiership. So my career could end without me refereeing a major final, and all because of my beloved Boro. I could live with that, but not if it was because of Sunderland.

The Carling Cup final was a joyous occasion. Goals from Joseph Job and a Bolo Zenden penalty gave us our first major trophy with a 2–1 win over Bolton. We benefited from what was technically a refereeing error by Mike Riley that day, but I defy anyone to criticise it. Zenden slipped as he took the penalty and in theory it should have been disallowed, because he actually struck the ball twice – though the gap between each contact was too brief to be measured and there is no way that a referee could have spotted it, though Bolton manager Sam Allardyce complained afterwards.

Meanwhile, some referees were looking beyond domestic honours. In the run-up to Euro 2004, it was clear that the top refs were desperately hoping that they were given the English nomination in the finals. When it was announced that Mike Riley was to be the chosen one, it went down very well with me and those colleagues I was close to, as Mike was popular among us. We liked him as a person as well as respecting him as a referee. It became clear how popular Mike was when some of us joined him for a party. The wine flowed and Staverton reverberated to the terrace chant of "England's, England's number one". The following day at training it was clear by the body language of other referees that they were disappointed at the nomination. I don't know how Graham Poll felt, for he wasn't at training that day.

My mind was soon focused on refereeing on the pitch, thanks in particular to Robbie Savage. Rarely has there been a player who gets as wound up as he does, and he refused to give me a moment's peace when I took charge of a Villa Park derby against Savage's Birmingham. Villa scored and tried to protect their lead. Savage was at me constantly, accusing the home side of time-wasting. I have never known a player ask so often how much time was left. He had clearly decided that the best way to help his side was to get me to agree to as much additional time as possible. But I stuck to my guns, stopping my watch only when I felt was it right to do so. I always used my own discretion as to how much time to add for substitutions, goal celebrations and so on. As it turned out, Birmingham grabbed a last-ditch equaliser and Savage, arms aloft, ran to me screaming, "Time's up. Blow the bloody whistle!"

I do tell players how much time is left, as I see no harm in doing so. But I wasn't always honest. As fourth official I used to love telling managers – when their team was a goal up – that there was to be at least seven minutes of added time. Stressed managers are the easiest people in the world to wind up. Down the years I annoyed enough of them when I wasn't trying to, so I must have a huge mischievous streak to want to do it deliberately.

Amid all the emotions of my final season, there were occasions when I couldn't help but admire the quality of the football. We are all drawn to football because it is the beautiful game, and perhaps one of the best performances I ever had the pleasure to observe from close quarters was the FA Cup quarter-final tie between

Arsenal and Portsmouth. Arsenal raced into a 5–0 lead with play of breathtaking quality. They were three goals up at half-time, and as we waited to start the second half, I said to Thierry Henry, a player who normally keeps himself to himself, "Sometimes you make the job difficult for me." He queried this statement as there hadn't been a moment's controversy. I explained that I was enjoying Arsenal's performance so much that it was easy to forget that I was supposed to be refereeing the game. He smiled, and then within a minute of the restart committed a foul, so I awarded Portsmouth a free-kick. He ambled up and smiled, "I was just checking that you were concentrating on your job." He was substituted later, possibly because Arsenal's supremacy was such that manager Arsène Wenger did not want to embarrass Portsmouth further.

However, even with Arsenal cruising, the ground reverberated to the sound of the Pompey chimes, as the club's magnificent fans ignored the scoreline and backed their team to the hilt. When they scored a late consolation goal, the fans made the biggest noise of the afternoon. At the end of the game I looked around the ground and felt both privileged and sad. I realised it was probably my last ever FA Cup tie, and after such a magnificent occasion I wanted to go on refereeing for ever.

Remaining ambitions were few, but there were still one or two grounds that I had not visited, and Keith Hackett, who had taken over as refereeing boss from Philip Don, kindly obliged insofar as he could. I refereed at Cardiff's Ninian Park then was handed a trip to the New Den for Millwall against West Ham. Both grounds have been the scene of violence among fans, and while the Cardiff game passed off peacefully, the trip to Millwall was more eventful. I had not awarded a penalty all season, but in this game, for good measure, I gave three, and sent off Hammers' keeper Stephen Bywater. The decision angered the Hammers fans so much that they started to invade the pitch, before being stopped in their tracks by determined policing. I have nothing against stewards, but the police are far more efficient in these circumstances, and the level of enforcement was considerably greater than it had been at Leicester a few weeks earlier.

After I'd turned down two penalty appeals – one for each side – in quick succession at Manchester City the following week, the commentator suggested that it was tit-for-tat refereeing. Commentators often claim that referees even things up, both on penalty decisions, and red cards. That has always annoyed me, because it is nonsense. Neither I nor any referee I know operates in that way. We give what we see. We all make mistakes, but evening things up is not part of the thought process. Once you make a decision, it's gone. If you dwell on it you cannot do the job properly. And that was something that I was determined to do, right to the end. I was determined to enjoy my final days too, but that didn't stop anger welling up in me whenever it was suggested that I had ulterior motives for decisions.

I was nearing the end of what sometimes felt like a farewell tour of the country. And a final visit to Merseyside was part of that itinerary. My game at Liverpool was scheduled for the Sunday and Lynette and I had been invited to the Grand National at Aintree, held the day before, by the *Liverpool Echo* newspaper. A few weeks earlier I had been a speaker at their big event, the Merseyside Sports Personality of the Year. The speaking and media engagements that were to become my future career were already part of my life. One of my regular radio appearances was on the *Wright and Bright* Saturday morning show on Radio 5 Live, and that Saturday we discussed the Grand National, as well as that weekend's FA Cup semi-finals.

A colleague rang me after the show, suggesting that I was to be appointed referee for the Cup Final. An article in one of that morning's national newspapers had speculated that the honour was coming, even though it would mean a break from the long-standing tradition of naming a FIFA referee. I wasn't a FIFA referee because (as I see it) it takes so long for refs in this country to be promoted through the leagues, unlike elsewhere in Europe, where they are often fast-tracked. Take Pierluigi Collina; he seemed to have been around for decades. I became a Football League linesman at the age of thirty, it took me six years to reach the Football League referees' list, and then another three years after that to get to the Premiership. That effectively ruled out FIFA duty for me.

I dismissed the story, as I had previously built my hopes up only to see them dashed. I didn't give it a further thought as I settled down that afternoon to enjoy the racing. I refrained from the booze as I was refereeing the following day and, aided by a clear head, picked three winners including Amberleigh House in the big race. The horse was ridden by Graeme Lee, who lives on the same Teesside estate as I do, at Ingleby Barwick.

Buoyed by a profitable afternoon, I was still in good spirits the next day as I set off for Anfield. Liverpool had the game sewn up by half-time, and it petered out. I could have done without that. Since I didn't need to be quite so much on my toes, my concentration levels eased and I began to get emotional, knowing that I would soon leave the famous turf for the last time. I reflected on the great Liverpool occasions, both uplifting and sad, that I had been involved in. The tragedy of Hillsborough, and the FA Cup final of 1989 when I was fourth official, came flooding back, and as the final minutes ticked away I could feel the emotions well up.

I had mixed feelings. On the one hand I wanted to finish the game a little early and get off the pitch before people saw big tough Jeff Winter burst into tears. Then again, I didn't want the game to end. Liverpool were 4–0 up, so it was in my hands. Nobody would care either way. In the end I played a little bit extra, waiting until play was at the Kop end, before sounding the final shrill blast – a bit like the Last Post. The fans behind the goal burst into spontaneous applause. It was longer and louder than normal, even for a big home win. Did they know it was my final visit? Was the applause for me? They are such knowledgeable football people, that it would not surprise me.

The tears streamed down my face as I left the field, head bowed. Back in the dressing room, Chris Foy, who had also been on duty with me that day, as on so many other occasions, understood how I felt. It was he who answered the knock on the door that came from Liverpool's Steven Gerrard when he delivered his autographed shirt.

My emotional state refused to subside and I was glad once the post-match formalities were over. I breathed a huge sigh of relief as I climbed back into the car and into my own world. It had been a fabulous weekend, but almost too much for me. I needed to get back home, put my feet up and spend some time in quiet reflection. The adrenalin rush that affects players had surged through me. Like an electric current, it needed to be earthed – in my case with a cool beer and some light-hearted television. Fat chance.

I was just beginning to come back down to earth as I reached that crazy spot on the M62 high over the bleak Pennines where the motorway splits into two to avoid the farm that is now sandwiched between the two carriageways. How the farmer stands the traffic noise I don't know. I'm told that he refused to move when the road was improved and, credit to him, he has stuck to his guns. You could write on the back of a postage stamp what I know about farming but I reckon he's as stubborn a character as I am.

Those who travel the route will know the place, and the distinctive nature of that spot means that it is etched on my memory as the point I was passing when the mobile phone rang. I recognised the voice immediately. It was Joe Guest, refereeing appointments secretary of the Football Association. He didn't have to say more than "Hello". There could be only one reason for the call. The rumours were correct. My dream had come true. "Jeff, you are invited to referee the FA Cup final." My reply was never in doubt. "Of course, Joe, it will be a pleasure." I was hardly going to say, "Sorry, Joe, I have a prior engagement."

After such an emotional couple of days, you would have thought that this brief conversation would have sent my mind spiralling out of control. But I felt an inner calm. This motorway was the highest in the country and I was on top of it at the highest point. I felt exalted, but in control. I sensed I was at the very pinnacle, and could look back with satisfaction on my career, knowing that the high point had been reached. Now all I had to do was experience it.

Just as on the day with Peter Mulcaster in the bank back in 1989, I'd been told not to tell anyone before the following day's press release. Lynette had travelled independently, and was ahead of me, but I couldn't ring her because she wasn't on a hands-free mobile. It wasn't much of a secret anyway. The rest of my journey was taken up with calls from people connected with the FA, congratulating me on my appointment. Maybe this time it took more than a day for the whole of Middlesbrough to find out, but quite a few of my close friends knew after I'd told Lynette and the rest of my family over a meal at the Fox Covert pub near our home that evening. I also realised that Cup Final day was going to cost me a fortune. I wanted my wife, children and their partners to be there, and while a simple jacket would suffice for me, it was clear that Lynette would need several outfits for the weekend. Fortunately, I had the experience of 1989, so knew what to expect in terms of functions and etiquette.

After the news broke, I was inundated with texts, phone calls, emails and letters. I knew that my refereeing colleagues would send congratulations, but what knocked me back were the letters from people like the groundsman at Crewe, and Gordon Nicholson, the former secretary of the Northern League who with the use of his battered old typewriter reminded me of my early days at Tow Law,

Whitby and Gretna. Those letters brought a lump to my throat. I replied to everybody. Emails, texts and phone calls were easy enough but the letters and cards were eventually answered after the final, because I wanted to enjoy the last few weeks of my career rather than get bogged down with correspondence.

I trained as hard as ever and, as was the normal custom, we finished a high-intensity session by warming down with a game of one-touch football. We all reckon we can play a bit. Andy D'Urso claimed to be in the same team as former West Ham star Tony Cottee at school, but when we saw Andy play we were not convinced. By rights we should have had a Premiership player in to referee us, just to redress the balance. Failing that, I should have done it, as it was not a good idea to risk injury. But I love playing whenever I get the chance, so Mike Riley took the whistle because he was one of the few who openly admitted that he was not a good player. Mike had the hardest job, because once we started playing we didn't hold back and were as aggressive as some Premiership players. Peter Jones broke a finger as a result of a challenge by Rob Styles.

I made a mistake by standing in front of keeper Mark Halsey for a free-kick. He is not only the fittest of referees, but probably also the most competitive. As the ball came in, he decided not to nip round me, but go through me. His knee caught my calf and I felt the most excruciating pain I have ever experienced. I fell to the ground, my leg going into spasms. The lads initially thought I was joking, but soon realised that I was in serious trouble. I had to be carried to the hotel. Mark is a good mate, and while it wasn't his fault, he felt dreadfully sorry. I feared I would not be fit enough for the FA Cup final, but he was more concerned about whether I would be ready for a game at Bolton in two days' time. As I lay on the bed, he suggested that I pack ice around the injury.

Before I had time to answer he came up with what he felt was a better idea. He went to the bath and turned on the cold tap. He then shouted at me to get undressed. I knew what was coming and was reluctant to take such drastic action but he laid the law down. He had to manhandle me into the bath, because I didn't fancy it at all. It wasn't only the pain but the shock of being immersed into near freezing water. He warned me to stay there for at least ten minutes, and then vanished with the slam of a door.

Pain, or no pain, I wasn't going to lie there shivering, but as I eased myself to the door Mark reappeared, screaming at me to get back in the bath. For the rest of the day I sought medical opinion, the upshot being that it was an impact injury that would ease fairly quickly, which it did. With my calf strapped up I took to the field at the Reebok Stadium and managed, with some discomfort, to get through the game. After I'd showered and changed I was invited, by the club chairman, to the boardroom.

It then became clear why Mark had been so keen to get me fit. He knew about the presentation of an enormous engraved crystal vase marking my last appearance at the Bolton ground. I even got a card from the Bolton tea lady. It goes to show that not everybody has a downer on referees. The warmth shown to me that day will live with me for ever. Team manager big Sam Allardyce, with whom I enjoyed a good relationship at the time, commented that my gift was richly deserved – even though Boro had beaten Bolton in the Carling Cup final. Sam even said that he wished I had refereed the game. For my part, I simply wished I'd refereed our training match.

Good wishes were flowing in, including from two Wolves players who managed to put to one side their disappointment at relegation. Alex Rae, having reached veteran status, came beaming up to me when I was fourth official for a game at Newcastle. He had realised a lifelong ambition by agreeing to join Scottish giants Rangers. He invited me to Glasgow for a game any time I wanted, an offer which I have since accepted. Paul Ince was another who spoke to me in glowing terms. I started the conversation by asking whether he was retiring, newspaper talk having suggested that he was. He said he had yet to decide, to which I replied, "Well one thing's for certain. I won't be around." Paul shook my hand and said, "I know. It's been a real pleasure, Jeff." I looked into his eyes, and knew that he meant it. Players have the choice of when to go and Paul decided to keep on playing. Referees have no choice, and many people have criticised that decision, saying how ridiculous it is. Boro goalkeeping coach Paul Barron made the same point to me, but put it rather differently. "Just when you buggers are getting the hang of it, they kick you out," he complained. I think I preferred Ince's tribute.

Personally, I agree with the "retire at forty-eight" rule. I wanted to carry on, but knew this would hinder the progress of younger referees and would hardly help refs get promoted more quickly, which to me was a major failing of the English system.

My final Premiership match came around all too soon. I was sent to the Valley to officiate Charlton against Southampton, along with my Cup Final assistants Tony Green and Roger East.

No disrespect to those two clubs, but I had hoped to be elsewhere in London that day, at the home of champions Arsenal for the game against Leicester. Refereeing chief Keith Hackett had hinted that I would bow out at Highbury, but I'm told that Premiership chief executive Peter Scudamore had a say on final-day appointments, and it was Paul Durkin who was given the honour of saying his farewells at the home of the title holders. This was the first I knew of Keith being manipulated from above. Both Charlton and Southampton made presentations to me, and I felt numb, sad and happy, an unlikely combination. Deep down it was perhaps fitting that I should blow my final Premiership whistle at Charlton, because the club is a bit like Boro. An also ran, but a key player in the family of football.

Just as Charlton are in the shadow of the London giants, so Boro are deemed to be in the shadow of Newcastle (but I'll never admit that).

As I travelled home I reflected on the wide-ranging character of the country's footballing towns. It had been a pleasure to visit them all and in my last season I had particularly enjoyed the derbies. Liverpool is perhaps the greatest of the footballing cities, because intense passion is interlaced with humour in a way that no other city can match. East London derbies at Millwall have a nasty edge while the animosity in Birmingham is of an intensity that would surprise a lot of people who haven't experienced it. Then there's Newcastle and Sunderland, both towns steeped in football tradition. But I don't think they can quite match up to Liverpool. Or Middlesbrough.

14

THE 2004 FA CUP FINAL
Byw'r freuddwyd (Live the dream)

As a supporter I had never seen major success in the FA Cup, and now the final was going to be my last ever professional game. I was determined to make the day memorable for all the right reasons, even though it was unlikely to be a classic as Manchester United ought on paper to be streets ahead of unlikely finalists Millwall.

The FA Cup has always been special. As a fan, I never failed to get that extra buzz from it, as it was my dream to follow Boro all the way to Wembley. There was a huge sense of anticipation when the day of the draw came, and I always believed that with luck each year would be our year. When I started refereeing, there was a special atmosphere even in the early qualifying rounds. Little clubs, even at that stage, want to call themselves giant-killers by knocking out somebody from higher up the ladder. For them, the first round proper is the goal, the chance to mix with the big boys in the national spotlight.

As I progressed through the Football League, I saw how much it meant to the minnows. The sight of Grimsby Town fans, complete with inflatable haddocks, taking more fans to an away tie than their usual home gate was one special memory. Then there was little Sutton United from the Conference beating Coventry City, cup winners just two seasons earlier; Hereford beating Newcastle with that memorable long-range goal from Ronnie Radford; Mickey Thomas scoring for Wrexham against Arsenal. They're all part of FA Cup folklore, and long may they continue to be so.

The final was, in the early seventies, the only club game that was covered live on television, so it was hugely anticipated, regardless of who was playing. I didn't leave the television from the start of the programme in mid-morning through to the winners' lap of honour. I even stood up once for the national anthem because I was got so carried away with the build-up.

As a fan, my hopes of going to Wembley were dashed with quarter-final defeats for Boro at Leyton Orient, Wolves and Birmingham. I thought that Charlton's champions were on their way to Wembley in 1975. They played Birmingham in the quarter-final, and we were all confident, having beaten them 3–0 both at home and away in the league. But Bob Hatton scored the only goal of the game for Birmingham and denied us a semi-final place against Second Division Fulham, who went on to lose to West Ham in the final. We would have fancied our chances against them. A few years later, when Boro, under John Neal, reached the sixth round against Wolves, we again missed out. After a draw at Ayresome Park, we came back from a goal down in the replay to equalise but, agonisingly, missed several chances for the winner before Wolves scored in extra time and earned a semi-final place against Spurs. The defeat at Molineux meant the end of an era, as the following season saw the break-up of John Neal's promising team, with David Hodgson, Mark Proctor, Craig Johnston and David Armstrong all leaving as the club struggled financially.

When it came to refereeing, the magic of the FA Cup held just the same power. It was a fantastic feeling to referee a game on a lower-league ground when one of the Premiership teams visited. That is what the FA Cup is all about. When I first refereed an FA Cup tie involving a Premiership club, between Walsall and Leeds, it had helped catapult me towards the Premiership list, while the 1989 FA Cup final had whetted my appetite, and inspired me for the rest of my career to referee the final.

I was mightily relieved when this dream became reality, because I was at the end of my career, and not a FIFA referee. So I finished my career on a high, but it had taken some firm words from Lynette to make me appreciate how lucky I was. My performances had become inconsistent once I'd realised that FIFA duty was to remain an unfulfilled dream, and even my Premiership place may have been under threat had it not been for Lynette telling me to focus on achievable goals and stop feeling sorry for myself. Despite the odds being stacked against me, my inner rebel made me believe that I could beat the English system. If I continued to meet the required standard on the pitch, then possibly I might be able to force the hand of those who make the appointments for big matches. Somehow I made the Cup Final by the skin of my teeth – and I was ready for the spotlight.

The media interest was immense, and because the BBC and Sky were sponsors of the Cup, the FA felt I had a duty to do interviews with them. Whether I spoke to the other media was up to me. I decided to defer all enquiries to my agent, SEM, who represented players such as Sol Campbell, Ian Wright and Ian Walker, as well as many other sports and entertainment personalities. It was decided that I would do a piece with the *Sun* for Cup Final day, but one of the *Sun*'s competitors, who had failed to get my story, suggested that the time had arrived when not only players but now refs too were wanting interview fees. Such insinuations didn't hurt me, because people close to me know it's not true, and they also know that I do a lot of charity work. My reason for being selective in my interviews was purely so that I could concentrate on the final. Three days beforehand, for example, I had been in London filming a *Superstars* special for Comic Relief, and didn't take a penny for it. Just like everybody else, I paid to get there out of my own pocket so that I could help a good cause.

While at the BBC, I received a phone call from Theo Paphitis, the chairman of Millwall. I'd met him once after a game at Burnley, when he'd asked me about the badge on my jacket, and I told him that I would swap it for the badge on his suit. "No chance," he said. "Yours only cost thirty bob, mine's a silver limited edition that's worth much more than that." Before the final, Theo merely wanted to wish me all the best for the game, and invite me and the other match officials to Millwall's after-match banquet, win, lose or draw, as it was one of the biggest days in their history. There was no attempt to try to influence me. He was being genuinely friendly.

As the build-up to the final intensified, I honoured an engagement on the Thursday evening at a fund-raising event in Derbyshire for friend and colleague Ray Gould. Sky TV filmed my after-dinner speech. It was an enjoyable night, and Ray was honoured for his role as an assistant referee in Boro's Carling Cup victory against Bolton. The stay in Derbyshire was good preparation for the final, because it broke up a 300-mile journey and allowed me to relax while at the same time helping to raise funds for the development of future referees. I would have got nervous sitting at home, so wanted to stay as active as possible.

I completed my journey to Cardiff the next day, with the aim of going through my normal match preparation. We were given a guided tour of the Millennium Stadium with the other match officials, and familiarised ourselves with the changing rooms and procedure for the following day. All four match officials then held a training session on the pitch. The stadium is unbelievable – the best I've ever visited – but I was concerned about the pitch. Every time we twisted and turned I could feel the turf move slightly, no doubt because it had just been re-laid.

After training, all the media wanted a piece of us, and several approved interviews were done. I managed to do some BBC radio interviews and one for *Soccer AM*, an offbeat programme on Sky that I'd watched many Saturday mornings in my hotel room before a game. It's the usual procedure on the night before the final for the host referees' society to hold a dinner, which referees from all over the country attend. Our visit was brief – obviously – so that we could be introduced and honoured by our hosts, but there was still an opportunity to say a few words. I wanted to make sure that this speech was particularly sincere. On arrival at the hotel, I'd found out how to say "good evening" and other pleasantries in Welsh, but one phrase I particularly wanted to learn was "live the dream".

I told the audience how I'd gone through the Cleveland Sunday League, the Northern League, the Football League and the Premiership, all the time dreaming that one day I would be FA Cup final referee. The following day, I was going to live the dream, or in Welsh "Byw'r freuddwyd". That phrase went down well with my hosts, and when I looked at my table, Lynette had tears streaming down her cheeks. The moment had got to her.

Now that there was a new head of the select group – Keith Hackett had replaced Philip Don as refereeing chief – the sex ban had been lifted for the night before matches, and I was allowed to share a room with Lynette. Despite the build-up and big day to come, I managed to get a good sleep. I was determined that the next day was going to be as normal as possible. I watched *Soccer AM*, and set off early for the ground. I wanted to take in every moment, because I knew that there would be no coming back.

The one thing I dreaded was making a controversial decision that would be debated for weeks afterwards. Usually, if something goes wrong in an FA Cup final, you can make amends afterwards, because you have time to redress the balance. But I was retiring and would not have that option. I didn't want to be remembered solely for an incident in my last game. In my final three seasons, no referee in the Premiership showed fewer yellow and red cards. I would struggle to keep this low count in the final, if the pundits were to be believed.

The game was billed as a clash between two of the game's hard men, Dennis Wise of Millwall and Roy Keane of Manchester United. However, I was encouraged by the words of Sir Alex Ferguson, who, I was informed, said that he was glad I was in charge of the game, because he believed that I was a strong referee. It may well have been more mind-games, but I was pleased he said it.

On arriving at the Millennium Stadium, I saw Dennis Wise's partner Clare, along with their family. I started to move across to talk to her as friends do. However, Joe Guest grabbed my arm. "Jeff, no!" he barked. I could understand his reasoning, but I felt it sad that I couldn't say hello to somebody I knew. Surely an inno-cent brief encounter wasn't going to influence a game. Yet I understood that people's perceptions can be strange. At least I was able to meet my sons, daughter and her partner Adam, to have a chat. I thought I was being calm, but my emotional reaction on seeing my family on that special day caused me to drop my camera – another expense on top of all the clothes and tickets I'd had to buy! I sensed myself welling up and I knew I was having problems keeping a clear head.

Back in the dressing room, the post was delivered. More cards from well-wishers, including one from my long-suffering room-mate at Staverton, Eddie Wolstenholme. It was one of those spoof cards that has a voice message when you open it. David Beckham's voice boomed across the room, "From one good-looking fit athlete to another!" Eddie got that bit right anyway. The next card took away the laughter. It was from Stuart Loudon, who had helped me at the start of my career, and he wrote, "Old Blue Eyes will be pleased and looking down on you." Old Blue Eyes, Harry Bage, was my early mentor, the man who had blasted me all those years ago for daring to turn down that first appointment because I wanted to watch the Boro. After that first telephone call, we became firm friends, and he followed my career closely until he died. That was it. I couldn't hold back. I tried to hide it the tears from my colleagues but it didn't matter that I couldn't. They knew what I was going through, because they felt the same as they opened their good-luck cards. It was a big day for them too, probably the biggest of their careers so far.

After a massage from Barry Phillipson, who looked after the select group, we went on to the field for the warm-up. It was no different from any other – shuttles, sprints and a few laps of the pitch – but this time I knew that the eyes of the world were upon me. The ground was almost full, even at 2.20. People had read the advice on the ticket, "Please be in your seat half an hour before kick-off." Even with so many people in the stadium, I could see Lynette on one side of the field and the kids on the other. I felt so proud that they were there. The Manchester United and Millwall players had their own supporters and families, and it was nice to know there was somebody there supporting me too.

As we left the field, I passed Millwall players Kevin Muscat and Danny Dichio, who were both standing wistfully in the tunnel. Kevin, who is a character, had played in the Millwall versus West Ham game I had taken charge of earlier in the season and after his team-mate Tim Cahill had been fouled had come charging towards me, demanding that I take some sort of action. Typically for my last two seasons, I shouted, "Shut the fuck up," to which he bowed and said, "You can't argue with that, Jeff." Unfortunately, he couldn't play in the final because of injury, while Danny couldn't play because he was suspended. Their body language told its own story. I went across to them and said how sorry I was they weren't playing.

A few encouraging words in the changing room with the other officials, a drink of Red Bull, and then for the very last time in my professional career, I pressed the buzzer, and could hear the noise echoing from the teams' dressing rooms. We began the long walk precariously downstairs and in that instant I thought of that Arsenal versus Barnsley game when I went arse over tit in 1995. I made sure I kept on my feet this time – I didn't want to be the first Cup Final referee to be carted off to hospital before the match had started.

The players were in the tunnel, waiting. A couple of minutes later, we were told to go on to the pitch. As we hit the daylight, I experienced an atmosphere unlike any I'd experienced before. That all-Merseyside Cup Final in 1989 was special for all sorts of reasons, but didn't prepare me for the wall of noise which met us at Cardiff that day. I'd witnessed the electric atmosphere at the Carling Cup final three months earlier, when the stadium roof was closed, but on pitch side the intensity was greater. Everybody was on their feet, cheering, singing and clapping. There was loud music playing and fireworks going off. It was absolutely deafening.

The stadium was deathly silent for the national anthem, another special part of the FA Cup. It sent a tingle down my spine because I knew then that the time had almost come for the biggest moment of my career. The anthem over, I went through the formalities with captains Keane and Wise. Even those two veterans showed some nerves as we shook hands, posed for photos and tossed the coin, a special one from Canada, given to me by the Saskatoon Referees Society from my good friend Gordon Quinlan. Before I was appointed to the final, he had sent me the medallion, and asked if I would use it to toss up at a game. They were stunned and delighted when I told him that this would be the coin I would use at the FA Cup final, because I wanted to show my appreciation for their hospitality and friendship. I blew the whistle to start the game, but it felt surreal. Maybe the Red Bull was kicking in, but my adrenalin was in overdrive. Those niggling imaginary aches and pains from my hamstrings and calves vanished, and I felt that I could run for ever.

The game was one-sided, but that didn't bother me. The expected aggression from Millwall towards Manchester United didn't materialise, apart from one slight exception. One of my favourite photos from the game is of Dennis Wise laughing as he is being lectured by me. Dennis, who had spent the week in Italy receiving treatment for an injury, was up to his old tricks. The flashpoint occurred midway through the first half when he had "helpfully" bent over to lift Ronaldo to his feet by using the old Wimbledon method of nipping his opponent's arms. That provoked an angry reaction from the United players, who confronted Dennis. I called him over to me. "Do that again, Dennis, and I'll nip your balls, not your arms," I said. He couldn't keep a straight face. I didn't have to make many major decisions. I correctly turned down a penalty appeal (thank God!) and gave another one correctly, from which Ruud van Nistelrooy scored. The football gods were smiling on me.

I showed just the one yellow card – to Dennis, who committed one foul too many. As I issued the card I said, "Please, please don't do anything else. I don't want to send you off, even though you took the piss out of me in La Manga." "Well, don't then," he replied with a smile. When United got their third goal with nine minutes left, the generous side of Dennis came out. He substituted himself to allow a young sixteen-year-old, Curtis Weston, to come on the field and become the youngest ever player in an FA Cup final.

I enjoyed myself so much that I wanted to stay out there all night, but at 3–0 and with no controversy, I decided to quit while I was ahead. I checked my watch, said to myself "Well, this is it," and blew the final whistle on my professional career. The whistle was met with elation for the winners, commiseration for the losers, and mixed emotions from me. What a way to bow out. Everything had gone well, all my major decisions were right, and there had been no real incidents. The same could be said for the other officials, who were just as proud of their day.

Sir Alex Ferguson walked on to the pitch and shook my hand.

"Good news on two fronts, Alex," I said.

He looked at me and said, "What do you mean?"

"You've won the FA Cup, and you'll never have me again."

There seemed to be genuine warmth in his smile, suggesting our fallouts had been no more than part of his mind-games.

There was a nice touch from Theo Paphitis when he met us after the game. He presented all four match officials with a golden Millwall FA Cup badge, and gave me the silver one, which I had admired earlier. He was magnanimous in defeat, but I didn't receive anything from Manchester United.

I was surprised to see the Sky cameras approach me for a short interview. We were then called up for our mementos, and as mine were presented, I heard a small amount of booing from the Millwall section. I hadn't done anything wrong, but I suppose old habits die hard. Instinctively, I kissed my medal as I left the podium, an action which was seen by millions on television – I didn't think the cameras were on me! My thoughts were then for my family. Before I left the field, I made sure that I waved to Lynette and the kids. I looked over my shoulder at United's celebrations and there was a tear in my eye as I left the pitch.

The match officials, our partners and members of the referees' committee went to a restaurant for a relaxing end to a perfect day. I can't remember much about it because I suddenly acquired a taste for champagne. Mike Riley had given me a bottle, Roger East, one of the assistants, also brought a bottle and some celebrating United fans sent one over. And to cap a wonderful evening, our families found us and joined in.

The following day should have been one of rest but instead I kept a long-standing promise to Peter Jones, an old colleague of mine, who had organised a charity match between referees and celebrities at Leicester. I drove there and played for half an hour in a kick-about. After that, it was back to reality and normality, whatever that was. I had lived the dream.

15

NEW HORIZONS

When the season had finished we let our hair down with a dinner at Staverton, where we hired a private room. I had seen many retiring referees say farewell there. Now it was my turn. Graham Barber and Paul Durkin also retired at the end of that season, and the three of us were presented with framed photographs of us in action, as is the Football Association's custom. My picture was of me and Steven Gerrard, one of my favourite players. I was delighted – and relieved, for over the years I had seen colleagues receive embarrassing photographs. Martin Bodenham, for example, was presented with one of him on a windy day, the breeze billowing his shirt out to make him look like Jimmy Five Bellies. Alan Wilkie fared even worse, the FA for some reason selecting a photo of him being carried off at the Carling Cup final. I'll never forget his face when he received his picture. I had to persuade him not to throw it in a skip outside the building, and I only managed that by telling him that the frame was worth a few quid. After my room-mates Howard Webb and Eddie Wolstenholme had made a moving speech packed with humour and warmth, I left Staverton feeling rewarded and appreciated.

Within a year my life had changed course, as two things happened. My involvement within the game diminished, and my media career took over. I didn't plan it that way, but it became increasingly clear that pursuing a media career and continuing to work within refereeing were incompatible.

Another series of *Superstars* brought light relief to that summer. Some of the same faces were there, and we were joined by others from the upper echelons of sport, including rugby league ace Elleray Hanley, another man whose sporting and social skills made him perfect for the event. Again, the footballers were there, but in competition they failed to hit the heights that the other sports stars reached. Bryan Robson insisted that he be allowed to do his squat thrusts at the end of the arena that was closest to the bar. Did he mean the one on the frame, or the one in the hotel? And I didn't expect John Barnes to invite me back on to his Channel 5 football show – not after I red-carded him for his single-handed attempt to wipe out every other competitor in the kayak event.

When I returned home I hoped to continue to play a part in football and was encouraged by Keith Hackett, who was look-ing to appoint regional managers to control Premiership referees and be in charge of a regionalised structure of referees through the Football League and below. He said he wanted me to take care of the North. At our annual conference I made a speech and presentation to Keith for his sixtieth birthday, urging referees to back his plans.

In the end I didn't get the role. The interviews were done in a formal way and we were encouraged to make a presentation using the PowerPoint facility. I wasn't comfortable with that, as technology is not one of my strong points. Instead I settled for giving my thoughts verbally. I felt that the attributes of the successful applicant should be an ability to man-manage, not computer skills. Two days after the first round of interviews Keith rang me to say that the interview panel of him, Joe Guest from the FA and the Football League's Jim Ashworth had not given me enough marks to reach the second interview. I tried to be philosophical, telling myself that it wasn't to be, and I congratulated Dave Allison, who was handed the northern post. Like the other two applicants, he had not refereed in the Premiership for ten years, but I had known him for a long time, wished him well, and told him to contact me if he ever needed any help.

Despite this setback I was still keen to stay in the game, so offered to become a match assessor, even though I knew I couldn't do it at Premiership level, because those posts were already taken. My offer was accepted and at the start of the 2004–5 season I received my initial appointments. But the rules stated that I had to first sit alongside an established assessor to see how the job was done before I could fly solo. I had to chuckle, in the space of three months I had gone from Cup Final referee to being nannied by someone who had never refereed in the Premiership and hadn't been on the pitch for fifteen years.

The appointed match was a Carling Cup tie between Leeds and Huddersfield. Despite the derby match atmosphere, I was now concentrating entirely on the performance of the referee. It was a different perspective from being a fan, or referee, and I was determined to get to grips with this "third dimension". If I'm honest, I was immediately uncomfortable with assessing, particularly the marking system. It had changed frequently over the years, and I was confused as to how it was to be applied. If a referee was marked at 85 or more out of 100, then a written explanation had to be submitted as to why the mark was so high. Within seconds of the final whistle, the assessor declared, "He gets 84." "How do you reach that figure?" I asked, and before he could answer, I fired another question, "Don't you have to spend more time analysing his performance?" The reply was stark, "He gets 84." The referee was Eddie Ilderton, one who I had always rated, and he had just lived up to my expectations. I would have given him more than 84 and enjoyed writing a report to back that up.

Before long I was sent to a game on my own. A young referee, who was well known to me, sent off a keeper in a game at York City, a decision that I felt was incorrect, but I found it difficult, despite all my own post-match experience with assessors, to tell him that in my opinion the decision was wrong.

I assessed just twice in the Football League, at Hartlepool and at Sunderland, where Scott Mathieson and Tony Leake both had good games. I thought Tony could have handed out stronger punishment in two incidents, and said so in my report. I hope he wasn't eating baked beans when he opened the letter. His coach phoned me to express Tony's dissatisfaction but a few hours later phoned me again and said that in hindsight, having viewed the video, Tony agreed with my comments. Despite the problems of adjustment I was slowly warming to assessing.

My media career was beginning in earnest too. My first big step was joining Tim Lovejoy and Helen Chamberlain for Sky TV's *Soccer AM* show. It gave me quite a buzz. I was both relaxed and nervous at the same time. Relaxed because I felt comfortable chatting about football but a little edgy because my new life started here and if I blew it on the first day my career might be over before it began. On the whole I felt ready for the role, largely thanks to Craig Mahoney, the psychologist who had been a huge help in my refereeing days. He had prepared me for life after football and I was up for it.

I had already had a brush with television, in an unlikely way. Early in my refereeing career, a few days before I was due to referee a Conference game between Halifax and Kidderminster, I was told that the game was going to be featured in an episode of the popular detective show *A Touch of Frost*. I thought it was a wind-up, but was assured that it wasn't. I then took it seriously and learnt that the plot was about a player being involved in a murder while the match was in progress. The idea was that during the actual game the film crew would take general crowd and action shots.

That all went to plan and a few days later I was invited back to shoot the "match" scenes, this time with the real Halifax players, and actors wearing the Kidderminster strip. Lynette was employed as an extra for additional crowd shots. She was paid £30 – £2 more than I got for refereeing the real game! The daft thing was that the Halifax players, who would normally do the simple things without any problem, just couldn't get it right. It took ten attempts to put a decent cross into the penalty area so that the plot could evolve. I managed to fulfil my role of showing a red card, as scripted, without any problem – I'd done it for real often enough that I didn't need much practice – but a few days later I got a phone call saying that I had been filmed without a crowd behind me, so I would have to produce another Oscar-winning performance at a remote farmhouse where they were filming another part of the programme.

I put on a ref's shirt, stood in the back garden of the farmhouse, and showed another red card. I wasn't an Equity member, so wasn't entitled to any royalties, but at least I can say that I've worked alongside David Jason. And no, it wasn't me who murdered the player.

Despite my brief drama appearance, it felt strange to be in the Sky studios. I was used to watching *Soccer AM* while loafing on a hotel bed before a game. But, helped by the friendly production team, I quickly warmed to it. The programme went well, and I was delighted to meet actor Ray Winstone, someone I had long admired. The more we chatted the more I liked him. We talked of our days as young fans, and I wondered whether we had ever squared up to each other on the terraces at West Ham. I reckon it would have been an even-money scrap, for he looks as if he can take care of himself.

Talk of the old days on the terraces reminded me that I had to dash. Boro were at home to Newcastle in a teatime kick-off, and I was free again to go to a game simply as a fan. The day could hardly get any better. But it did. Boro grabbed an underserved draw against Newcastle, Dutch striker Jimmy Floyd Hasselbaink scoring with an "arm-assisted" header – missed by the ref – late in the game. Newcastle's luck on Teesside was still out. The dubious goal was not my fault but nor had it been my fault a couple of years earlier when a game between Boro and Newcastle had been postponed – though I'm blamed to this day by Newcastle fans. Heavy snow had put the game in doubt, and the day before it was due to be played, I was asked to inspect the pitch. I gave it the thumbs-up. However, the decision was taken out of my hands. The safety supervisor and local police were not happy because the approach roads, pavements and underpasses outside the stadium were treacherous from the snow and ice. For that reason alone the game was postponed. The Boro squad was decimated by injuries but when the match finally took place, some of the stars were back, and Boro won 1–0. You can imagine how that went down on Tyneside. Ever since I have rubbed Geordie noses in it. Whenever I have an after-dinner speaking engagement in Newcastle, I wind them up, even in midsummer, by saying, "I nearly didn't make it tonight. The snow in Middlesbrough is terrible."

My media career was now gathering pace, and I was soon back in London for another Sky appointment; this time on their *Soccer Monday* programme. Keith Hackett had recommended me. Before long I was working with Sky, Radio 5 Live, Talk Sport, *Zoo* magazine and the *Sun*. Keith often complimented me on my work as I continued to support referees and was using my role to give them a platform that had previously been unavailable. But if I was to retain my credibility, I could not stick up for refs with blind loyalty. There were times when I had to admit that the referee was wrong, though I always sought to explain the problems from the referee's perspective – never more so than on one particular occasion when Manchester United striker Wayne Rooney had won a penalty against Arsenal. Referee Mike Riley, like many before him in games between the two clubs, was in a no-win situation. Feelings between the two clubs were running particularly high at this time, so much so that the media hype before the game had built it up into World War Three. Arsène Wenger was fuming when the penalty was given. He claimed that Rooney had dived.

Sky presenter Andy Gray screamed "penalty" the second he saw it and only after half a dozen replays from as many different angles could we conclude from the studio that Rooney had made the most of minimal contact from defender Sol Campbell. Mike Riley saw it once. He gave an honest decision and I didn't condemn him, despite admitting that it was a close call. I used my comments after the game to blast the double standards of managers. I pointed out that early in Arsenal's unbeaten run of forty-nine games, a Premiership record, Robert Pires had appeared to dive to win a penalty against Portsmouth and salvage a game Arsenal might easily have lost. Wenger did not complain about that decision.

Keith Hackett was soon on the phone in a far from chatty mood, to warn me that I had upset people in high places. Within days I received a letter saying that I had been removed from the referees' assessors' panel for failing to heed verbal warnings from Keith about my media work. I was flabbergasted. There had been no such warnings. In fact, quite the reverse – he had encouraged me and recommended me to media organisations. For me this was just another example of how the big clubs are running the game. You criticise Arsenal or Manchester United at your peril.

Two days later Yorkshire Television phoned asking me to work for them. I asked them how they had got my mobile number. I was almost speechless when they said "Keith Hackett". I wrote to the Professional Game Match Officials Ltd, stressing that my media work had been done with Keith's approval. The reply was to the point. It said that as I would not promise to cease media work without getting prior approval for articles or interviews my involvement in the professional game was over. The revolving door which had drawn me into the world of refereeing had thrown me unceremoniously back on to the street.

I resolved to put it behind me and focus on my new career. Controversy was never far away. I was at Boro when Bolton striker El Hadji Diouf was accused of spitting at a supporter, and was asked to do a newspaper article about the match. Out of courtesy, and as I had enjoyed a good relationship with Bolton and especially manager Sam Allardyce, I spoke to his assistant Phil Brown to tell him what to expect in the newspaper. By coincidence, within days, I met Bolton secretary Simon Marwood at a sportsman's dinner. He told me to expect a letter. I expressed surprise, but was shocked when the letter arrived from a firm of solicitors, stating that the word "obnoxious" was a slur on the character of El Hadji Diouf. I dug out the dictionary and found that the Pocket Oxford gives the definition of obnoxious as "offensive" "objectionable" "disliked." I stood by my use of the word. The matter was referred to the newspaper's lawyers, as the buck stops with the paper. I heard no more about it.

Up to this point I had always found Bolton officials to be open-minded. Allardyce had once attended one of our Staverton meetings to put across his views. He used his "big club, small club" argument by which he believes that the less fashionable teams don't get the rub of the green. I feel in terms of refereeing decisions that he is wrong but he made a fair point about the big clubs' grip on the game. Some referees felt that he had turned up at Staverton to try and win favour for his team. I didn't agree with that, and stuck up for him. We often hear that there is a huge gulf between referees and managers so it is good to communicate whenever we can.

I also liked the technology and training methods that Sam installed at Bolton. One of our top referees, Mark Halsey, occasionally trained with Bolton. The offside rule was revised at around that time, stating that players who were not deemed active could not be flagged if they were in an offside position, and there were claims that Bolton used Mark's presence to quiz him on how they could push the law to the limit. Bolton used a free-kick routine in which they had a couple of players standing well offside to distract the defence. The players then ran onside just as the kick was taken. I have no evidence that Mark advised them on that ploy. Besides, it was within the law. Others wouldn't leave it alone though, and some clubs made noises about Mark refereeing games which involved teams placed close to Bolton in the Premiership table. It shows that referees can't win. If they keep their distance they are accused of being aloof and if they are close to players and managers they are accused of bias. Mark worked at Bolton to improve his fitness and understanding of the pressures that players and managers face. Anyone who believes that he would deliberately give decisions against Bolton's rivals has a vivid imagination.

It was against this background of support for Allardyce and his club that the manager turned on me. The relationship between myself and Bolton has not recovered. I had been due to speak at a couple of pre-match hospitality functions, but I was banned by the club.

The Bolton boss soon had company in Birmingham manager Steve Bruce. In a volatile Birmingham derby with Aston Villa in December 2004, Blues midfielder Robbie Savage appeared to poke Villa's Olof Mellberg in the eye during a mêlée involving several players. At the time, the media were running articles with an "anti-Savage" theme. I was asked my opinion of his actions in the Villa match. The article was printed after the forty-eight-hour watershed following the game – the time by which the FA have to charge a player if they are going to.

Bruce was irate and produced the following outburst: "When have we ever been interested in Jeff Winter? He was hopeless at refereeing and absolutely despised by most of the professional players because of his attitude and thinking that he was bigger than any other player. Who is interested in what he writes? What was he – a bog-standard referee who loved himself? He drives me nuts. An absolute prat – and you can print that as well. For him to comment on anything like that, well, he has got about as much personality as a bag of chips. I disagree with what he has said. I just think it is someone making a few quid and, as I have said, who the hell is interested in Jeff Winter. He was disliked immensely for the way he was as a referee, the way he conducted himself, the way he portrays himself."

Strong stuff, but rather than annoy me, it amused me, because I thought when I retired from refereeing that I would no longer annoy managers and yet I was still at it. A couple of days later I spoke to Savage, who was not charged. Despite his reputation I like him. He has a wholehearted style, speaks his mind, and carries his heart on his sleeve. And I had sympathy for him when he was in trouble with the authorities for using the referee's toilet before a match. The referee in question was not one of my favourite people. In fact anyone who craps in Graham Poll's toilet can't be all bad. I explained my newspaper comments to Savage and he said, "Fair enough, but I'll tell the papers that you are a hopeless after-dinner speaker." We laughed. There were no bad feelings. And nor have there been from most people in the game.

Despite being on the outside now, I could not escape the problems inside the game. Throughout the season I took calls from many referees and some of the conversations were less than upbeat. The picture they were painting of life inside the job was dismal. The brave new world of refereeing had not materialised. In fact, things were worse than they had ever been.

The scramble among referees to be the top dogs was intensifying, as they eyed being England's representative for the 2006 World Cup. I found it interesting being on the outside looking in. Mike Riley was in the driving seat after his successful appointment to Euro 2004 and I knew that he was ahead of Rob Styles in the pecking order, because Keith Hackett had told me that Styles had received a letter telling him that his FIFA place would be under threat if his performances did not improve. The small group of referees at the top now appeared to be down to three – Mike Riley, Graham Poll and Steve Bennett. Hot on their heels was Matt Messias, who had been promoted to the FIFA list. Yet from the start of the season the biggest games seemed to go to Poll and Styles, with Messias rarely featuring. This surprised me, as several conversations I'd had with Keith Hackett had convinced me that these two referees were not his favourites.

An early season incident waiting to happen occurred when Steve Bennett sent off Everton's Tim Cahill for a second yellow-card offence – removing his shirt in celebration after scoring. Steve's decision was, according to the law, correct. Personally, I think that unless a player provokes opposition supporters he should not be cautioned. But the rules make no allowance for that.

The match assessor Jim Ashworth supported Steve's decision, as did Joe Guest, the FA's referees' officer. Yet Steve was instructed by Hackett to withdraw the caution, so had no choice but to deal with an impossible situation as best he could, agreeing to issue a statement saying that he "reluctantly" agreed to withdraw the second yellow card. By saying "reluctantly" he was making it quite clear that he was making the statement under duress. At the next meeting of assessors I'm reliably told that Hackett berated Ashworth, Guest and Bennett for their stance. Steve was due to referee a match the following weekend but was demoted to fourth official and didn't take charge of a game for four weeks. Morale among referees was sinking and the lower it got the more phone calls I took from referees who needed to vent their anger.

To their credit, the referees continued to impress with their performances. Graham Poll's handling of Arsenal against Manchester United, when there was an altercation between the two skippers, Roy Keane and Patrick Vieira, in the tunnel before the game, was exemplary. Close-up television revealed how much authority Graham had as he calmed a tense situation by having a firm word with the aggressors. The one blot on his copybook that day was his refusal to show Wayne Rooney a red card for continuous foul and abusive language. There was media comment that the chance to tame Rooney should have been taken. Yet I was told that at a refereeing get-together two of the best up-and-coming referees, Howard Webb and Mark Clattenburg, were handed some advice by Graham who suggested that Mark should book more players, and that Howard, in a forthcoming televised cup tie between Manchester United and Southampton, should do referees a favour by sending off Rooney should he use foul and abusive language.

In early 2005 I took a call from the press asking for my views on the referees selected for the 2006 World Cup. I told the reporter that it was disappointing that England had just one nominated referee. Unsurprisingly, considering all the big-game appointments he had been given, it was Poll. I added that I could see the value of referees working together in preparation for such a big tournament but felt that to name them so far in advance was ridiculous. For referees such as Mike Riley and Steve Bennett, one major incentive to maintain and improve their standards had been taken away.

To their credit, they never have dropped their heads, and continue to be among the best referees we have. If I'd had a say in it, Mike would have got the call. I can't believe that he wasn't chosen. If it was purely down to refereeing ability I can't see how the authorities could look beyond him. Ideally, I would have chosen him along with Steve and Graham. I think all three are easily good enough to officiate at the World Cup.

Towards the end of each season referees get letters from the FA, Football League or PGMOL about their performance. One Premiership assistant referee, who was within two months of retirement, was told that his place was under threat unless his performances improved. What was the point in that? This was an example of standard letters being sent out without thought as to their impact. The personal touch has gone.

It hurt me when referee and friend Mike Dean was "exposed" for his part in a horse-racing ownership syndicate. His involvement in racing was open, and many referees had enjoyed a day at the races with him. But when he advertised on a website, inviting people to join the syndicate, a story appeared in the *News of the World*. Mike was out of luck in that his involvement was made public just after a German referee had confessed to match-fixing. As horse racing carries an association with betting, Mike was suspended as a referee. He missed almost three months of the season before the hearing into his behaviour was held. By that time he had lost match fees and had been fined. His "crime" was that he had entered into a legitimate business, with the knowledge of his football employers. The punishment caused bad feeling among the referees. Some breaches in behaviour and protocol it seemed were punished and others went unpunished. Our feeling was, it was one law for some and one law for others in the group.

It wasn't just those inside the game who were in the doghouse, as I found out early in 2005. As I had refereed the 2004 Cup Final I was invited by the Cardiff referees' association to be guest speaker the following year at their eve of the Cup Final rally. But early in 2005 I received a call from an embarrassed secretary from Cardiff who said that the FA and national referees association didn't want me to speak. By now the president of the referees' association was David Elleray. I tried to get in touch with him to ask why I had been ditched but I haven't heard from him since.

Nevertheless, the media work came thick and fast in the build-up to the 2005 FA Cup final between Arsenal and Manchester United. There was media talk of the showpiece game degenerating into a personal feud between the two skippers. Rob Styles had been named as referee and there were media suggestions that he was not up to the job, mainly because of the number of yellow and red cards he tended to issue, and partly because he was inexperienced at the highest level. So comment pieces were required from me.

I said that while I believed that there were more experienced officials who could have been handed the game, Rob was up to it. Sadly, as is often the way with newspapers, the headline did not match the story. "Styles not up to it", blasted one, though the story made no such claim. I was in the Millennium Stadium for the final and I felt he had a good game, though I would not have sent off Arsenal's Jose Antonio Reyes – even though he committed two yellow-card offences – because the second came in the last seconds of extra time. The final whistle could have brought this matter to a close without drawing attention to the referee. It certainly would have happened that way had it been in the previous year's final.

I was taken aback when Sky asked me to referee a game in which players in the penalty area could not be ruled offside. I agreed, though I thought the idea was a non-starter. It had been proposed by the Welsh Football Association. Sky had heard about the idea and decided to put it to the test in a game between two top non-league sides. The plan was excellent; far more practical than sitting round a table to discuss it in theory, and I would have changed my mind if, after the game, I thought the idea had merit. But I didn't get the chance. Out of the blue the FA told me that the game could not go ahead, even though I had got the go-ahead after phoning John Baker, who by then was the FA's head of refereeing. They claimed they hadn't realised it was to be televised, and didn't want to risk the current rules of football being ridiculed. Why they thought a television company should be involved in a project that was not to be screened is beyond me. The football authorities appear frightened of the media.

I wish I had a pound for everyone who has asked me if I enjoy retirement. They don't realise that I work harder than ever, and am away from home more often. One of the things I enjoy most is meeting fans who used to hurl abuse at me. And I'm still capable of being star-struck, as I was when I was invited to speak at the *Liverpool Echo*'s Merseyside Sports Personality Awards. When I looked at the 600-strong guest list my heart missed a beat. The room was filled with a who's who of Liverpool legends. Everton manager David Moyes and ex-Liverpool boss Gerard

Houllier were on the same table as me. In the two hours that we chatted that day we understood each other better than we ever had on the pitch.

I work alongside lots of former managers, players and senior football officials, and the camaraderie among us is better than it was when I was inside the game. Some of the most enjoyable occasions are those on my own doorstep. Not just the dinners, but radio work – if I can call it work. Our local TFM Radio has a kind of radio equivalent of *Soccer AM*. As well as covering the fortunes of our local teams, Ditchy, Dave, Giles and myself get up to all sorts of nonsense – including penning our own words and singing them to the tune of popular songs. We also have a spoof "referees' wives" feature. Without station manager Colin Patterson I would never have broken into the world of local radio. And fellow pundit, former Boro star Terry Cochrane, has his uses. He blames every problem under the sun on referees, so defending the profession keeps me on my toes. I've now got my own radio show, a phone-in, which is half serious and half fun. We address the football issues of the day, whenever possible with a slice of humour.

I also help refereeing at grass-roots level in the local referees' academy that I set up. Thanks to Middlesbrough Football Club, the county FA and the Referees' Association, we've attracted, trained and encouraged a number of young referees. I'm proud to say that one of our academy pupils has, at eighteen, progressed to within one step of the Football League's assistants' list. There are others to follow. And if Steve Bruce, Fergie or any other manager gives them a hard time in the future, they will have me to answer to.

The football world they are entering is perhaps changing for the better. It seems that the FA, under the leadership of Brian Barwick, at last appears to be addressing the wrongs. After an error when the FA appointed a head of refereeing, but then had to reconsider because they'd appointed from within without asking for applications, John Baker's successors as head were announced. Baker has been an excellent figurehead for grass-roots football, but wasn't as respected in the professional game.

The new head of refereeing role has been split into two, with Ian Blanchard to oversee grass-roots and non-league football (no doubt his reward for lending me his shoes that time at Old Trafford) and Neale Barry as the head of refereeing of the professional game. Neither suffer fools gladly, and are honest and straightforward. Jim Ashworth is in his last season as the Football League referees' appointments secretary. I hope that Eddie Wolstenholme gets that job as I think he will be a man who treats everybody equally.

In the Premiership, Keith Hackett has a couple of years left before retirement and, despite my experiences with him, I believe that if unhindered from above he could have been the man in the short term to carry refereeing forward. I'd like to see Steve Bennett replace him. Whoever gets the role needs to be strong on man-management and fairness. The qualities that are foremost in any referee on the pitch must be applied with regard to the treatment of referees off the pitch. Consistency must also be paramount. Whoever is to take refereeing in this country forward has got to have the respect of all referees. It will be a difficult decision. I hope the authorities make the right choice. With young referees like

Martin Atkinson and Andre Marriner coming through, then perhaps one day we may see an English referee emulating Jack Taylor and taking charge of a World Cup final. Maybe it will be a referee from my academy.

As for my future, I'm not looking beyond today. It's early Saturday afternoon, and last night's speaking engagement went well. I've shaken off the tiredness, it's stopped raining, and the pale winter day with its watery sunshine is beckoning me out of doors. I think I'll nip down to some playing field and take in a junior league game. I'll seek out one that's being refereed by one of our academy youngsters. I won't say a word. I'll just let him get on with it. He'll appreciate that, because if he makes the grade there'll be abuse galore in the years to come. Another Bastard in the Black perhaps.

16

AM I MISSING IT?

Football, like life, never stands still, and those of us who are optimists always believe that things will get better. Sometimes they don't, and I'm sad to say that the game of football is in a worse state today than it was when I retired – though I don't link my departure with the downturn in the game. I may have an arrogant side to me, but I'm not that conceited! However, there is no doubt that recent events in the game have made my split from it much more palatable, and each day, on reflection, I wake up pleased that I'm not tied to it any more.

In the last twelve months, the image of football and refereeing of the game, in particular, have been rocked by allegations of incompetence, corruption and bribery. Firstly, there has been the biggest ever match-fixing scandal the European game has known in Italy, centring on the former Juventus sporting director, Luciano Moggi, and his alleged setting up of a network of referees who favoured his club in key matches. In return for favours on the pitch Moggi, along with his fellow director Antonio Giraudo, was accused of wining and dining referees and giving them half-price deals for cars made by Fiat, the company controlled by Juve's owners, the Agnelli family. Moggi was also alleged to have discussed refereeing appointments with senior Italian Football Federation officials. Several referees faced charges, including Massimo de Santis, who was set to officiate at the World Cup but was pulled out after being drawn into the investigation. Moggi and Girando were eventually suspended from football for five years on grounds of 'sporting fraud'. De Santis was banned from refereeing for four and a half years.

Football has also been rocked by the match-fixing revelations of German referee Robert Hoyzer. Ironically, he had honed his skills in a pre-season friendly in Germany involving Middlesbrough, who were annoyed about some of his decisions in the game, but they just put his performance down to bad refereeing, and never dreamed of the drama that would unfold around him. His career came to a sudden end when he was suspected of betting on a first-round German cup tie between Paderborn and Hamburg SV. Hamburg took a 2–0 lead before the referee, who was only twenty-five, sent off Hamburg striker Emile Mpenza, then awarded Paderborn two dubious penalties, which helped them to a 4–2 win. He denied allegations, then dramatically admitted them, and was handed a lifetime ban from refereeing. And it got worse for him, because the police launched an investigation into allegations that he had fixed other games. Another referee was implicated, and Hoyzer was jailed for two years and five months after admitting the charges. The other referee Dominik Marks was jailed for eighteen months, and the betting ringleader Ante Sapine was handed two years and eleven months. The German FA imposed a blanket ban on betting on football matches by anyone – players, coaches, referees and officials – who was involved in the sport.

Despite these cases, I've always found it difficult to grasp that a referee could act in this way. I have always thought that if a referee accepted a bribe, then it would be blatantly obvious over the course of a game if some of his decisions influenced the result. In the case of Hoyzer it did become clear; and it does make you wonder how often it happens, though despite these high-profile cases, I'm pretty sure it is not a deep-rooted problem in the game. But I didn't think it would happen at all, so was evidently wrong about that.

I've been asked on many occasions if I've ever been offered a bung. Shall I say that the absence of a personal yacht berthed underneath the Transporter Bridge on the River Tees in Middlesbrough should be enough to answer that question! I can categorically say, hand on heart, that I have never heard of any sort of serious belief of any referee in the domestic game being corrupt. Unfortunately it has surfaced abroad, and let's be honest, where there's money, there can be problems, and the huge amount of money at stake on major matches increases the possibility of temptation, bribery and even coersion. Whilst all these matters are unpalatable, and drag the image of football through the mud, it is more practical, everyday refereeing matters closer to home that have concerned me.

At the start of the 2005–6 season two referees, Matt Messias and Andy D'Urso, weren't even offered Premiership refereeing appointments. Even though they attended the fortnightly get-togethers at Staverton and showed full commitment to the cause, the only action they saw was as fourth officials in the Premiership and refereeing in Football League games. Consequently, they also lost their places in this country's elite FIFA group, leaving Graham Poll, Mike Riley, Steve Bennett, Rob Styles, Mike Dean, Mark Halsey, Howard Webb, Mark Clattenburg and Martin Atkinson. During the course of the season, several referees picked up long- term injuries but still Matt and Andy were snubbed and denied Premiership matches, to the extent that eventually Matt could take no more and walked away from refereeing, a tremendous waste of a talent that could have served the national game, and perhaps international football, for many years. Andy has gone back to the Football League. At the same time, Dermott Gallagher was granted an extension beyond the normal retirement age. Whilst I am delighted for him as an individual and as a referee, it was a decision forced upon the bosses due to their inability to bring on younger referees and use others whose faces did not fit.

The final ignominy regarding the lack of thought and consideration for referees was the appointment of the 2006 FA Cup final referee. As I well know, the appointment is the most important domestic honour a referee can have bestowed upon him, but on this occasion it became an embarrassing fiasco. With Boro involved in the semi-finals and facing a game against West Ham for a place at Cardiff (the new look Wembley still not being finished), I had more than a vested interest in the competition I have always loved. About a week before the semi-finals, I received a phone call from one of my local academy refs, telling me that Graham Poll and Mike Riley were refereeing the games, and Mike Dean had been appointed to the final. I took the announcement of the final referee with a pinch of salt, because I knew from experience that the appointment was never announced until the finalists were decided. Once again, though, I was wrong. For whatever reason, the FA referees' committee had broken with tradition and had made the appointment public before the semi-finals. Mike was obviously elated by the appointment.

On semi-final day, along with 15,000 other Boro fans, I travelled to Villa Park to watch us play West Ham – back with the boys, enjoying being on the road again with my beloved Boro. The first half didn't go to plan mainly because of a string of missed chances and an injury to our keeper Mark Schwarzer, who was accidently caught by robust Hammers' striker Dean Ashton. It was obvious it wasn't going to be our day. But then I received a text at half-time that knocked me sideways, and distracted me in the second half. The missed opportunity of a day out at the FA Cup final was surpassed by the news that Mike had been taken off the Cup Final because of Liverpool's win over Chelsea in the other semi-final the day before. All of a sudden, Mike's home in the Wirral was deemed to be too close to Liverpool for him to officiate the Anfield club. Yet he had always lived there and the clowns who had announced the appointment were surely aware of this. It was basic common sense that if there was any doubt as to the wisdom of appointing Mike to referee a Liverpool match, they should have waited until after the semis – or did they think that Liverpool would lose to Chelsea? By ditching him, the referees' committee, predominantly of former referees, had given Mike the biggest kick in the teeth imaginable.

Let's hope he gets the 2007 FA Cup final, unless Liverpool or Everton are in it, of course. Mind you, in previous years the appointment of David Elleray of Harrow, to referee the Manchester United v Chelsea final had not been changed. Another case, it would seem, of rules for one and not another.

The problem was made even worse when Alan Wiley was handed the final. Alan is a more than capable referee and equally worthy Cup Final referee, but to my follow my lead as a non-FIFA Cup Final referee has surprised me, and disappointed others even more. David Elleray had previously stated that a non-FIFA referee should not referee the Cup Final, but the referees' committee on which he sits supported the appointment just two years later. Don't get me wrong, I'm delighted that after I broke the trend, officials are now appointed on ability. But the problem for me was that Alan had already refereed the Carling Cup final between Manchester United and Wigan earlier in the season, and I was always led to believe that an official wouldn't get two major cup finals in the same season. To me, it was another blow to the other officials, especially for somebody like Mark Halsey, whose face doesn't seem to fit with the hierarchy, and he is constantly overlooked, even though to my mind he is probably the fittest referee and the most in tune with the players.

So that was the end of another season that had me shaking my head in disbelief at officialdom, but there was little time to dwell on it, for that carnival of football that happens only once every four years was upon us. If ever a World Cup arrives without me feeling excited, then I will know it is time to totally turn my back on the game.

My working schedule had been arranged around the tournament, with corporate events being hosted and the remaining games being watched at home in front of the television. And it was partially work related for me, because from my column in the *Evening Gazette* to my views in the *Sun* newspaper, and on radio and television, my opinions would be in demand, and you can't pass credible comment if you haven't watched the games. Well, that was my excuse for indulging in hour after hour of football, and Lynette seemed to accept it, so harmony descended on the household.

We all have preconceived ideas, and ahead of the tournament mine was of concern – even trepidation – that the officials would overreact and we would have yellow and red cards galore leading to spoiled games. My fears were borne of the fact that referees have no leeway any more. The edicts from FIFA must be obeyed. Yet in the early stages of the competition I was pleasantly surprised. The football was flowing, open and attack-minded, and while referees were quick to clamp down on diving – which has become the scourge of the domestic game as well as the world stage – the games were flowing freely.

I thought this was a positive step. We have always blamed foreign players for the increase in diving in the English game, yet here in the World Cup it was being curtailed. The referees were firm and consistent in stepping in with calm authority whenever shirts were pulled, dissent shown, or lunging tackles committed from behind. I even got to thinking that maybe a new era was dawning when the domestic game might benefit from the example shown at the World Cup. But maybe that was fanciful, because managers and clubs in this country will never accept high card counts and suspensions of star players, and would try to pressurise referees into managing situations without issuing cards. I had learned in my career in the middle that you had to consistently apply the laws to earn respect before you could hope to use discretion to man-manage situations. But any such notions of mutual respect between managers and players on the one side, and referees on the other, were soon to be blown away.

Enter our own Graham Poll. He was on World Cup duty with Glenn Turner and Phil Sharp, officials he had worked with during the previous season in the Premiership. Phil, in particular, has a wealth of experience, having run the line in the World Cup final of 2002. This time Poll would not have the excuse he had previously used in the 2002 World Cup, when he felt that he had been let down by a Danish assistant. On the whole I felt Poll did reasonably well in his first game, even though he issued a couple of harsh and, in my view, unwarranted bookings. One of the players was subsequently sent off for a second bookable offence and he did issue the cards in the wrong order for the sending off, showing first the red, then the second yellow. In his second game he did very well and looked to have overcome the blip in the earlier match. Referees, like players, can get nervous and take a while to settle into a tournament, and it seemed that he was now in control. So was it onward to the later stages and possibly the final itself? But after his third game, the only way he would be reaching the heights was on the plane home. He took charge of the deciding group F match between Croatia and Australia on 22 June. For much of the game he was in control in a low-key manner, with his ability, experience and confidence keeping a potentially explosive match under control. But as Philip Don often used to say: "You have to get the big decisions right."

Australia's captain Mark Viduka was assaulted in the penalty area, being hauled to the ground, yet Poll waved appeals aside. He did well to spot one handball in the penalty area, but missed a blatant one, so awarded only one penalty when there should have been three. Ironically, the foul on Viduka was committed by Josip Simunic, a name that Poll will never forget. As the game heated up, he booked the Croatian defender THREE times before finally showing him a red card following the final booking moments, after the final whistle. By the time the red card was belatedly shown, the damage had been done. It was a nightmare for Poll; one of the biggest mistakes a referee can make. The game was building towards a dramatic climax as Croatia needed to win to qualify for the second stage, while Australia needed a draw to reach the knockout stage for the first time in their history. Liverpool's Harry Kewell equalised for the Socceroos eleven minutes from the end with a goal that looked suspiciously offside. He had drifted in at the far post, and beyond the last defender, a split second before the ball was headed into his path.

That goal left Croatia frantically seeking a winner, and tempers frayed. In the heat of the drama – and to be fair the heat of the day, for referees, like players, find it harder to concentrate in stifling conditions – Poll obviously didn't realise he had already booked Simunic when he thrust a second yellow at him. The player appeared to be trudging disconsolately off the pitch when he realised that the red card had not been shown. He stopped in his tracks and got on with the game. As it turned out there were no further goals, so in terms of the smooth running of the competition, the referee's error made no difference. But had the Croatians scored there would have been unprecedented repercussions and FIFA would have had to order a replay. In fact, they admitted as much.

It was the sort of error you could perhaps get away with in local football or a lesser league, but not on the world stage. Poll was subsequently sent home from the World Cup, when FIFA sat to make their decision six days later. Within days he announced his retirement from international tournaments. I thought that was a clever move on his part, because he anticipated what was perhaps inevitable. He would probably not have been selected again anyway, but he made it look as if it was his decision and not that of the authorities. He said he considered retiring altogether, but decided to continue officiating in the Premiership. But as everyone knows, referees are scapegoats and fans have long memories.

In the days after the fateful game, the media crucified him. I tried to be rational in my comments, though the scale of his error meant that I was unable to defend him. The *Sun* ridiculed him in a front-page lead story, and they, along with other papers, splashed Poll across several pages. Whether he bothered to read them in his hotel or on the plane home, I don't know, but wouldn't have blamed him if he shut his eyes when passing newsagents' stands. You are up there to be shot at, he knows that, and has proved that he can handle it.

Some people felt that it would have been the honourable thing for Simunic to walk off the pitch because he knew he had been booked twice. But we are talking footballers here. As the referee didn't show him the red card, he stayed on the pitch and got on with the game. I was interested to read Viduka's comments to the media afterwards. Apparently, he suggested to Poll at the time of the second booking that Simunic had already had one yellow, but Poll said it was his first caution. The referee later admitted he thought he had earlier booked the Australian number 3 and not Simunic, who was wearing number 3 for Croatia.

However it happened, there can be no excuses. I was asked whether the assistant referees or fourth or fifth officials (they had fifth officials at the World Cup) were in any way responsible, the theory being that they should have contacted Poll over his head-set. I said that I didn't think that they were in any way to blame. They can be up to fifty yards from the incident, and when players surround the referee – as they invariably do – it's impossible for somebody on the sidelines to be sure who has been booked and why. The buck stops with the referee.

So there we are. The brave new world had not materialised. The same old antics of players continue, and as the World Cup progressed the behaviour worsened. Players took dives, argued with referees, tried to get opponents sent off by brandishing imaginary cards at the referees, and even patted referees on the back when they obliged. It was all so unsavoury. I particularly felt for referee Valentin Ivanov, of Russia, who issued a World Cup record of four red cards and sixteen yellows in the match between Portugal and Holland for a place in the quarter-final. I thought he handled the game as well as he could in near impossible circumstances. What can a referee do when it seems that most of the players from both sides are intent on kicking lumps out of each other? Yet the official got no support from FIFA president Sepp Blatter, who suggested that Mr Ivanov should have given himself a yellow card. With "support" like that from the top brass, what hope is there? My answer to a lot of the problems at the World Cup would have been simple: red card for Blatter.

Meanwhile, my life has been good. Before the rest of the country focused on Germany and the World Cup, I had some great days in Europe with Boro, culminating in the UEFA Cup final against Sevilla in Eindhoven. The stunning comebacks we enjoyed in beating Basle then Steau Bucharest after being three goals down in both games are never to be forgotten, though in typical fashion it was to end in despair with a 4-0 final defeat. However, I'm flourishing on the after-dinner speaking circuit and loving the radio work, so life away from the politics of refereeing is great. Am I missing it ? To use a well-known Teesside phrase: "Yer jokin', aren't yer!"

INDEX

Adams, Jimmy 229
Ajax 132
Al Fayed, Mohammad 145
Aldridge, John 156, 175
Allardyce, Sam 258, 267–8, 291–3
Allison, Dave 285
Aloisi, John 144
Amberleigh House (horse) 262
Anderton, Darren 199
Andrew, Eric 11
Anfield 133, 137–8, 147, 164, 204, 263
Angie (Pilates instructor) 194
Armstrong, David 273
Arsenal FC 109, 116–18, 125, 155, 170, 173, 179–81, 195–6, 199–203, 205–6, 212, 217–19, 224, 257, 260, 269, 272, 279, 290–1, 296, 298–9
Arsenal (women's team) 103
Ashworth, Jim 193, 215, 257–8, 285, 295, 301
assessors 45–6, 56–7, 88–9, 125–7, 136–8, 142–3, 174–5, 248–9, 285–6, 290–1
Aston Villa FC 19, 59, 74, 79–80, 108–9, 117, 135–6, 147, 149, 153, 157, 165, 196, 210–11, 242, 255–6, 259, 293
Atkinson, Martin 172, 302, 306
Ayresome Park 2, 6, 10–12, 17–18, 29–30, 33–4, 36, 38, 48, 74, 80, 92, 103, 272–3

Babski, Dave 225
Bage, Harry ('Old Blue Eyes') 25–6, 65–6, 277–8
Bailey, Mark 242
Baker, John 299, 301
Baker, Zoe 229
Baldwin, Peter 24–5
Ball, Kevin 133
Bam Bam, Frankie 20–1
Banik Ostrava 20
Banks Group Northern Youth League 61
Barber, Graham 108, 176, 192, 224, 283
Barnes, John 284
Barnsley FC 72, 101, 116, 147, 279
Barron, Paul 268
Barry, Neale 301
Barwick, Brian 301
Baulch, Jamie 228
Bayern Munich 232
Beagrie, Peter 242
Beardsley, Peter 55–6
Beasant, Dave 56, 227
Beckham, David 115–16, 169–70, 198–9, 210, 224, 277
    boot-flying saga 218
Begg's coach company 15
Bellamy, Craig 171
Belle Vue, Doncaster 47–8
Bennett, Steve 221–2, 226, 295, 296–7, 301, 306

Billingham Social 36
Billingham Synthonia FC 167
Birmingham City FC 156, 165, 176–8,
    224–5, 242, 259, 272, 293
Biscan, Igor 183
Blackburn Rovers FC 52, 120–1,
    133–6, 147, 180–1, 202–3, 205,
    219–20, 233
Blackhall CW 51–2
Blackmore, Clayton 167
Blackpool FC 47
Blake, Nathan 233
Blanc, Laurent 199
Blanchard, Ian 145, 301
Blatter, Sepp 313, 314
Blyth Spartans FC 39
Boa Morte, Luis 212
Bodenham, Martin 194, 283
Bodley, Dave 24–5
Bolton Wanderers FC 104, 136–7,
    197–8, 209, 246, 258, 267, 275,
    291–3
Booth, Russell 219, 234
Bootham Crescent 85, 115
Boothferry Park 53
Borussia Dortmund 166–7, 168
Bosnich, Mark 147
Boston United FC 41–2
Boundary Park 99–100
Bournemouth, AFC 156, 226
Bowyer, Lee 172, 195, 210
Bradford City FC 88, 90, 162–4
    fire 62–3, 162–3
Bramall Lane 222
Brazil, Gary 156
Bristol City FC 226
Bristol Rovers FC 104
Britannia Stadium 233
British Broadcasting Corporation (BBC)
    164, 222, 224, 274, 275
Brooking, Trevor 19
Brown, Phil 291
Bruce, Steve 115, 157, 242, 245, 293–4,
    300
Brunton Park 82, 134
Burnley FC 39, 87, 88, 101, 161–2,
    203–4, 208, 274
Bury FC 104, 212, 226
Butler, Andy 202–3
Butt, Nicky 198
Bywater, Stephen 261

Cahill, Tim 278–9, 295
Cambridge United FC 97, 174, 202
Campbell, Darren 228

Campbell, Kevin 112
Campbell, Sol 200–1, 212, 274, 290
Cantona, Eric 115, 127, 256
Carbone, Benito 133
Cardiff City FC 86, 226, 260–1
Cardiff referee's association 298
Cargo Fleet 127
Carling Cup 171, 205, 209, 212, 227,
    246, 251, 257–8, 267, 275, 279, 283,
    285–6, 308
Carlisle United FC 83, 84, 134, 174
Carroll, Dave 70–1
'Celebrities versus Legends' games 117
Celtic FC 1
Central Boro crew 16–17
Central League 28, 56, 61–2, 63
Chamberlain, Helen 287
Champions League 169
Channel 5 284
Charlton, Jack 8, 38
Charlton Athletic FC 144, 221, 253,
    268–9
Charlton's Champions 8, 11, 174
Charnley, Doug 72–3
Chelsea FC 13, 18, 74, 109, 111–12,
    119–20, 130, 143–4, 160, 171–2,
    180, 219, 228, 245
Chester City FC 87
Chesterfield FC 129–30, 163, 223,
    225
Chorley FC 57
Christie, Linford 177
City Ground 109
Claridge, Steve 131, 227
Clark, Frank 110, 112
Clarke, Wayne 83
Clattenburg, Mark 296, 306
Clement, Neil 199
Cleveland League 31, 127
Cleveland Nomads FC 26–7, 75
Cleveland Sunday League 26, 276
Clifton Hospital 34
Clough, Brian 44, 49, 76–7, 110
Coca-Cola Cup 84, 131
Cochrane, Terry 13, 300
Cole, Andy 199
Collina, Pierluigi 262
Collins, Steve 227
Comic Relief 274
Conference games 70, 74, 78, 92, 272,
    287
Conroy, Nikki 94–6
Cook, Paul 208
Corden, Steve 39–40
Cottee, Tony 266

County Durham youth team 40–1
County Football Associations 41, 46
Courtney, George 32, 35, 50, 72–3, 79–80, 88, 126, 142–3
Coventry City FC 62, 106, 108, 143–4, 171, 272
Craggs, John 10, 38
Cramman, Kenny 120
Crewe Alexandra FC 104
Croft, Annabel 229
Cross, Paul 147–8
Croxteth and Gilmoss British Legion 51–2
Cruyff, Jordi 127
Crystal Palace FC 135–6, 256
Cummins, Stan 19
Currie, David 'Kid' 49–50

Dabizas, Nikos 154, 155
Dagenham & Redbridge FC 131
Daley, Tony 59
Dalglish, Kenny 254
Darlington FC 36, 48–50, 61, 81, 97, 147, 253–5
Davies, Kevin 129
Dean, Mike 192, 197–8, 297–8, 306, 307
Deepdale 171
Dell, The 127, 128, 184, 205
Derby County FC 178–9, 184
Devine, Jim 152
Di Matteo, Roberto 131
Dichio, Danny 278–9
Dilks, Roger 77, 106, 107
Dinning, Tony 159
Dinosaurs 165–6
Diouf, El Hadji 291
Don, Philip 126–7, 137–8, 142–3, 150–1, 174, 184, 186–91, 197, 200, 204, 208, 222, 225–6, 232, 236–7, 241–2, 248–51, 260, 276, 310
Doncaster Rovers FC 76
Doncaster youth team 86
Dorigo, Tony 74
Dorman Long ground 28–9
Dotchin, Dicky 20
Dublin, Dion 242
Dunn, Steve 192
Durkin, Paul 124, 182–3, 192, 205–6, 269, 283
D'Urso, Andy 192, 266, 305, 306

East Riding youth team 40–1
East, Roger 268, 282
Edghill, Richard 113–14

Eland, Bernard 28, 31–2
Elland Road 97, 141–3
Elleray, David 78, 101, 104, 124–5, 129–30, 185, 188, 194, 199, 224–5, 232, 298, 307, 308
England football team 19, 37, 164
English, Dave 35, 36
Euro 96 110, 24
Euro 2000 164
Euro 2004 258, 295
Evans, Alan 136
Evening Chronicle (newspaper) 146
Evening Gazette (newspaper) 46–7, 61, 93, 186, 309
Evenwood 36
Everton FC 62, 64, 112–13, 118–20, 158–9, 174, 183–4, 210–11, 221, 243, 245–6, 295, 299

FA Cup 23, 51, 57, 60, 69, 78, 119, 120, 136, 163
  1970 160
  1974 174
  1982 37
  1985 41–2
  1986 48–9
  1989 93, 263, 265, 273, 279
  1991 72–3
  1997 128–31, 228
  1999 145
  2001 175, 181–3
  2002 201–2, 219, 220, 221, 224
  2004 86, 253, 254–5, 259–60, 262, 264–5, 271–82, 298, 306, 307
  2005 298–9
  Women's 102–3
FA Premier League Academy 147
FA Referees' Committee 52
FA Trophy Final 131
FA Youth Cup 152
Feethams 49–50
Ferdinand, Les 108, 198
Ferguson, Sir Alex 78, 115–16, 122, 128, 145–6, 154, 170, 174, 184, 206, 210, 218, 233–41, 245, 251–2, 277, 281, 300
Ferguson, Darren 174
Ferguson, Duncan 121
Ferryhill FC 39
FIFA (Federation Internationale de Football Association) 86, 125, 191, 224, 262, 273, 295, 306, 308, 309, 312, 313
Finlandia Company 246
Finney, Jim 86

First Division 104, 180, 224, 226, 257–8
Fitzharris, Tom 49, 50
Fleming, Curtis 167
Flitcroft, Gary 120–1
Foakes, Peter 104
Football Association (FA) 41, 52, 60, 63, 89, 99–101, 123, 127, 133, 136, 174, 180, 196, 207, 235–6, 247, 256, 264–5, 283, 285, 293, 295, 297, 298, 299, 301
  disciplinary hearings 145, 236, 237–41
  dismissals/booking reviews 172
  fines 153, 171
  official's transport system 150–1
  professional referees 188, 189
  referee directives 148–9
Football League 28, 35, 36, 44, 47, 52, 54–6, 69, 70–1, 75, 78–80, 85, 87–9, 92, 99–104, 110, 118–20, 134, 138, 169, 173, 186, 188, 189, 191, 193, 203, 208–9, 213, 215, 232, 262, 272, 276, 284–6, 297, 300–1
Foster, George 48–9
Fox, Bill 52, 60
Foy, Chris 263
Frankland, Graham 208–10
Frickley Athletic FC 41–2, 57
Fulham FC 145, 205, 212, 238, 272
Futcher, Ben 242

Gallagher, Dermot 124, 192, 306
Gascoigne, Paul 57–8, 163, 254
Gavin, Jason 168
Gerrard, Steven 164, 263, 283
Gibson, Terry 183
Gigg Lane 226
Giggs, Ryan 115, 234, 240
Gillingham FC 253
Goggins, John 101
Goodison Park 118, 175, 246
Gould, Ray 244, 275
Grand National 261–3
Grangefield Youth Club 27
Grant, Bobby 144
Gray, Andy 290
Green, Tony 268
Gregory, John 135–6, 149
Grimsby Town FC 36, 92, 272
Guernsey football team 225–6
Guest, Joe 182–3, 264, 277, 285, 295
Guinness 40
Guisborough youth side 61
Gullit, Ruud 110, 150

Habron, Andy 167
Hackett, Keith 136, 142–3, 260, 269, 276, 284–5, 289, 290–1, 295, 301
Halifax Town FC 76, 87–92, 287–8
Hall, Andy 188–9
Hall Garth School incident 93–6
Hall, Kenny 20
Halsey, Mark 192, 196, 266–7, 292–3, 306, 308
Hankin, Ray 39, 62
Hanley, Elleray 284
Hansen, Alan 144–5
Harold Wilson Recreation Ground, Thornaby 26–7
Harper, Tommy 23–4, 60
Hart, Robbie 50
Harte, Ian 196
Hartlepool United FC 82, 147, 286
Hartley, Ged 167
Hartson, John 163
Hasselbaink, Jimmy Floyd 288–9
Hatton, Bob 272
Hatton, Ricky 228
Head Wrightsons 35
Heilbron, Terry 174
Hemley, Ian 76
Henderson, Paul 45, 46–7
Hendrie, John 92, 103
Henry, Thierry 155, 170, 196, 199, 217, 260
Hereford City FC 88, 90–1, 272
Heskey, Emile 131, 153
Highbury 12, 195, 269
Highfield Road 144
Hill, Clint 156
Hillsborough 219–20, 263
  tragedy 62–5, 147
Hine, Mark 36
Hodgson, David 38, 254, 255, 273
hooliganism 1–3, 12–14, 18, 24, 51–2
Hooper, Brian 228–9
Houllier, Gerard 183–4, 217, 299–300
Howard, Jon 129
HoyzerR <obert 304, 305
Huddersfield Town FC 61–2, 74–5, 88, 157, 223, 285–6
Hughes, Mark 112
Hull City FC 8, 53, 84
Hurst, Glyn 223

ICI Wilton 29
Ilderton, Eddie 120, 286
Ince, Paul 71, 219–20, 222–3, 241, 268
Inland Revenue 247

Institute of Banking 8
Inter City Firm 18
Ipswich Town FC 169–70, 176–7
Ironworks Road, Tow Law 37
Irwin, Denis 38–9, 198
Italy football team 19
ITV Digital 203
Ivanov, Valentin 313

Jacks, Brian 229
Jason, David 288
Jeffers, Francis 217
Jersey football team 225–6
Job, Joseph 258
Johnsen, Erland 112
Johnsen, Ronnie 184
Johnson, Andy 177
Johnston, Craig 273
Jones, Dave 219
Jones, Peter 132, 192, 232, 266, 282
Jones, Vinnie 163
Juninho, Pernambucano 129

Keane, Roy 71, 127–8, 218, 277, 280, 296
Keegan, Kevin 19, 38, 108, 122, 145, 155
Keele University 194, 225
Kelly, Ned 154–5
Ken (bus driver) 15–16
Keown, Martin 201
Kerr, Paul 74
Kewell, Harry 141–2, 311
Kidd, Brian 160
Kidderminster Harriers FC 287
Kilbane, Kevin 171, 172
Kinder, Vladimir 129

La Manga 226–9
Lambert, Malcolm 27
Lampard, Frank 245
Lawrence, Lennie 167
Le Saux, Graeme 171–2, 219
Le Tissier, Mark 226
Le Tissier, Matt 226
League Cup 12, 23, 115, 116
League Managers' Association 249
Leake, Tony 286
LeBoeuf, Frank 160
Lee, Francis 113, 114
Lee, Graeme 262
Leeds United FC 25, 34, 38–9, 72–3, 88, 97, 118, 136–7, 141–3, 160, 172, 195–6, 210, 213, 215, 219, 221–2, 243, 255, 273, 285–6

Leicester City FC 82, 131–3, 158–9, 197, 243, 255–6, 261, 269, 282
Leyton Orient FC 272
Lightfoot, Chris 87
Lilley, Geoff 44–5, 46
Limpar, Anders 113
Lincoln City FC 174, 242
Linderoth, Tobias 245
Lindin 37–8
Little, Brian 81, 211
Littlewoods Cup 79–80
Liverpool Echo (newspaper) 262
    Merseyside Sports Personality
        Awards 262, 299–300
Liverpool FC 38, 62, 64–5, 109, 133, 137–8, 153, 164, 181–3, 195, 204, 215–17, 243–4, 254, 261–4, 299–300
Liverpool (women's team) 102–3
Livingstone, Steve 62
Lodge, Steve 77, 131
Loftus Road 212
Longstaff, Dave 7
Loudon, Stuart 28, 31–2, 277–8
Louis-Jean, Matthieu 146
Lovejoy, Tim 287
Lucic, Teddy 221
Lupton, Ken 47–8
Luton Town FC 103
Lynch, Terry 45, 46–7

McAllister, Gary 183
McAuley, Jim 53
McCall, Stuart 163
Macclesfield Town FC 201–2
McDermott, John 167
McDonald, Neil 59
McGhee, Mark 97
McGrath, John 54
Machin, Mel 156
McManaman, Steve 251
Mahoney, Craig 231–2, 287
Maine Road 1
Mallon, Ray 20
Manchester City FC 1–2, 76, 113–14, 120, 139, 159, 165, 178–9, 216, 227, 241, 246, 251–2, 254–5, 261, 296, 298
Manchester United FC 12–13, 108–9, 115–16, 117, 122, 127–8, 145, 152, 154–5, 165, 169–70, 172–3, 184, 198–9, 205–6, 209, 217–19, 224, 233–41, 251–2, 256, 271, 277–82, 290–1
Mansfield Town FC 36–7, 48–9, 213–15

Marriner, Andre 302
Marseille Football Club 37
Marwood, Simon 291
Match of the Day (TV show) 144, 201
Mathieson, Scott 286
Meadow Lane 109
Mellberg, Olof 293
Merry, Catherine 229
Messias, Matt 295, 305, 306
Michelle (school friend of Emma
    Winters) 95–6
Middlesbrough FC (Boro) 2–3, 6–20,
    23–6, 29–30, 33–4, 38–40, 46, 49,
    62, 69, 71, 73–4, 80, 85, 89, 92,
    100–3, 128–31, 139, 163, 166–8,
    186, 196, 215–16, 226–8, 254,
    257–8, 267–9, 271–3, 275, 278,
    288–9, 291, 300
Middlesbrough and District Sunday
    Morning League 27
Middlesbrough Referees' Society 28, 32
Middlesbrough Supporters' Club 14
Midgley, Neil 121
Midland Senior League 97
Millennium Stadium 177, 224, 226,
    275, 277, 279–80, 298–9
Mills, Danny 144, 195–6, 221–2
Millwall FC 18, 161–2, 260–1, 271,
    274, 277–82
Mirandinha 55–6, 58–9
Moggi, Luciano 303, 304
Molineux 222–3, 273
Moncur, John 201
Mourinho, Jose 180
Mowbray, Tony 38, 177, 178
Moyes, David 221, 299
Mulcaster, Peter 59–60, 265
Mullins, Geoff 6
Muscat, Kevin 278
Mustoe, Robbie 166–8

Nattrass, Wally 70
Neal, John 272, 273
Neville, Gary 127, 128, 169, 251–2
Neville, Phil 128
New Den 260–1
Newcastle United FC 34, 37, 55–9,
    71–2, 74, 80, 85, 108, 113, 128,
    134–5, 145–51, 154–5, 197–8, 204,
    224–5, 232–4, 239, 243, 258, 272,
    288–9
Newcastle United youth team 152
News of the World (newspaper) 297
Nicholson, Gordon 39, 265–6
Ninian Park 260–1

North Riding Football Association 23,
    25, 30, 37–8, 40, 45, 239
North Riding Junior Cup 33–4, 36
North Shields FC 39
Northallerton FC 62–3
Northampton Town FC 53
Northern Echo (newspaper) 49–50
Northern Intermediate League 34,
    38–9
Northern League 27–8, 36, 39, 62, 69,
    276
Northwich Victoria FC 78
Norwich City FC 62
Nottingham Forest FC 15, 44, 49, 62,
    64, 77, 109–12, 119–20, 146, 197–8
Nottingham Forest reserves 76
Notts County FC 109, 156, 213–15,
    256
Nunthorpe Athletic FC 31
Nunthorpe juniors 34

O'Brien, Andy 234, 235, 240
O'Hanlon, Kelham 83
Old Trafford 12, 78, 115, 129, 145,
    154, 172, 208, 209, 217–18, 251
Oldham Athletic FC 99–100
O'Leary, David 196
Oliver, Alan 146
Omoyinmi, Manny 157
O'Neill, Martin 158–9
Ord, Dickie 167
Osborne, Tommy 35
Osborne, Wayne 35
Ossie's Bar 37–8
Oxford United FC 167

Pallister, Gary 38, 115
Paphitis, Theo 274, 281–2
Parkinson, Andy 156
Parry, David 32
Parry, Derek 32
Parry, Ronnie 32
Partridge, Pat 126
Patterson, Colin 300
Paylor, Eric 93
Pearce, Stuart 110–11, 227
Perez, Lionel 202
Peterborough United FC 36
PGMOL (Professional Game Match
    Officials Ltd) 247, 291, 297
Phillips, David 112
Phillipson, Barry 278
Pires, Robert 196, 290
Pitman, Paul 167
police 161–2, 175, 256–7

Poll, Graham 124, 192, 194–5, 205, 249, 259, 294, 295, 296, 306, 310, 311, 312
Pollock, Jamie 159
Pontins Central League 69, 71, 74
Portsmouth FC 99–100, 260, 290
Premier League 236, 250
Premiership 71, 79, 83–4, 91, 101–12, 115–19, 122, 123–5, 127–8, 132, 136–8, 141–3, 152, 155, 159, 165, 168–9, 172–3, 176, 178, 183–4, 185, 189, 197–8, 201, 210–11, 213, 215, 224–6, 236, 258, 266, 268–9, 273, 276, 284–5, 290, 292, 297, 301
Press Complaints Commission 146
Preston North End FC 54, 104, 171
Pride Park 178–9
Prissick Base, Middlesbrough 27–8
Proctor, Mark 273
Professional Footballers' Association 249
Prutton, David 158
Pugh, David 186, 196–7, 212

Queens Park Rangers FC (QPR) 13, 119
Question of Sport, A (TV quiz show) 164
Quinlan, Gordon 280
Quinn, Micky 72

Racecourse Ground 174
Radford, Ronnie 272
Radio 5 Live 262, 289
Rae, Alex 208, 241, 268
Rangers FC (Glasgow) 1
Ravanelli, Fabrizio 129
Rayner, Amy 194
Reading FC 97, 104
Real Madrid 224
Real Zaragoza 118
Redknapp, Harry 157–8
Redmond, Derek 228
Reebok Stadium 136–7, 267
Regis, John 228
Reid, Peter 152, 179, 243–4
Rejer, Paul 77
Rennie, Uriah 133–4, 148, 149, 151, 192, 233–5
Repka, Tomas 201–2
Reyes, Jose Antonio 298–9
Reynolds, George 254
Ricard, Hamilton 168
Richards, Dean 198
Ridden, Ken 120, 124

Riise, John Arne 217
Riley, Mike 84, 242, 258, 266, 282, 290, 294–5, 296–7, 306
Rioch, Bruce 178, 179–80
Riverside Stadium 103, 139, 166–7, 232, 257
Roberts, Ben 131
Robinson, Eric (Ernie Ragbo) 20
Robinson, Paul 244
Robson, Sir Bobby 204
Robson, Bryan 102, 254, 284
Rochdale 54, 69, 77, 87, 106
Roker Park 53
Ronaldo 280
Rooney, Wayne 155, 210–11, 290, 296
Rotherham United FC 74–6, 84, 213
Royle, Joe 118–19
Ruddock, Neil 'Razor' 141–3
Runcorn FC 70, 74

St Alphonsus 27
St Andrew's 176–8
St Cuthbert's Boys' Club 24
St James's Park 57–8, 59, 71, 72, 80, 85, 106, 107–8, 148, 151, 204, 224–5, 232
Sanchez, Lawrie 181–3
Saskatoon Referees Society 280
Savage, Robbie 242, 259, 293, 294
Schmeichel, Peter 116
Scholes, Paul 218
Scott, David 113
Scudamore, Peter 269
Scudamore, Richard 250
Scunthorpe United FC 76, 157, 242
Seaman, David 196
Second Division 104, 115, 174, 226, 272
Sellars, Scott 38–9
SEM 274
Sharp, Phil 225, 310
Shay, The 90
Shearer, Alan 146, 149–51, 155, 234
Sheffield, Alan 163
Sheffield United FC 213, 215, 221
Sheffield Wednesday FC 10, 16, 17, 133, 136, 219–20
Sheringham, Teddy 198–9
Shildon youth side 61
Simpson, Shaun 20
Simunic, Josip 311, 312
Sky 114–15, 117, 122, 235–6, 274–5, 282, 287–90, 299
Slaven, Bernie 74
Slovenia 118

Smith, Alan 160–1, 172
Smith, Geoff 33
Smith, Jim 100
Smith, Kevan 81
Smith, Malcolm 12
Smith, Tony 15
Smiths Dock Park 28
Smoggies (Teessiders) 5
Soccer AM (TV programme) 275, 276, 287, 288, 300
Soccer Monday (TV show) 289
Souness, Graeme 203, 220
South Bank, Teesside 47, 167
Southampton FC 78, 112–13, 120, 127–8, 158, 184, 205, 224, 246, 268–9, 296
Southend United FC 101
Southgate, Gareth 153–4
Spennymoor FC 39
Sportsnight (TV programme) 25
Stadium of Light 132–3, 151–2
Stam, Jaap 169
Stamford Bridge 12, 119–20, 160, 219
Stapleton, Simon 70–1
Staunton, Steve 210, 211
Staverton training camp 190–1, 193, 197, 209–10, 244, 247, 250, 258–9, 277, 283–4, 292
Stevo (old friend of Jeff's) 20
Stockport County FC 159
Stockton 39
Stoke City FC 222–3, 233
Stokesley League 118
Strachan, Gordon 73, 143–4, 171, 246–7
Styles, Rob 192, 243, 250, 266, 295, 298–9, 306
Sullivan, Neil 163
Sun (newspaper) 134–5, 136, 274, 289
Sunday League 239
Sunday People (newspaper) 97
Sunderland FC 9, 17, 34, 53, 71–2, 74, 132–3, 150–2, 167, 171–2, 220, 257–8, 286
Sunderland youth team 152
Superstars (TV sports competition) 222, 224, 226, 227–9, 236, 243, 274, 284
Sutton, Alan 97
Sutton United 272

Talk Sport 289
Taricco, Mauricio 224
Taylor, Graham 152
Taylor, Jack 302

Teesside and Cleveland Junior League 28, 30
Teesside Junior Alliance 29
Ternent, Stan 208
Terry 35–6
TFM Radio 300
Third Division 53, 104, 226, 242
Thomas, Ewan 228
Thomas, Mickey 272
Thorn, Andy 56
Todd, Colin 179–80, 183, 184
Toms, Wendy 194, 205
Toon Army 149
Tottenham Hotspurs 18, 37, 58, 121–2, 125–7, 130, 134, 179, 198–9, 200–1, 205, 215–16, 224, 254–5, 273
Tow Law 36–7
Tranmere Rovers FC 101–2, 119, 156, 174
Tring Triads 192
Turf Moor 87, 203–4
Turner, David 78
Tyldesley, Peter 72
Tyler, Martin 131
Tyne Tees Television 133
Tyson, George 54

UEFA Cup 20, 118, 314
Ukraine football team 164
Upson, Matthew 225

Valley Parade 162–3
van Nistelrooy, Ruud 199, 218, 281
Vase, Muratti 225
Venables, Terry 160
Veron, Juan Sebastian 199
Verona, Chievo 232
Vickers, Steve 139
Viduka, Mark 311, 312
Vieira, Patrick 196, 218, 296
Villa Park 80, 181, 210–11, 259
Villains 165, 232

Waddle, Chris 37
Walker, Ian 255–7, 274
Walsall FC 83, 273
Watford FC 152
Watkins, Maurice 238–9
Watson, Albert 7–8
Watson, Dave 118
Watson, Gordon 120
Webb, Howard 213, 283–4, 296, 306
Welsh Football Association 299
Wembley 19, 60, 61, 64–5, 130, 132, 164, 228, 271, 272, 306

Wenger, Arsène 116, 260, 290
West Bromwich Albion FC 199–200, 203–4
West Ham United FC 17–18, 79–80, 121–2, 125–7, 137–8, 141–3, 150–1, 157, 195, 201–2, 260–1, 272, 278, 288
Weston, Curtis 281
Weston, Matt 204
Whinney Banks 36
Whinney Banks juniors 34
Whitby Town FC 55–6, 167
White Hart Lane 137, 198, 216, 224
Wiley, Alan 139, 192, 308
Wilkie, Alan 74–5, 146, 283–4
Wilkinson, Stephen 95, 96
Williams, Paul 171
Willington ground, County Durham 47
Willis, Peter 50
Wimbledon Crazy Gang 111
Wimbledon FC 40, 157, 162–3
Windass, Dean 84, 164
Winstone, Ray 288
Winter, Betty (Jeff's mum) 3–5, 8, 9–10, 18–19, 46, 68–9
Winter, Craig (Jeff's son) 38, 67–8, 93, 101–2
Winter, Elaine (Jeff's first wife) 19–20, 33, 38, 64–6, 67, 93–4, 96
Winter, Emma (Jeff's daughter) 33, 67–8, 93–6, 97, 143, 144
Winter, Jeff
  as after-dinner speaker 147–8, 252, 262, 294, 302
  as assessor 285–6, 290–1
  on assessors 45–6, 56–7, 88–9, 125, 126–7, 136–8, 142–3, 174–5, 248–9
  banking career 8, 9–11, 23–4, 75
  days as a boot boy 1–3, 11–20, 24, 64
  childhood 3–8
    birth 4
    education 7–8
    jobs 6–7
    love of football 4–9
  children see Winter, Emma, Winter, Craig, Winter, Mark
  on the current status of referees 294–7, 300–2
  divorce from Elaine 66, 67
  drinking 14–15
  as financial advisor 75–6
  fourth official work 60–6, 202–3, 205–6, 209, 221–2, 224–5, 233–5, 242, 246, 254, 259

  friends of his youth 20–1
  likes a bet on the horses 144
  as linesman 28–9, 36, 41–2, 44–50, 52, 57–9, 69, 72–7, 79–80, 203
  marriages
    first wife Elaine 19–20, 33, 38, 64–7
    second wife Lynette 66–7, 93–4, 96, 106, 175–6, 195, 204, 221, 227, 231–2, 261–2, 265, 273, 276, 282, 287
  media career 284, 287–8, 289–94, 298–300
    appearance on A Question of Sport 164
    co-presenter of Soccer AM 287, 288, 300
    co-presenter of Soccer Monday 289
    radio appearances 262, 275, 289, 300
    rumours of TV documentary of his final season 236–7
    stars in A Touch of Frost 287–8
    Superstars commitments 222, 224, 226, 227–9, 236, 243, 274, 284
  media interest in 46–7, 49–50, 114–15, 216–17, 244, 274, 275, 282
  perma-suntan 221
  as referee 24–42, 50–7, 61–3
    in Canada 165–6, 232
    early career
      on bad organisation 40
      clangers 61, 70–1
      commitment grows 29–30
      on corruption 40–1
      first match 26–7
      on having fun 57–8
      on the hostility towards referees 45
      hungry for promotion 69–72, 74–9
      promotions 38–9, 42, 43–4, 50–2
      qualifies as class 3 referee 25–6
      reputation as a 'bastard' grows 30–1
      on respect 35
      thinks about becoming a referee, enrols on a course 24–5
    for the FA Cup final, 2004 262, 264–7, 271–82
    and the FA Trophy Final, 1997 131

injuries 78–9, 136–7, 147, 148, 208, 266–7
League career 79–80, 81–92, 97, 99, 102–3
  appointment 79–80
  debut 82–3
  eyes on the Premiership 83–4, 99, 102–5
  fans take against his decisions 99–101
  first game as sick cover 74–5
  first season 81–92
  simultaneous to Premiership work 173–4
  pre-season matches 167–8
Premiership service 123–8, 132
  appointment 105–7
  on bad language 155–6, 223–4
  clangers 112–13
  confidence 168–9
  critics 145–6
  on dealing with stars 141–64, 170, 220
  on diving 117
  fairness 153
  first match 107–8, 109–12
  first season 105–22, 123
  and his linesmen 112–13
  on the importance of privacy 146
  last ever game at Anfield 164
  media coverage 114–15
  on the pressures of the appointment 173, 247–8
  on pundits 144–5, 181, 201, 210
  on referee egos 123–4
  self-doubt 132–9
  sixth season, 2000-1 168–84
  turning professional 184, 185–95
    begins to doubt his fitness 207–8
    clangers 212–13
    final match 268–9
    final season, 2003-4 231–52, 253–69
    first season, 2001-2 195–202, 203–5
    gains extra years service 207
    looses self-employed status 247
    media interest in 216–17, 244, 274, 275, 282
    on the mentoring system 196–8
    preparation for retirement 231–2
    on racism in the game 214

second season, 2002-3 208–26
on the secrecy regarding the game 195
serves his last red card 215–16
sex ban before matches 190, 276
training 186, 190, 191, 192–4, 197, 204–5, 266
wages 188
training 24–5, 31–2, 74, 186, 190, 191, 192–4, 197, 204–5, 266
reputation as football hooligan 2–3
retirement 283–302
Winter, Jim (Jeff's father) 3–6, 8, 9–12, 18–19, 42, 46, 68–9
Winter, Lynette (Jeff's second wife) 66–7, 93–4, 96, 106, 175–6, 195, 204, 221, 227, 231–2, 261–2, 265, 273, 276, 282, 287
Winter, Mark (Jeff's son) 52, 67–8, 232
Winter, Peter (Jeff's brother) 3
Wise, Clare 228
Wise, Dennis 110–11, 120, 227–8, 277, 280–1
Wise, Henry 228
Woking FC 131
Wolstenholme, Eddie 104, 187, 213, 277, 283–4, 301
Wolverhampton Wanderers FC 199–200, 208, 219–20, 222–3, 233, 241, 268, 272–3
Wood, Darren 38
World Cup
  1994 126
  2002 205
  2006 294–5, 296–7, 310–14
Worthington Cup 134, 157, 176, 197–8, 213, 219, 221
Wrexham FC 174, 272
Wright and Bright (radio show) 262
Wright, Ian 117, 155, 274
Wycombe Wanderers FC 70–1, 181–3, 202

Yarm FC 26–7, 75
York City FC 34, 35, 84–5, 92, 97, 115–16, 286
Yorke, Dwight 169
Yorkshire County Savings Bank, Thornaby 9
Yorkshire Television 291

Zenden, Bolo 258
Zenith Data Systems Trophy 73–4
Ziege, Christian 198, 215–16
Zoo magazine 289